A BUILDING

HISTORY OF

NORTHERN

NEW

ENGLAND

A BUIL
HISTO
NORT
NEW
ENGLA

DING

RY  OF

HERN

ND

James L. Garvin

University Press of
New England

HANOVER AND LONDON

University Press of New England, Hanover, NH 03755

© 2001 by University Press of New England

Printed in China

5 4 3 2 1

Library of Congress Cataloging-in-Publication Data

Garvin, James L.

    A building history of northern New England / James L. Garvin.

      p.   cm.

    Includes bibliographical references and index.

    ISBN 1–58465–095–8 (cloth)

    1. Building—New England—History. 2. Architecture—New

England. 3. Historic buildings—New England—Dating. I. Title.

TH23.15 .G37 2001

690'.837'0974—dc21   00–010536

This project received support from Furthermore,

the publication program of The J. M. Kaplan Fund.

CONTENTS

PREFACE

I arrived in Portsmouth, New Hampshire, in the summer of 1963 to become the second employee of Strawbery Banke. Now a respected outdoor museum, Strawbery Banke was then only a paper corporation that hoped to become the redeveloper of an urban renewal area containing dozens of eighteenth- and early-nineteenth-century houses.

The local urban renewal authority was then acquiring from private homeowners the area that is now Strawbery Banke Museum. After several years of intense negotiations, the housing agency had agreed to preserve twenty-five early buildings for eventual resale to the museum. The rest were to be demolished.

Soon after I arrived, it became my regimen to rise before daybreak, gather my tools, and head for the towering boom of the wrecker's crane. That looming shape foretold the day's demolition and marked the place of my pre-dawn work. I would salvage all the doors, paneling, and mantelpieces I could and carry my sad trophies to a place of safety as the wreckers arrived to start the engines of their machines. A quick change of clothes, and I was ready for my nine-to-five office job. By evening, the house from which I had watched the sunrise would be a pile of debris.

But what had I saved? As I started to inventory the scores of doors, paneled walls, sections of moldings, and hardware that I had snatched from the wreckers, I realized that I had become the curator of a collection of artifacts from a culture that was unknown to me. I could see differences among these artifacts, but which were earlier or later? Why were they different? Did their differences derive from changes in style or technology, or both?

Later, as I directed the restoration of several buildings for Strawbery Banke Museum, I was forcibly impressed with the urgent need to understand how buildings change over time. It is impossible to date a building, to evaluate its significance in relationship to other structures, to perceive and appreciate the changes that succeeding generations have made to it, or to restore or rehabilitate it intelligently without understanding its mute but eloquent language.

The ability to understand that language is crucial to the preservationist, but it is equally a need of the private homeowner, the public official who has responsibility for an old building, the volunteer member of a historic district commission, the contractor, and the student of architecture.

In 1963, I could find only one source to help me in my quest to make sense out of the complex artifacts that lay before me. This was a slim pamphlet called *The Dating of Old Houses*, which had been written in 1923 by Dr. Henry Chapman Mercer of Doylestown, Pennsylvania. Happily, the Bucks County Historical Society had recently reprinted it. A bit later, the American Association for State and Local History published Lee H. Nelson's *Nail Chronology as an Aid to Dating Old Buildings*, which refined some of Mercer's conclusions of forty years earlier. For a broader context, I had the help of Fiske Kimball's *Domestic Architecture of the American Colonies and of the Early Republic* (1922) and of J. Frederick Kelly's *Early Domestic Architecture of Connecticut* (1924), two enduring classics that were reprinted in the 1960s.

I began my task with these simple tools. It was a task of self-education. It was an act of communion with the materials of construction and with the minds, hands, and tools of long-departed craftsmen. It was a slow, arduous, and humbling quest that will never end for me or for anyone who loves history and old buildings.

Many people have pursued that quest over the past forty years. A glance at the bibliography at the end of this book will hint at the effort and intelligence that were focused on old buildings during the last decades of the twentieth century. Collectively, these sources are the fruit of immense labor, the distillation of thousands of hours spent in investigating, and sometimes solving, a multitude of vexing puzzles. Anyone beginning the task of understanding old buildings today is accompanied in spirit by an army of colleagues, not by just one or two voices from the past.

Yet this amount of literature, much of it hidden in professional journals, can be daunting and confusing. It is the purpose of this book to condense and simplify the bewildering array of discoveries that have been made by many people over the past years and to make those discoveries available in a single source.

This is not a book about restoring old buildings. It is a book about the necessary prelude to preservation or restoration. It is a book about understanding old buildings. Whether duty or pleasure brings us together with an old structure, our first obligation is to try to understand that building. To begin to alter it without understanding it would be an act of ignorance, perhaps of barbarism.

This book is written for all who may have occasion to understand old buildings. It is especially addressed to homeowners, who are often the people most in need of information, the people least equipped to find the needed answers, and, in the aggregate, the people most likely to do harm or good to old buildings.

It would be splendid if a single book could outline the history of buildings throughout North America or at least throughout the area encompassed by the original British colonies. Unfortunately, this is not possible. Like the accents of human speech, buildings betray regional variations within relatively short distances. No single book,

unless vastly larger than this one, could address all the many localized construction practices, stylistic preferences, and vernacular building forms that make our architectural landscape so varied and interesting.

This book therefore focuses on one relatively small and understudied region: northern New England—Maine, New Hampshire, and Vermont. That region has many connections with other areas, especially with eastern Massachusetts and the lower Connecticut River valley, the original homes of settlers who migrated to unsettled northern regions during the 1700s. But the distinctive geology and forest cover of the northern states, together with the cultural isolation that typified all of inland New England before the advent of improved transportation, quickly shaped the buildings of that region into somewhat different forms than we see in southern New England. The architectural distinctiveness of northern New England was erased only after the arrival of the mail-order house plan, and eventually the pre-cut house, beginning in the late 1800s.

This book will therefore be of greatest use to those who live in northern New England. Some of its statements—especially those that deal with the evolution of architectural styles—will be applicable over a much wider region. But the reader should use increasing caution in proportion to his or her increasing distance from Maine, New Hampshire, and Vermont. Perhaps this book will encourage the writing of comparable guides for other regions.

January 2000   J.L.G.

A C K N O W L E D G M E N T S

This book represents the evolution of a series of articles— "Merciful Restoration of Old Houses"—that I wrote for *New Hampshire Profiles* magazine in 1976. The book could not have assumed its final form without the forbearance of my colleagues on the staff of the New Hampshire Division of Historical Resources (the State Historic Preservation Office), who patiently tolerated my inattention to daily duties over a three-month period as I brought the manuscript and illustrations to final form. In particular, I offer thanks to Van McLeod, Commissioner of the New Hampshire Department of Cultural Resources, who allowed me to place the book ahead of my other departmental obligations; to Nancy C. Dutton, New Hampshire State Historic Preservation Officer, who shielded me from the daily requests of a public whose needs we feel acutely; and to Linda Ray Wilson, Deputy State Historic Preservation Officer, with whom I taught courses on the care of old houses years ago and who offered encouragement and help as I learned to set aside ruling pen and india ink and draw with the computer.

I am grateful to photographer Bill Finney, who graciously postponed other tasks to devote himself to the many photographs that bear his name as well as to much of the copy work in this volume. I thank the New Hampshire Historical Society for providing access to their rare-book collection during production of illustrations for this volume.

Furthermore, the publication program of the J. M. Kaplan Fund, provided subvention for the cost of publication of this book through a generous grant to University Press of New England. A donation to the New Hampshire Division of Historical Resources from the Eva Gebhard-Gourgaud Foundation of New York, through the kindness of Robert A. Sincerbeaux of Woodstock, Vermont, provided early encouragement and underwrote the cost of providing illustrations for the volume. I thank the staff at the University Press of New England for their trust, patience, and skill during transformation of an incomplete draft to a finished book.

I owe special thanks to Thomas Durant Visser, director of the Historic Preservation Program at the University of Vermont. Professor Visser set aside many pressing duties to critique and improve an early draft of the manuscript. He greatly enriched the final text and was especially generous in sharing his deep familiarity with the distinctive architectural traditions of western Vermont.

I am happy to acknowledge the help of Gary Thomas Lord, the Dana Professor of History at Norwich University in Northfield, Vermont. Professor Lord was a partner in many architectural adventures when we were both young employees of Strawbery Banke Museum in Portsmouth, New Hampshire. His friendship over the years has been a fixed point in a changing life. To him I owe what I know of central Vermont.

Finally, I thank my wife, Donna-Belle, who knows the full cost of this book.

A BUILDING

HISTORY OF

NORTHERN

NEW

ENGLAND

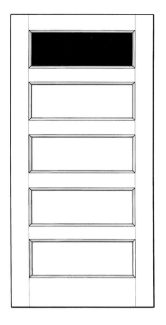

Introduction

If you have enjoyed the shelter of an old house during a hard rain, a gusting wind, or a driving snowstorm, you know that such a dwelling is like a living thing. A strong wind buffets the structure. Its frame, formerly supporting only the weight of the house and its contents, now creaks and shifts as the stresses build in each timber and the skeleton resists the lateral pressure of the wind. The wind whistles over the roof. The rafters are pressed downward on the windward side and momentarily lifted by the comparative vacuum on the leeward side. The stresses in the collar ties shift and change with each gust, and the joints at the feet of the rafters are tested. The snow adds its weight. The fabric of the house adjusts to the new burden. The turbulent wind rumbles over the chimney tops. The air currents in the flues shift from a moaning suction to a down-draft that puffs smoke through the stove doors.

If you have lived long enough in an old house to have heard its groans and snaps on wild nights, you have learned by observation that a dwelling must wrestle with the elements to remain standing. But a house is alive in more subtle ways. It breathes as the smoke rises from its chimneys on cold nights. It sweats as the moisture within pushes out through each crack, condensing as hoarfrost on the storm windows and on the points of every nail in the frigid attic. It expands as each timber and board absorbs humidity from the summer air, swelling with dampness;

and it contracts, drying and cracking, as the artificially heated air of autumn desiccates everything it touches. Old fissures in the woodwork and plaster, healed for the summer, reappear to admit the chill air of winter.

A house constantly responds to its environment and, if well maintained, resists for centuries those forces that seek to break down everything in nature. The engineering embodied in an old house is often ancient and intuitive in nature, having evolved from experiments, both successful and unsuccessful, over many generations. What has survived the test of time and nature is a series of craft practices and principles of proven soundness. By understanding these principles, you can glimpse the world and your own house through the mind of the original builder. You can develop sympathy with your dwelling and its era. This sympathetic understanding can provide you with a sound guide to the needs of the house and to the technologies that are appropriate to meet those needs.

What is true of the fabric of the house is also true of its appearance. Each house originally possessed a distinct character. Whether the dwelling started life as a pre-Revolutionary merchant's mansion on the coast, a farmhouse in a newly settled township, or a contractor's speculation house of the 1920s, its builder gave it a characteristic floor plan, characteristic proportions, and characteristic detailing. Each house, particularly if it has been treated sympathetically over time, stands as an artifact of its era. If you can see the plan and detailing of a house as they were created by the original builder or owner, you gain an accurate sense of the taste and aspirations of a time other than our own.

Few old houses survive without some alteration. The older the house, the greater the likelihood that it will have needed some major repair or will have come to be seen as hopelessly old-fashioned by some unsympathetic owner. Either circumstance is likely to have led to some change to the original design.

Alterations to an old house can be sympathetic and can even add something to the original character. Alterations can also violate the integrity of an old house, destroying its personality with an agglomeration of jarring and inharmonious elements. Whether an alteration adds to, detracts from, or blends invisibly with the original character of an old house depends entirely upon the thought and sensitivity that are invested in the change.

Like your predecessors, the earlier owners of your old house, you have the right to make changes to your dwelling. This right is yours legally, within broad limits of safety and reason. It remains yours even when your taste and judgment may puzzle or offend your neighbors. It remains yours, though to a more limited extent, even if your house falls within the bounds of a locally established historic district. Both custom and law expect you to make your house a home, and to be free and secure in its enjoyment.

Once you have title to the property, there is usually nothing to prevent your taking even the most ancient house and stripping it to its frame, slashing great holes through its sides to accommodate whatever additions your need or whim may dictate, and substituting the most up-to-date design and materials for whatever had survived of the old fabric. Many owners have done this, or worse. Most houses built before the Civil War have been demolished deliberately to make way for something newer.

It is frequently noted that poverty is the friend of preservation. Where people are too poor to afford the luxury of remodeling or replacing their dwellings, old houses survive, provided that the roof is kept reasonably tight. We owe the survival of some of the most intriguing neighborhoods of our old coastal cities and of some of our most pristine farmhouses to hard times prolonged over several generations. If you can find an old house that has been owned by people of modest means, you stand a good

chance of finding a home with architectural integrity. If you are a person of modest means, you could be the ideal custodian of such a house. You will be spared the temptation of making changes that are driven by mere fashion and that could spoil the building for a future owner.

Though you may have the legal right to treat your old house in any way you wish, both prudence and your innate sense of responsibility suggest that you should invest a little time and thought before you begin to rip and remodel. It is prudent, first, to understand what you are dealing with before you invest hard-earned money in it. This book will attempt to provide at least a general understanding of old houses from the eighteenth century to the twentieth.

It is prudent to protect your financial investment. For most of us, buying our home is the single greatest financial transaction of our lives. Unless you live in a changing neighborhood where dwellings are looked upon merely as an obstacle to commercial development, careful preservation of the original qualities of your house will invariably enhance its resale value.

It is prudent to take advantage of the innate character of a building rather than to work against that character. You may not care to live as did your predecessors of 1850 or even 1920. But if you can appreciate and find enrichment in the comforts and the beauty they provided for themselves, you have gained some measure of contentment in your home without having to resort to extensive and perhaps destructive remodeling.

It is prudent to husband the resources you own. By ripping out the work of earlier generations, you are tossing aside an investment of human energy that may have cost your predecessors months or years of their lives. That investment lies latent in the fabric of your house. It would cost money to undo those months or years of work, and it would cost still more money to replace that work with new work. By accepting and preserving the artifact your predecessors created, you add the value of their labor to your own life, freeing yourself to go about your other business. If, on the other hand, you spend time and money to undo rather than to enhance what others have done, you waste your limited resources on a job that is already finished.

If these arguments make no sense to you, perhaps you should not own an old house. Some people buy old houses because that is all they can afford, not because they wish to live in a building with a history. Such owners may long for a brand-new house, with the freedom from care that new things seem to promise. They may think that a few remodelings and the application of some synthetic coverings will transform their tired old dwelling into the house of their dreams.

This is almost never true. A heavily remodeled old house usually becomes a denatured old house. It never achieves the look or feeling of a new building, because it is the product of a different time and a different vision and cannot be transformed without its virtual destruction. At the same time, a remodeled house loses the integrity of its own period, and so becomes less than it was before the remodeling.

If you yearn for a new house and are condemned to live in an old one, this book may still be of use to you. Bide your time and carry out responsible repairs. Take the time to understand and preserve the characteristic features of your dwelling. If you preserve whatever integrity you find in an old house, a buyer will eventually appear who will be willing to pay a bit extra for this well-maintained character. That is the time to sell and fulfill your dream of buying or building a new house.

Whether you love or merely tolerate your old house, it is well to approach the building with one truth firmly in mind. Human life is short. The life of a house is potentially limitless. Even in the youthful United States, we have houses that have been sheltering families for three hundred years or more.

Barring disaster or imprudent neglect, your house is destined to outlive you. You are but one in a long line of custodians of the property—a line that extends backward through the decades or centuries and forward to an indefinite future. You may have received a deed conveying your house to you and your heirs and assigns forever. But it is your heirs and assigns, not you, who will probably have the property in a few decades. Whatever your legal title, your human mortality guarantees that you are in truth only a temporary custodian of your house.

That being the case, let the changes you make to your property be additive rather than subtractive in nature. If you need a new kitchen or bathroom or furnace, install it. But wherever possible, install it in such a way as to preserve original features or fabric or at least to preserve evidence of original features. Try to make your work add to the legacy of the past so that you can pass a dwelling of even greater value and comfort to the future. Remember that the number of old houses is finite and diminishes each year. It is a privilege and a responsibility to own a piece of the past.

Until very recently, houses were built entirely from natural materials, either organic or mineral. Technology was applied to transform and shape these materials from the raw products of the earth to the finished components of the house, but that technology was relatively simple. While it took years of apprenticeship and hard physical labor to learn to become a joiner, a blacksmith, a mason, or a painter, we of today can understand the basics of those and similar trades even though our hands and brains may lack the ability to practice them.

The first essential product of house building is wood. The forests of New England and the rest of the northeastern United States are typically mixed forests, containing both hardwoods (deciduous trees) and softwoods (conifers), depending on varying conditions of elevation, soil type, prevailing wind, and sunlight. Wood has been used in buildings as logs, as hewn framing members, as sawn boards, planks, and timbers, as shingles, as clapboards, as lath for plaster, as insulation, as planed and molded joiner's work, and as glued plywood. The means of shaping wood have evolved over the years, beginning with the simplest of hand tools and ending with the factories and mills of the gigantic forest products industry of the twentieth century.

It is striking, however, that in house preservation no technique of woodworking has become truly obsolete. While the great majority of wooden architectural elements have for a long time been the products of mechanized industry, there is still an important place for hand tools in the maintenance of eighteenth-, nineteenth-, and twentieth-century houses. Anyone undertaking the preservation of an old house today has the happy choice of using hand tools, power tools, ready-made elements, or a combination of several or all of these, as circumstances may dictate.

If you take your responsibility seriously, you may find that part of the skill of living happily in an old house lies in adjusting your outlook as to what is desirable or possible in a dwelling. You may have to accommodate yourself to some of the expectations, limitations, or desires of another time—something that human nature is often reluctant to do. Yet the discipline of doing this is usually rich in its return of broadened understanding, of new perspectives on the world, and of the exhilarating ability to move in one's mind—and one's dwelling—freely from the present to the past and back again.

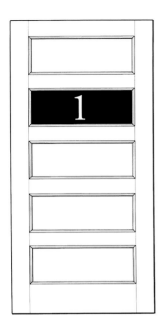

How a House Is Built: The Evolution of Building Technology

Log Buildings

The log cabin is a powerful symbol in the mythology of the United States. From the presidential campaign of 1840, in which candidate William Henry Harrison answered his detractors by proudly proclaiming his birth in a humble log house, Americans have equated the log structure with pioneering settlement and with frontier virtues.

For settlements made in forested country after the mid-1700s, the image of the log building as a pioneer's house is largely an accurate one. The memory of such settlements undoubtedly did much to confirm the accuracy of the log cabin image in the minds of nineteenth-century Americans and to entrench that image as an American icon to this day. Renewed interest in the log cabin in the early twentieth century contributed to a powerful movement to build log structures as camps and summer homes, a movement that spawned almost as extensive a literature as did the bungalow, another favorite small house type of the same period. That love of the log cabin persists and has grown into a virtual industry. The last decades of the twentieth century saw a multitude of competing manufacturers of pre-cut log home kits and of custom-designed log houses. In many parts of the country, log construction became a valid alternative to framed construction.

But the first settlers of New England were ignorant of the log house. Possibly a few settlers had seen such structures in travels to the Baltic regions before their departure for the New World. Most, however, would have known nothing of such construction, and all evidence of the first wooden houses to be built in New England confirms that these structures were framed buildings of the general type discussed in the following pages.

The false image of the log cabin as the home of the first settlers of New England had become so pervasive by the early twentieth century that Harold R. Shurtleff, a researcher at Colonial Williamsburg and a graduate student at Harvard, devoted the last years of his life to an extensive study to disprove the supposed connection between log structures and seventeenth-century settlement in the Northeast. Shurtleff agreed that log construction had been brought to New Sweden (centered on the Delaware River) by the first settlers there in 1638. But he marshaled strong arguments to show that no such buildings had been constructed in New England before the mid-1600s and then mostly as specialized structures, often as fortified places of refuge or defense. Shurtleff died before finishing his work, but his book was published posthumously in 1939 under the title *The Log Cabin Myth*.

The earliest recorded log building in northern New

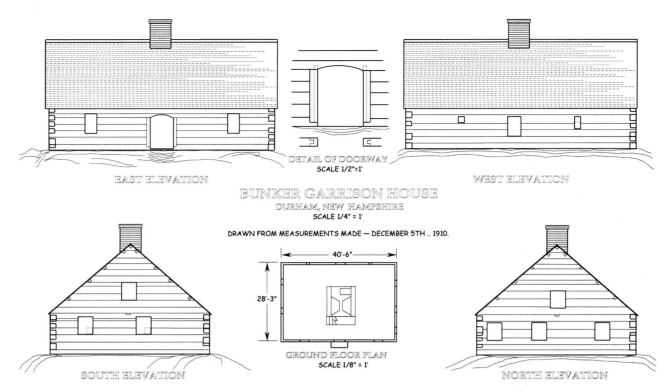

Copy of 1910 drawing by Charles R. Wait of the Bunker Garrison House, Durham, New Hampshire. Built before 1694 and in ruins by the early twentieth century, the Bunker Garrison was an example of a coastal log house built with notched corners and small windows, which were later enlarged. Many coastal log buildings were built of mill-sawn logs. Drawing by author.

England was a meetinghouse in Portsmouth, New Hampshire, built in 1659. A number of log structures are documented in coastal New Hampshire and Maine from the 1660s onward, many of them apparently serving as garrisoned houses or places of refuge during the recurring hostilities with Indian raiders from the north. Several log garrison houses survive in this region. Researcher Richard M. Candee has documented the fact that many of these structures were built of logs or thick planks sawn in water-powered sawmills, not hewn. Never more than a small minority of the structures standing in the coastal communities, these sawn log buildings were the product of an advanced technology. They represented an exploitation of the same industry that was rapidly reducing the forests of the coastal region to merchantable timber and lumber.

The situation apparently changed rapidly as the New Hampshire and Massachusetts governments granted the first inland townships in the 1720s. Early records of Londonderry, New Hampshire, settled by Scotch-Irish immigrants in 1719, make several references to log houses. While settlers in the new townships undoubtedly used sawn logs when they could obtain them, building contracts from the 1730s and later reveal that a number of these log structures were built of hewn timber.

By the 1760s, when the first detailed listings of house types were compiled in New Hampshire, the majority of buildings in the frontier settlements were "logg" or "poll" houses and barns, with framed houses in the minority. In 1771, for example, the town of Wolfeborough had seven framed houses (including Royal Governor John Wentworth's forty-by-one-hundred-foot mansion) and nineteen log houses. In 1771 the town of Limerick (later Stoddard), New Hampshire, contained fourteen log houses, twenty pole houses, three "camps," and six framed houses. It is likely that "log" houses were built of squared timbers, while "pole" houses were built of natural tree boles. In the same year, Washington, New Hampshire, had thirteen log houses, one pole house, and seven framed houses. Records from Maine suggest that some 60 percent of the dwellings in new settlements at the same period were log structures.

Wall detail, Pendergast Garrison House, Durham, New Hampshire. At the right is the wall of the original log house of circa 1735, showing the mill-sawn logs and dovetailed corner joints. At the left is the wall sheathing of a framed addition, showing sawn boards with beveled and lapped edges. Photograph by L. C. Durette, 1936. Library of Congress, Prints and Photographs Division, Historic American Buildings Survey, Reproduction Number HABS, NH, 9–DUR.V, 1.

Writing in 1792, New Hampshire historian Jeremy Belknap described the common house in new settlements as

a square building of poles, notched at the ends to keep them fast together. The crevices are plaistered with clay or the stiffest earth which can be had, mixed with moss or straw. The roof is either bark or split boards. The chimney a pile of stones; within which a fire is made on the ground, and a hole is left in the roof for the smoke to pass out. Another hole is made in the side of the house for a window, which is occasionally closed with a wooden shutter. . . . Many of these first essays in housekeeping, are to be met with in the new plantations, which serve to lodge whole families, till their industry can furnish them with materials for a more regular and comfortable house.

Clearly, these structures were regarded as temporary in nature. They were supplanted by larger and more permanent framed houses as soon as possible, and their replacement was regarded as proof of progress in any settlement. Inspecting the improvements that had been made in New Boston, New Hampshire, in 1759, one observer noted a family living in a house of round logs. Nearby, however, was the "frame of a house . . . with 4000 feet of boards lying at said frame . . . and a Cellar under the same," promising a more comfortable future for the family. In visiting General Henry Knox's Boston-inspired mansion at Thomaston, Maine, the duc de la Rochefoucault Liancourt remarked in 1795 that "the dwelling houses around are frequent; and out of a hundred that may be seen at the General's residence, there are hardly half a dozen log-houses."

For this reason, relatively few early log houses are to be found in northern New England. A number were mentioned and even photographed in the late nineteenth century, but most have since disappeared. Those that remain have often been covered with clapboards, and their identity has been hidden from the casual observer. Surviving log houses, including several in Maine and a number in Vermont's Champlain Valley and on the islands of Lake Champlain, provide rare glimpses of once dominant building traditions and technologies that have nearly vanished from the landscape.

Framed Houses

Wall Framing. In the northeastern United States the two genera of trees of essential importance in early building are the pines and the oaks. In constructing house frames, carpenters in the region north of the Merrimack River tended to choose pine, while those working south of that river preferred oak. Later in the eighteenth and early nineteenth centuries, as settlement extended north and inland, spruce was widely used as well, for both framing and sheathing.

Each region frequently used a combination of woods. With knowledge of native species gained over several generations, carpenters of the eighteenth and early nineteenth centuries departed from their routine when confronted by special circumstances. When building large dwellings or meetinghouses, for example, carpenters in the pine-framing region of northern New England sometimes turned to oak for their posts, knowing that extra strength

Eldridge Berry House, Campton, New Hampshire, said to date from 1775. Built of hewn logs pinned together with treenails at the corners, this house stood until the 1940s in a remote location in the foothills of the White Mountains. Its fireplaces were formed from upright slabs of flat stone, with a brick stack (removed before this photograph was taken) rising through the center of the roof. Photograph by L. C. Durette, circa 1937. Library of Congress, Prints and Photographs Division, Historic American Buildings Survey, Reproduction Number HABS, NH, CAMP.V, 1.

---

was required. Similarly, carpenters in the oak-framing region used pine where timbers of great continuous length and straightness were needed, as in the wall plates of a frame.

Framing was the province of the carpenter. The carpenter chose the trees for his timbers, cut them, shaped them, carried them to the building site, joined them, and erected the frame. Frames for buildings became a commodity, sometimes fabricated in roughly standardized sizes and prepared for center-chimney or center-entry houses and then offered for sale through newspaper advertisements or word of mouth. Such frames were even shipped from New England along the coast or to distant points within the British Empire. In the five years preceding the Revolution, for example, carpenters at the port of Piscataqua, the entrepot for the great timber region of

New Hampshire and Maine, exported 147 house frames to the West Indies.

Although the carpenter fabricated a house frame, it was usually the joiner or finish woodworker who actually planned a house and designed any special features that might be required in the frame, working with the carpenter to be sure that the frame matched the plan. Even where a house was built according to a drawn plan, however, it is not uncommon to find empty pockets and mortises in its frame. These reveal that the framers provided for regularly spaced joists or studs, which were ultimately omitted from the frame because of some unforeseen need—the placement of a chimney, for example. These empty pockets are frequently mistaken for evidence of later alterations to a building. In reality, joiners and bricklayers probably began to adjust a standardized frame soon after beginning their work on the house.

A house frame is a heavy and complex piece of craftsmanship. The skeleton of a three-story dwelling may contain thirty-five thousand board feet of timber or more and weigh some forty tons if made of pine, twice that if hewn from oak. In spite of their weight and bulk, house frames were routinely transported over long distances. In town dwellings, particularly, frames were usually fabricated at a carpenter's yard some distance away and then freighted to the building site for final assembly and raising. In 1781, for example, two traders in Rochester, New Hampshire,

Hewn pine timber, Old New Hampshire State House, Portsmouth, New Hampshire, 1758. As shown by its rippled surface, this timber was smoothed with an adze. The thin wedge inserted in the cut on the top was apparently intended to increase the camber, or crown, of the timber. Photograph by author.

agreed to supply a mariner in Newburyport, Massachusetts, with "a Good Frame done workmanlike, Forty feet in length & Nineteen in width, to be Delivered at Newburyport . . . According to a plan drawn by a Suitable man for Such a frame." The frame for the Governor John Langdon mansion in Portsmouth, New Hampshire, was hewn in 1784 in Stratham, a town fifteen miles distant, and probably transported largely by water. The frame of the three-story Amos Blanchard house of Andover, Massachusetts, was fashioned in 1819 in Temple, New Hampshire, and carried overland to its destination more than forty miles away.

From the late 1600s to the early 1800s, house framing techniques tended to become standardized in each region of the Northeast. Evidence suggests that the house frames built by immigrant carpenters from England during the seventeenth century were complex, reflecting a mature carpentry tradition in the mother country. Over the years, as the older generation of British-trained carpenters died and were supplanted by their American-born apprentices, framing sometimes became even more ambitious. But by the early 1700s (the date of the earliest houses likely to be encountered as private dwellings), framing practices had generally reached a norm from which they would not substantially depart until the end of the century. This is why it is difficult to date a house from its frame alone. Carpentry evolved too slowly through the 1700s in most locales to provide good benchmarks for dating. Unaffected by con-

cerns of changing style or fashion, individual carpenters tended to adhere to old habits that they might have learned as apprentices decades earlier.

The frames of houses built before the 1830s or 1840s, whether large or small, generally exhibit many features in common throughout most of northern New England. Such frames are based on English precedent and follow the general principle that all stresses in the frame are transmitted to the ground through relatively few principal posts. In most houses that are two rooms in width, either with a central chimney or a central entry or stairhall, these posts are usually eight in number. Other European traditions, especially Dutch and French, used many more than eight posts in their frames, and these posts were placed much more closely together than was the custom for English carpenters. Such traditions may occasionally be reflected in early buildings in western Vermont and northern Maine.

The major timbers of a house frame, whether oak or pine, are typically shaped by hewing with broadaxe or adze. This method of squaring encourages the use of large timbers. It begins with a length of tree trunk, which is transformed from round to square by cutting away the outer portions. Once the largest possible squared section has been achieved in a log of a given diameter, it clearly costs more in time and labor to reduce the dimensions of the timber still further. This encouraged the "over-engineering" of early house frames with timbers that were often much larger than necessary to carry the stresses encountered in small buildings.

In general, the members of house frames tended to become somewhat lighter over the years, with more and

White pine timbers being hewn. Iron staples, or "dogs," hold the logs in place as they are squared with a broadaxe. Photograph by author.

more of the timber being hidden behind the plane of the walls and ceilings until practically none of the skeleton projected into the rooms of the house.

In contrast to the hewn principal members of a frame, the smaller framing elements—the studs, diagonal braces, and often the floor joists—were typically sawn on an "upright" or reciprocating water-powered saw, even in the 1600s. As the eighteenth century drew to a close, it became more and more common in the sawmill regions of New England to saw the larger framing members as well. The sawing of major framing members had been technically possible since the introduction of water-powered sawmills in the early 1600s but was seldom resorted to. The earliest dwelling so far known to have a fully sawn frame, including posts and girts, is the Wentworth-Gardner house of 1760 in Portsmouth, New Hampshire. By the 1790s it was not uncommon to see rafters and other roof framing members sawn in both city and country houses. Sometimes the rafters were sawn with a taper, being deeper at the bottom than at the ridge, even though this required a careful skewing of the timber in the sawmill carriage.

The principal framing members of seventeenth-century houses—the posts, girts, and summer beams—were usually planed (or more roughly smoothed with an adze) after hewing. They were frequently decorated with molded chamfers on their exposed corners or arrises. These members were intended to be exposed to view.

After 1700, with few exceptions, the framing members in dwellings were intended to be covered, either by wall or ceiling plaster or by casings of planed one-inch boards. It is almost always a mistake to strip away such a covering and expose any part of the skeleton of an eighteenth- or nineteenth-century house in the belief that the builder intended this.

Except for rude frontier shelters, all of which have probably been consumed by the elements long ago, houses were always underpinned with some kind of stone foundation. Before the late 1700s, this foundation would have consisted of irregular stones, usually glacially rounded fieldstones used as found or split by impact and laid either loosely or in mortar to form a footing or a cellar wall. After granite splitting and quarrying techniques became widespread in the late 1700s, the portion of a foundation that lay above grade was often capped by a curb or underpinning of "hewn stone"—granite slabs that were split with wedges to chosen dimensions and often smoothed to a "true face" or plane surface with a toothed or textured hammer.

Sawn pine rafters, Ffrost Homestead, Durham, New Hampshire, circa 1800. By the late 1700s, as sawmill carriages increased in length, sawn framing elements often supplanted hewn members. Rafters were sometimes sawn on a skew so that they taper from eaves to ridge. Photograph by author.

Laid atop the foundation walls are the sills, the lowest members of a house frame. These horizontal members provide a base for the vertical framing elements and also a resting place for the first-floor joists. The joists of the first floor, sometimes referred to as sleepers, are commonly a series of rounded logs, ranging in diameter from six inches to a foot and hewn flat only on the upper surface, where the floor boards are nailed. Little labor was expended upon such joists except at the ends, where they were squared to form cogs that rest in notches in the sills. Such joists were often left unpeeled, and their still adhering bark will permit those familiar with trees to make quick identification of the species used to form them.

Standing upright on the sills are a series of bents or

A modern floor of sleepers (1993). Sleepers are straight tree trunks that are hewn flat on the top but otherwise left in their natural condition. Sleepers are the common framing members of the first stories of buildings built before the mid-1800s. Photograph by author.

transverse frames. In a two-story house built in the English tradition, a bent is an H-shaped framing unit consisting of two posts connected at their midpoint by a horizontal beam, called a girt, which runs through the house from front to back. The typical eighteenth-century house frame, whether intended for a central chimney or for a central hall, has four bents: one at each end and two near the middle of the house. If the house is a center-chimney dwelling, the chimney will stand in the space between the two inner bents. The posts of these bents are then called chimney posts, and the girts that run through the house on each side of the chimney are called chimney girts. If the house is laid out with a central stair hall (or "entry," as our predecessors called it), then the inner posts of the frame are called hall or entry posts and the girts that connect them become hall or entry girts.

One will occasionally encounter a house whose frame consists of a series of evenly spaced bents, with no sign of accommodation at the center for a chimney or entry. This

Corner of frame of an eighteenth-century two-story house with a purlin roof frame. Such houses typically have heavy posts at the corners and intermediate points. The posts carry most vertical stresses, with studs serving mainly to frame wall openings and to support the horizontal sheathing boards that are nailed to them. Diagonal braces strengthen the connections with horizontal members. Drawing by author.

type of frame often proves to have started its existence as a warehouse or shop. Such a building typically had no internal subdivisions and, if originally heated at all, had a chimney placed wherever convenient. Many such utilitarian structures were eventually converted to dwellings in the old coastal cities of New England, and deeper investigation of such an atypical house will often reveal that it began as a commercial structure.

The feet of the four bents of the typical house frame are anchored in the sills, usually by tenons. At the second-floor level in a two-story house, the bents are connected to one another along the front and rear walls by a second series of girts, which run along the front and rear walls midway up each post. This combination of posts and girts creates a boxlike skeleton locked at its feet by the sills and at its midpoint by a grid of girts running along the front and back walls and through the house.

This leaves the tops of the eight principal posts needing

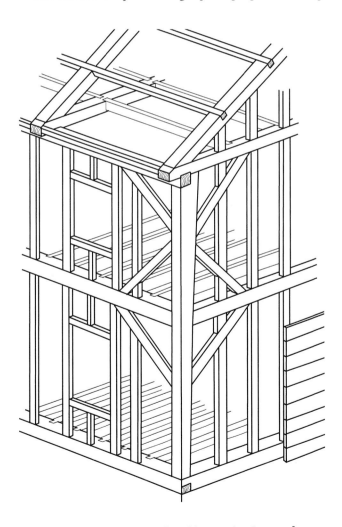

House frame, Deerfield, New Hampshire, circa 1800. Two-story houses that are built two rooms deep often have prick posts in their end walls, between the corner posts. These posts usually support the ends of beams that run longitudinally through the house just behind the chimney stacks. Photograph by author.

some form of connection that will lock them together and provide support for the roof structure. The tops of the posts are typically cut and tenoned by the carpenter into the most complex set of joints in a house frame. The tops of the posts must receive, first, a long timber that locks the upper ends of the posts together along the length of the building. This timber, called the wall plate, is, wherever possible, a single stick, forty or more feet long in a large house. Second, the tops of the posts must receive a series of transverse beams that serve two functions. Called tie beams, these timbers lock the back and the front of the frame together. Equally important, they serve as the bottom chords of the triangular frames that make up the roof system. Because the joints that accomplish all these functions are complex and require the cutting away of much

wood, the top of a post needs to be larger than the bottom, which merely needs to stand on the sill. For this reason, the tree trunk that is hewn into a post is often stood on its head, with the larger bottom of the tree forming the top of the post. In very early frames, the top of the post may have been hewn into a dramatic flare; nowadays, such a feature is popularly referred to as a "gunstock" post.

Roof Framing. With the plates in place atop the posts, the frame of a house becomes nearly a box. What are missing are front-to-back ties at the attic floor level and the roof itself. The tie beams, which provide this front-to-back connection, are typically placed (in northern New England construction at least) above each of the four bents of the house, with two additional ties halfway between each end-wall bent and each chimney or entry bent. These tie beams are locked to the top of the wall plates by dovetail joints on their undersides; additionally, in some carpentry traditions, those that fall above the four bents of the house are held down by tenons projecting upward from the very tops of the posts.

The typical full-length house built in northern New

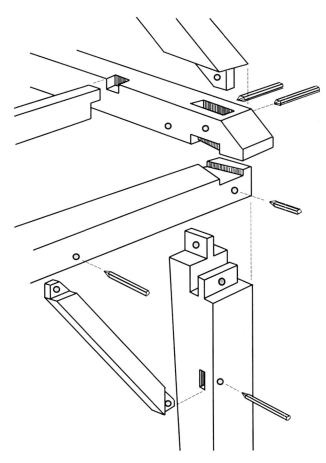

Upper corner of a typical eighteenth-century house frame. Exploded diagram showing the intersection between the rafter and tie beam (*top*), the wall plate (*middle*), and the corner post (*bottom*), with treenails (pins) and brace. Drawing by author.

(*Right*) Diagrams of (*top*) a purlin roof (purlins omitted from the rear slope of the roof for clarity) and (*bottom*) a common rafter roof. Common rafter roofs were often used in the upper Connecticut River valley during the 1700s and are found throughout northern New England after about 1830. Drawing by author.

England during the early to middle 1700s has six tie beams beneath its attic floor, with six sets of rafters rising from them. The feet of the rafters are tenoned into the tops of the tie beams, and thus the rafters and ties compose a triangular truss, capable of resisting almost any wind pressure. Through the addition of collar ties, which are additional horizontal timbers placed halfway up each rafter, the rafters may be strengthened against any tendency to bow under wind or snow loads.

After the mid-1700s, as settlers progressed northward through the Connecticut River valley and westward into Vermont, they brought somewhat different carpentry traditions with them from Connecticut and western Massachusetts. As settlers arrived in southwestern Vermont, they absorbed certain traditions from the Hudson River valley to the westward. This mixture of traditions began to introduce variations from the house-framing traditions described above.

The most notable departure from the eastern New England tradition lay in methods of roof framing. The traditional roof frame in coastal New Hampshire and southern Maine and in the areas settled by migrants from those regions was composed of a few sets of rafters, often spaced seven or eight feet apart. These sets of rafters are linked together at their base by tie beams and are connected to adjacent rafters by purlins that run along the length of the roof. In such roofs the sheathing boards are applied vertically, running from eaves to ridge.

By contrast, the roof frame that was favored by settlers traveling north from Connecticut or from western Massachusetts was composed of a series of closely spaced "common" rafters. Like the heavy rafters common in the coastal tradition, these are hewn in buildings dating before 1800 or so, after which they may be sawn. Common rafters tend to be somewhat lighter than those in rafter-and-purlin roofs. They are spaced at regular intervals, often from two to four feet apart. With such rafters, roof sheathing boards are nailed horizontally, running parallel to the

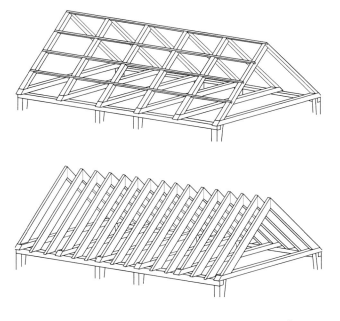

Roof frame, Sampson Doe House, Newmarket, New
Hampshire, circa 1706. The rafters of this roof frame
are supported at their midpoints by collar beams, a
common feature. The two summer beams supporting
the attic floor act as bridging members and receive the
ends of common joists. The house originally had a
central chimney that rose through the floor in the foreground. Photograph by L. C. Durette, circa 1937. Library of
Congress, Prints and Photographs Division, Historic American
Buildings Survey, Reproduction Number HABS, NH, 8 –
NEWM, 1.

Purlin roof, Deerfield, New Hampshire, circa 1800.
Purlins are long, straight tree trunks that are hewn flat
on top and let into the upper faces of the rafters.
Sheathing boards on purlin roofs run from ridge to
eaves. The rafters of this house were hewn with a broadaxe but not smoothed with an adze. Photograph by author.

A common rafter roof in the William Jones House, Claremont Plains, Claremont, New Hampshire, 1847–1850. Photograph by David S. Putnam.

eaves or ridge. Common rafters may be stiffened at their midpoints by collar beams. Common rafters rest on the wall plates, many of them at points distant from any tie beams in the upper frame. Since their feet are not tied together, common rafters may have a tendency to push the wall plates outward. For this reason, their collar beams may sometimes act as tension members, helping to restrain the spreading tendency of the unrestrained feet of the rafters.

Knee-Wall Frames. In a one-story house, like the typical "Cape Cod" cottage, the posts are only one story high, and the wall plates sit on their tops. Tie beams run across the wall plates from front to rear, linking the feet of the rafters and providing support for the attic floor. By the 1830s, however, the advent of the Greek Revival style brought with it a new type of one-story house, one in which the wall plates are supported a few feet above the attic floor at the tops of knee walls. These buildings are often referred to as "raised Capes" or "classic cottages."

In such a frame, the feet of the rafters rest on the plates without any tie between them. Not being connected to one another, the rafter feet tend to spread apart under wind and snow loads, pushing the front and rear walls outward. To resist this outward pressure, the timbers that run through the depth of the building under the attic floor must tie the front and rear walls of such houses together. It is unusual for floor timbers to be placed so

strongly in tension, and carpenters devised a variety of special joints to allow these floor joists to lock the front and rear walls together against the outward bending force of the rafter feet.

Both Dutch and French Canadian carpenters had brought knee-wall house framing traditions from continental Europe to North America in the 1600s. These timber framing traditions favored the story-and-a-half house, without the full second story that was common in British dwellings. Instead, houses built on these continental models had a garret, often covered by a gambrel roof in the Dutch settlements, that was given extra height by the knee wall that extends above the garret floor.

Whether covered by gable or gambrel roofs, these early knee-wall houses had to resist the spreading pressure exerted by the feet of the rafters pressing outward on the wall plates. To accomplish this, continental carpenters employed a multitude of closely spaced bents in their wall frames. Like bents in an English house, these are H-shaped units. Unlike the typical English two-story bent, the posts in a continental frame rise only a few feet above the crossbar of the "H" to create the knee wall. The crossbar is not a moderately sized girt tenoned simply into its two posts. Continental bents are called anchor bents, and they are connected by an anchor beam that is heavier than the common girt and is more solidly attached to the

Left: one form of Dutch anchor bent framing, seen in eighteenth-century buildings in the Hudson River valley and western Vermont and in Shaker meetinghouses built by Moses Johnson in the late 1700s. *Right*: one form of knee-wall construction, seen throughout New England by the 1830s. Drawing by author.

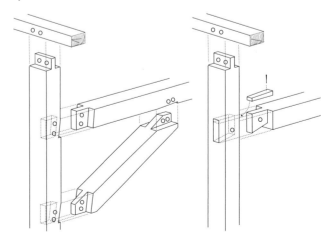

Roof frame, Matthew Harvey House, Sutton, New Hampshire, circa 1784. Large roof frames were often stiffened by diagonal wind braces that connect rafters and wall plates, preventing racking under wind loads. National Register of Historic Places photograph by Robert S. Bristol, 1992.

posts at its ends. In the Dutch tradition, anchor beams sometimes have tenons that extend fully through their posts. These projecting tongues are pinned on the exterior sides of the posts, allowing the beams to act as strong tension members and to resist the spreading forces of the roof above. Typically, joints between posts and anchor beams are further strengthened by curved knee braces or diagonal braces at each joint in each bent, not just in the end walls of the building as in the English tradition. By spacing a multitude of these anchor bents along the length of the building, carpenters in the Hudson River valley and in

Québec created staunch knee-wall frames that were well adapted to the one-and-a-half-story houses that were favored in those areas.

Though lying close at hand in New York and Québec, this tradition was seldom borrowed in northern New England during the 1700s and early 1800s. The most conspicuous adoption of the method was seen in the gambrel-roofed meetinghouses that carpenter Moses Johnson built in ten Shaker villages in New York and New England between 1785 and 1794. By employing braced anchor bents, Johnson was able to create undivided first-story halls in these buildings while providing residential spaces under the gambrel roofs, above the anchor beam level, for the Shaker elders. On a smaller scale, examples of anchor-bent construction are found in dwelling house framing in western Vermont, where they reflect Hudson River valley traditions.

Under the same influence, many barns in western Vermont employed anchor-bent framing (often referred to as dropped-girt framing) from the late 1700s onward. Unlike houses, which may employ a number of anchor bents along their length, these western barns usually employ only four such bents.

The advent of the Greek Revival style in New England brought with it a reason to build knee-wall houses. The high wall above the first-story windows could be covered with a deep Greek entablature, making the house a somewhat convincing replica of a small temple. Many knee-wall houses were built without this architectural embellishment simply to take advantage of a heightened garret.

The late acceptance of knee-wall construction in northern New England forced carpenters to adopt or reinvent some of the carpentry traditions that had long lain just outside the region. Rather than employing the traditional heavy anchor beam, with its diagonal bracing projecting down into the rooms below, New England carpenters devised methods by which the joints between posts and beams could resist considerable tension. Sometimes they employed only four bents in their house frames, in the time-honored English tradition; sometimes they employed a multitude of heavy wall studs that became, in effect, the posts of a series of light anchor bents.

Braces. Sills, posts, girts, and wall plates are the major elements of a typical timber house frame of the eighteenth or early nineteenth century. Yet no frame would be capable of supporting the thin skin of an ordinary house without more substance than this. Of primary importance, first, are a series of diagonal braces that lock most of the timber intersections on the outer envelope into miniature triangular trusses, keeping the frame square and staunch against racking. In roofs of large span, the rafters, too, may be connected to one another or braced against their intersecting purlins by long diagonal "wind braces," which keep the roof membrane from twisting in high winds.

The prevalence of these many diagonal braces distinguishes an early house frame from other types that followed in the nineteenth century. Thus, it was natural that some twentieth-century authors, in seeking to describe such a frame in texts on building construction, referred to it as the New England braced frame. In some conservative locales, prevailing custom or local building codes required that wooden houses be constructed with versions of the braced frame well into the twentieth century. These later versions of the traditional frame employed sawn posts,

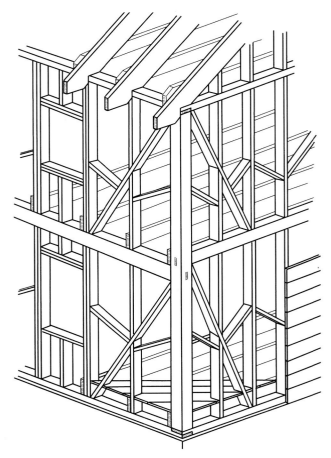

The New England braced frame. In contrast with other parts of the country, which adopted the balloon frame by the mid-1800s, some conservative builders in New England continued to employ an adaptation of the eighteenth-century house frame throughout much of the nineteenth century and occasionally into the twentieth. Drawing by author.

girts, joists, and other members but connected the posts and girts with mortise-and-tenon joints. These frames included diagonal braces to stiffen the frame in the traditional manner. Even today, carpenters' framing squares reflect the long prevalence of this ancient form of carpentry. The better squares retain brace-measure tables on their blades, giving the length of a forty-five-degree brace, having its mortises located at various distances from the post or girt.

A house frame also needs an infilling of smaller members to hold its roof, wall, and floor sheathing or boarding. The smaller members of the roof are called purlins. Usually composed of long, partly squared poles of spruce or pine, purlins run horizontally from rafter to rafter, resting in trenches cut into the upper surfaces of the rafters.

The smaller members of the wall are called studs. Studs are usually of square, sawn stock that was called slitwork and was not unlike the two-by-four-inch studs of modern times. The ends of studs are typically set into mortises cut into the sills, girts, plates, or tie beams.

The smaller members of the floors are called joists.

Except on the first floor, where rounded sleepers typically appear, joists are usually either hewn square or are sawn. Sawn joists, which became common in larger buildings by the mid-1700s, are usually two-inch planks with their ends supported by notches cut into the main horizontal members of the frame.

Sheathing. Both the outer frame of the house and the floor membranes must be covered with a skin of sheathing or boarding. Boards of eastern white pine have always been a major item of manufacture and export in the northeastern United States, where water-powered sawmills were set up as early as the 1630s. By 1718 almost a million board feet of pine boards were being shipped each year from the port of Piscataqua alone; by the period just before the Revolution the average annual export of sawn boards and planks from the same port had risen to over fourteen million board feet. Thus, it is natural that one-inch rough

Saw blade, frame, and carriage of the Nichols-Colby Sawmill, Bow, New Hampshire, first quarter of the nineteenth century. The "rag wheel" at the right advances the carriage on every down-stroke of the saw frame. This typical upright or "up-and-down" water-powered sawmill operated into the twentieth century and was destroyed in the hurricane of 1938. Historic American Buildings Survey photograph, circa 1936, courtesy of the New Hampshire Historical Society.

white pine boards (supplanted by spruce in more northerly regions) remained the normal material for house sheathing for centuries in northern New England.

Eighteenth-century pine boards were divided into three principal grades: clear, merchantable, and refuse. Each town appointed a surveyor or culler of lumber, usually someone who was thoroughly familiar with wood, to ensure that boards were properly manufactured at each sawmill and that they were properly measured in board feet when offered for sale. Clear boards were required by law to be at least a full inch thick and square-edged. As the name denotes, they were free of any significant knots, sap streaks, or other defects and were fit for use in finished joiner's work. Merchantable boards likewise had to be at least a full inch thick, square-edged, and fit for use in normal construction, but they could contain knots and other minor defects. Refuse boards were those of an inferior grade, culled out by the surveyors but still of some value and use in rough construction.

Depending on the quality of construction in an old house, boards of the merchantable or the refuse grades will be encountered as sheathing. The latter are knotty boards with waney edges. They are commonly seen as roof sheathing, where the gaps that occur naturally between their irregular edges are beneficial in allowing moisture to evaporate from beneath the wooden shingles.

Refuse lumber also may be found as subflooring and exterior wall sheathing. It was commonplace, however, for joiners to try to give each exterior wall sheathing board a straight edge and then to lap the horizontal joints with bevels that served to shed any water that might find its way behind the clapboards. Wall sheathing will therefore often be found to have been originally of fairly high quality, though it will commonly have become split and deteriorated by repairs, re-nailing of clapboards, and protracted leaks around window and door openings.

Upright or Reciprocating Sawmills. Until roughly the mid-1800s and later in some neighborhoods, boards were cut on reciprocating, or upright water-powered mills. Such mills had been known in Europe before the settlement of North America. Though rare in Great Britain because of the influence of guilds of hand-sawyers, water-powered (and occasionally wind-powered) mills were introduced in New England at the time of settlement. The first is said to have been erected at present-day South Berwick, Maine, in 1630. Thus, few New England houses

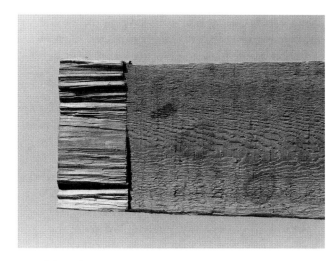

Detail, board sawn in an upright sawmill, early nineteenth century. Lumber sawn on upright mills retains parallel marks that record the forward motion of the log at each down-stroke of the blade. The sawmill carriage stopped before the blade reached the end of the log, and each board was snapped off, leaving a split end. Photograph by author.

of the eighteenth century or later will reveal any evidence of hand-sawn boards or framing members.

Mill-sawn boards, planks, joists, or larger framing members are readily recognized. The upright sawmill has a reciprocating, coarse-toothed saw blade stretched within a wooden frame. The teeth of the blade, like those of any rip saw, are set and filed to cut on the downward stroke. As the blade descends, the log is automatically advanced on its carriage about a quarter of an inch. The resulting board has a rough surface with obvious parallel striations spaced about a quarter of an inch apart. Close examination will reveal the presence of many torn wood fibers at each cut, giving the surface of the board a slightly fuzzy texture.

In any mill the length of the carriage that carries the log against the saw determines the maximum length of any board or timber sawn in that mill. In an upright mill, the carriage automatically stops when the blade has cut to a point about three inches from the end of the log. The sawyer then snaps the board off the log and returns the carriage to begin another cut. The split ends of sawn boards that have been used full-length are often seen in attic flooring or are revealed when subflooring is exposed to view.

The carcass of the New England house long retained its identity as a hewn frame (not uncommonly with some mill-sawn joists or braces), covered and floored with mill-sawn boards. During the 1790s, possibly because of the introduction of mills with longer carriages, sawn rafters and other major framing elements began to make their appearance in some areas.

Scribe Rule and Square Rule Framing. Beginning approximately in the 1830s, further changes began to manifest themselves and to signify an evolution in the thinking of New England carpenters. During this era, the traditional craft of the building framer began to move toward greater standardization. The older method of framing, used since the seventeenth century without radical change, began to give way to a new method. Writers of the nineteenth century, recalling the change, described it as the abandonment of the "scribe rule" method of framing and the adoption of the "square rule."

The scribe rule was the name given in the early nineteenth century to the "old-fashioned" method of framing that had persisted with only minor change since the days of first settlement. In using this traditional method to build the type of frame already described, carpenters laid out the entire frame on the ground, scribing each joint with dividers and a sharp awl or knife and then carefully cutting the mortises and tenons with a variety of augers and chisels. Because a hewn timber might not be perfectly square along its length, carpenters also frequently had to true up the faces of timbers at points where the tenon of an intersecting member joined, thus ensuring that members would meet at right angles. Using a chisel or a tool called a race knife, carpenters then marked the adjacent ends of intersecting members of the frame with identical numerals, similar to Roman numerals. These marks gave a unique number to each joint, allowing the frame to be reassembled on the building site exactly as it had been laid out and cut in the carpenter's building yard. In this method of framing, each joint was slightly different even from comparable joints elsewhere in the same frame.

The new square-rule method of framing, by contrast, produced a frame that tended toward standardization of parts. In this method, greater care was given to the drafting of a framing plan and the compilation of a timber schedule (a list of needed timbers) than had previously been common. With these aids, rafters, joists, studs, and other framing members could all be cut to needed sizes at different sites. When using the square rule, carpenters also prepared patterns for each type of joint, applying the pattern so that all mortises, tenons, pin holes, and other fea-

Framing numerals from a dwelling in Deerfield, New Hampshire, circa 1800. Each framing joint in a building constructed according to the "scribe rule" is unique. Each intersection is therefore marked with numbers, similar to Roman numerals, so that the joints fashioned by the carpenter in his yard can be reassembled when the frame is raised at its permanent site. Photograph by author.

---

tures of joints of the same type would be interchangeable. The timbers in a frame might not be of exactly the same width and depth (especially if hewn rather than sawn), but carpenters using the square rule applied their patterns with reference to lines drawn on each timber. By this means, each joint bore an identical relationship to others in the frame, even if the timbers varied somewhat in their dimensions.

Square-rule framing required that the seat of each joint be chiseled down below the irregular surface of the timber so that all seats would be equally distant from the lines drawn on the timber. The result is a noticeable cutting away of the outer surface of the timber at each joint—a clue that the carpenter was using the new, standardized framing method.

By this method of layout, all joints could be expected to fit perfectly when the framing members were brought together and erected. The term *square rule* probably derives from the dependence of the system on carefully squared joints laid out with a framing square and having standardized details. Often, especially after 1830 or so, the laying out of such joints was eased by the fact that framing timbers were mill-sawn rather than hewn and thus were perfectly regular in cross-section.

Introduction of the square rule did not do away with the traditional mortise-and-tenon method of joining timbers; it merely standardized the procedure so that each joint was no longer a unique feature. Other construction methods were introduced during the 1820s and 1830s. These likewise tended toward standardization of framing. Most important was the ever-increasing use of sawn timbers, joists, rafters, and other components. Houses built after 1830 not infrequently have wholly sawn frames.

Details of square rule framing in the upper corner of a house with a knee wall frame, circa 1830. Seats for joints are brought to a uniform distance from the center of the timber through the use of saw cuts and chiseling. Drawing by author.

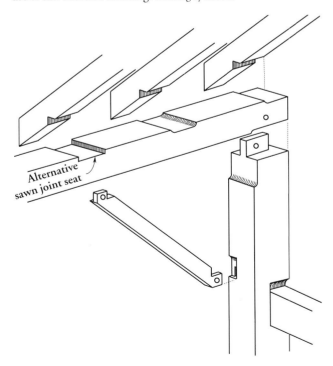

Floor and roof membranes also tended to become regularized during this period. Roofs framed entirely with common rafters, in the modern manner, began to appear. Floor joists increasingly became two-inch-thick planks, often spaced at the modern interval of sixteen inches on centers, sometimes at twenty-four inches. In general, it is clear that during the 1830s carpenters became increasingly concerned with standardization and less devoted to the traditional practices of their trade.

Plank Houses. An increasing use of the sawmill in house construction is revealed in another phenomenon: the plank house. Such houses appear in many variations throughout the northeastern United States, their precise form varying with their date and their location. In all of them, however, the wall studs and their horizontal one-inch sheathing boards are omitted from the frame. In the place of studs and sheathing, the frame is clad with thick, sawn, vertical planks that extend from sill to plate. The planks bear some or all of the stresses found in any exterior wall and also hold the frames of windows and doors, taking the place of the studs that usually define wall openings. The planks constitute the principal wall fabric, having clapboards applied directly to their outer surfaces and lath and plaster applied directly to their inner faces.

House frames covered with sawn planks or boards, applied vertically, were not uncommon in New England during the seventeenth century. The Jackson House in Portsmouth, probably the oldest dwelling in New Hampshire, was built in this fashion about 1664. This method of enclosing a frame appears to have been especially prevalent south of Boston in Plymouth County, Massachusetts, where the Pilgrim settlers may have introduced the concept from Holland. The practice spread south and west into Rhode Island and Connecticut, where a substantial number of early homes are enclosed with vertical planks. From there, the tradition appears to have spread up the Connecticut River valley all the way to northern New Hampshire and northern and western Vermont, where it provided an alternative to the stud-and-sheathing method of walling a house.

Perhaps in the late 1700s, and certainly by the early 1800s, a significant evolutionary step took place in the planked house. Whereas older examples had possessed a full frame, capable of standing on its own (and required to do so while the planks were applied to it), the newer form of plank house dispensed with all posts or other vertical

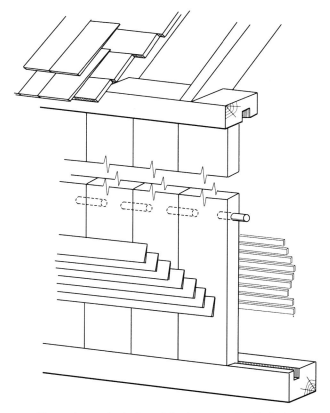

Alternative method of attaching bottoms of wall planks

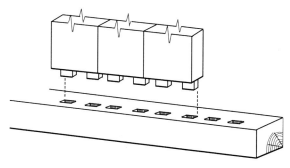

Wall section of a plank house, seen from the exterior. Vertical planks are often doweled together to prevent the wall membrane from racking under wind loads. Planks may be nailed or pegged to the outside of the frame, or their tops and bottoms may be let into trenches cut into sills and wall plates or tenoned. Drawing by author.

Plank-walled house, Epsom, New Hampshire, circa 1820. In this house, vertical planks are attached to the outside face of the frame, one of several methods of employing planks in wall construction. Photograph by author.

framing members. In such dwellings the walls are a solid membrane of planks, affixed in various ways to each other and to a sill at their feet and a plate at their tops. Such fully developed plank houses have attracted attention in the upper Connecticut River valley and northeastern Vermont, but they can also be found elsewhere throughout much of New England.

Sometimes, homeowners fail to realize that they live in a plank house until an electrician tries to snake wires through the wall cavities, only to find that there are *no* wall cavities. In other cases, owners know that their house has plank walls but assume that this is the usual way in which old houses were built. In most regions of New England, plank houses do not constitute the majority of old dwellings but represent a rather rare type. In all cases, the appearance of such houses suggests the one-time presence of a strong local lumber industry, where heavy planks, sometimes as much as three inches thick, could be purchased and transported economically.

A second form of plank construction is occasionally encountered in northern New England. This is the use

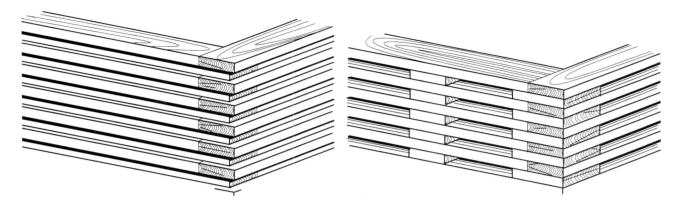

of planks, or one-inch boards, laid horizontally atop one another, like miniature logs in a log house, and nailed together to form a wooden wall without cavities. Sometimes, alternate courses of wall boards are laid in a staggered fashion that produces horizontal grooves in the wooden surface, permitting plaster to adhere to the inside of the wall. Sometimes, wide and narrow boards are laid in alternate courses to provide the same effect. Occasionally, the planks or boards are stacked at the corners but left with voids between them along the lengths of the walls, with a few blocks for intermediate support. The exteriors of such walls are covered with clapboards, shingles, or occasionally vertical boards and battens.

This "board wall" method of construction was first publicized in 1848 by the popular author and phrenologist Orson S. Fowler, who stated that he had earlier observed the method of construction in central New York. In his book *A Home for All; or a New, Cheap, Convenient, and Superior Mode of Building*, Fowler recommended board walls as both inexpensive and adapted to house plans of any shape, including Fowler's favorite — the octagon. This method of construction was also within the capacity of many homeowners, freeing them from the need to hire a professional carpenter. Fowler again described the method in the second edition of *A Home for All* in 1853, but by then he had become enamored of the "gravel" wall, composed of a lime-based concrete, and relegated his description of the board wall to the back of the volume.

Like the older and more common vertical plank construction, horizontal board or plank walls depend on plentiful and cheap supplies of sawn lumber. As Fowler noted, however, the board wall can make advantageous use of almost worthless knotty or waney-edged lumber that could "generally be procured just for the drawing of

Two types of wall construction using stacked boards or planks: (*left*) staggered boards; (*right*) spaced boards. Such walls are usually covered with clapboards or shingles but may be exposed to view and painted to imitate brick construction. Drawing by author.

the logs and sawing." This made the board wall potentially advantageous to anyone who had a woodlot and lived close to a sawmill.

The Balloon Frame. Despite the appearance of plank walls in some houses, the traditional braced frame remained the standard in New England for a long time. Examples of braced framing commonly appear until after the Civil War, and building codes in some communities required the use of this type of frame for certain kinds of structures into the twentieth century. During this same period, however, two factors were working against the braced frame.

The first was style: after the mid-nineteenth century, houses typically became more elaborate in plan and outline, with bay windows, towers, and complex, intersecting roof planes supplanting the simple, boxlike shapes favored in earlier years. The rigid, rectilinear skeleton of the braced frame was ill-adapted to the needs of such buildings.

The second was technology: machine-made nails were common and cheaper after 1800, and the introduction of the circular saw made the production of sawn boards and scantling (light framing timbers) quick and inexpensive. These new factors offered the promise of speed, economy of labor and materials, and flexibility of plan. With a burgeoning American population creating an unprecedented need for new housing, it was virtually guaranteed that some alternative framing method would appear by the mid-1800s.

The alternative that appeared was radically different from any framing method previously seen in North America. This was the so-called balloon frame, named in derision by traditional carpenters, who saw it as having no more strength and rigidity than the silk balloon of the period. The balloon frame is composed of a multitude of sawn two-by-four-inch studs, each extending from the sill to the plate of the frame. To these studs is attached a ledger board called a ribband or ribbon, and upon the ribband rest the ends of sawn joists, placed beside and at the same interval as the studs. The roof is framed in a similar manner, using only sawn common rafters.

Since the eighteenth century or earlier, laths for plaster had been sold in a standard length of just over four feet. By spacing the members of a balloon frame so that a four-foot lath would extend across three stud, joist, or rafter intervals, carpenters arrived at a standard spacing of sixteen inches for all elements of a balloon frame—an interval that has remained unchanged to the present day for all American framing.

The clear advantage of such a frame is its simplicity. It can be erected without complicated joints, being fastened together by nails only. Where sawn scantling is available, the framing members can be cut to size using only a framing square and hand saw. The two-by-four-inch studs and two-by-eight or two-by-ten-inch joists and rafters can be taken directly from the sawmill and used with only a few cuts to their ends, since they are small enough in cross-section to be fastened by nails alone.

Such a frame demands only that the carpenter have an ample supply of nails and scantling. It requires no large timbers and no complicated joints. It permits rapid construction, not only because it is merely nailed together but because every stud, joist, or rafter is the same as every other, except where openings for doors, windows, staircases, or chimneys may occur. Its sixteen-inch spacing of framing members guarantees a nailing surface for laths, for boards that are cut to standard lengths of eight, twelve, or sixteen feet, and (more recently) for expanded metal lath, gypsum board, and plywood, which retain the four-foot width of eighteenth-century laths.

Being assembled from a multitude of small members, the frame is easily adaptable to a plan that might include porches, bay windows, towers, and complex, intersecting roofs. As the carpenter's traditional two-foot square slowly evolved during the nineteenth century into the sophisticated framing square, with its many scales and

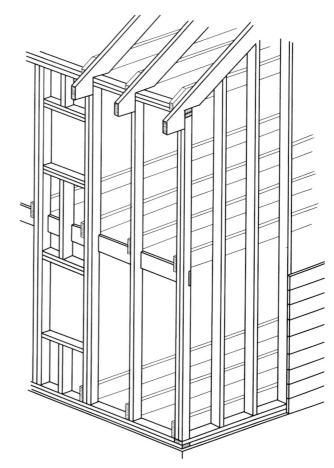

Balloon framing, early method. Early balloon frames were lightly constructed, with no firestops in their wall cavities and with horizontal sheathing that provided little resistance to racking. Drawing by author.

tables, an intelligent carpenter could solve almost any problem posed by a complicated house design with this tool alone.

The disadvantages of the frame were equally clear to the traditional carpenters who ridiculed it. Being held together merely with nails, the balloon frame had no inherent rigidity. Being assembled with scantling, the floor and roof membranes might easily be framed too lightly to support normal loads. And as experience quickly showed, the continuous stud spaces of the frame, running from cellar to attic, provided dangerous, hidden flues that could quickly carry a fire in the lower parts of the house to the upper rooms and the attic. In comparison with the traditional frame, with its substantial timbers and its bracing, the balloon frame seemed insubstantial indeed.

Improvements to the Balloon Frame. Many of the problems of the balloon frame were overcome by thoughtful experimentation. Despite its flimsy appearance, the frame was found to be surprisingly rigid once it was sheathed. Carpenters had long known that a traditional braced frame was made even more rigid once the skeleton began to be covered with boards. It now became apparent, in a similar way, that the multitude of small members of the balloon frame, once linked together by a skin of sheathing, began to act as a single membrane. The effectiveness of this membrane was found to be enhanced when the sheathing was applied at a forty-five-degree angle rather than horizontally, thus providing a diagonal bracing effect that carried wall stresses directly down to the sills and

---

Balloon framing, mature method. Fully developed balloon framing includes firestopping in the wall cavities and diagonal wall sheathing and subflooring to resist racking. Bricks are sometimes employed as firestops above the sills. Drawing by author.

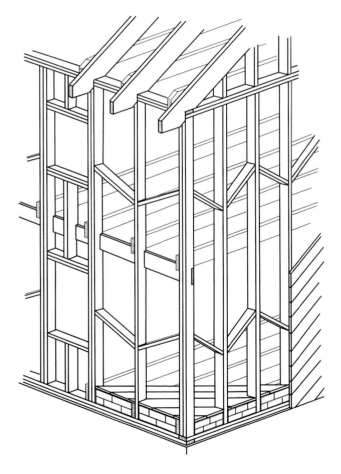

foundation of the house. Lath and plaster on the inside of the frame, of course, increased the effectiveness of the walls as membranes.

Carpenters also discovered that floors framed with light scantling could be strengthened by simple expedients. The nailing of a row of bridging (crossed bracing members) at the midline of a floor greatly enhanced the solidity and strength of the floor by stopping the lateral flexing of the individual joists. Similarly, the laying of subflooring at a forty-five-degree angle to the joists transformed each floor of a house into a stiffened horizontal membrane within the structure.

Finally, a remedy for the fluelike effect of the stud spaces of the balloon frame was easily provided by mortaring a few bricks between the studs at the cellar level and by inserting scraps of studding as a line of wooden firestops at intervals up the wall. These wooden barriers stopped not only the hot gases of a house fire but also the normal convection currents that made the walls colder in winter. They also acted as stiffeners in the walls, comparable to lines of bridging in the floors.

The balloon frame was not invented in the eastern states, which had a long tradition of heavy framing. According to widely accepted tradition, the balloon frame was developed out of necessity in Chicago, by George Washington Snow (1797–1874), who had moved west from Keene, New Hampshire. Snow supposedly used this makeshift method of framing a waterfront warehouse in 1832 when he presumably could not obtain enough heavy timbers for a normal frame. Some researchers say that the first appearance of the frame was in a small Catholic church building erected in Chicago in 1833 by Augustine D. Taylor, a local carpenter. In either case, the method was quickly adopted in the timber-poor prairie states and is credited with meeting the almost insatiable housing needs caused by the great westward expansion of the mid-nineteenth century.

If Snow was, in fact, the first to use the balloon frame, it may be that he was inspired to attempt this light framing method by some of the developments he had observed near Keene. Southwestern New Hampshire appears to have seen the use of all-sawn house frames, with common rafter roofs, by 1830 or earlier. The same region has many plank houses, some of them walled entirely with sawn planks, without posts or studs, thereby suggesting the feasibility of eliminating the traditional heavy frame.

Despite such experimentation, however, New England

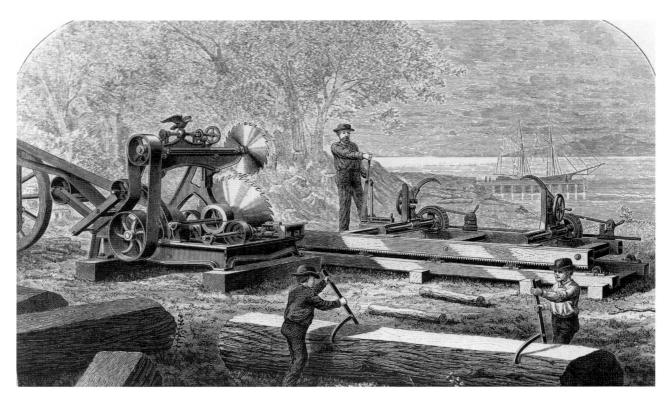

was slow to give up the principle of the braced frame. As late as 1843, New England author Asher Benjamin published a book illustrating a light form of the braced frame that used two-inch-thick sawn joists but still relied on heavier posts and mortise-and-tenon joints. Although other books began to illustrate the balloon frame by 1860, examples of the type are rare in New England until after the Civil War. Even then, New England balloon frames often reveal oversized sills, corner posts, and plates, sometimes connected to one another by pinned mortise-and-tenon joints in the time-honored manner. Such frames differ from older types only in having ribbands instead of girts and in having wall studs that extend in one piece from sill to plate.

Adoption of the balloon frame depended on two factors: cheap nails and cheap scantling. Inexpensive nails began to appear just before 1800, when machines were introduced to supplant the ancient method of forging nails by hand. Inexpensive two-inch-thick lumber, on the other hand, did not appear until later. The economical production of small-dimension lumber depended largely on the speed of the saw. As long as slow reciprocating saws remained in use, the production of a multitude of two-by-four-inch studs, for example, remained a time-consuming (and hence an expensive) process. That is why the studding

Circular sawmill. This portable sawmill operated on the same principles as permanent water- or steam-powered mills. In both cases, a carriage advanced the log against a rapidly revolving toothed disk. In this case, two blades were employed to permit the mill to saw large logs without the need for a blade of great diameter, which tended to vibrate. From *Appleton's Cyclopaedia of Applied Mechanics* (New York, 1885).

of older houses is often found to consist of wide planks (sometimes roughly split into narrower ones) instead of two-by-fours of the modern type (see figure, page 66).

Circular Sawmills. Faster sawing of lumber resulted from two developments. The first was the widespread adoption during the early nineteenth century of the water-powered turbine in place of the vertical water wheel. With its high speed of rotation, the turbine proved to be the ideal power source for woodworking machinery of all kinds.

The second revolutionary development was the introduction of the circular saw. Unlike the upright or reciprocating saw, which cuts only on the downward stroke of a flat toothed blade, the circular saw cuts continuously. Depending on the diameter and speed of the blade and the rapidity with which the carriage is advanced against the saw's teeth, the circular saw can cut a board in seconds. An upright saw, cutting about a quarter-inch on each stroke, might require ten or twelve minutes to cut a board from a sixteen-foot log.

The circular saw is a toothed iron or steel disk, mounted in a vertical plane and rotating at high speed. Such saws had been the subject of experimentation and patent in eighteenth-century England and were known in the United States by the early years of the nineteenth century. In their earliest commercial uses in New England, during the 1820s and 1830s, such saws seem to have been restricted to such uses as the cutting of shingles, clapboards, and small-dimension millwork rather than being employed in the large-scale production of lumber. As late as the 1870s and even into the twentieth century, many of the smaller and older sawmills in the lumber country of northern New England were still using upright saws.

At the same period, however, many advances in the design and metallurgy of circular saw blades, as well as the introduction of steam to power very large sawmills, made cheap, circular-sawn scantling easily available in all areas and encouraged the adoption of the balloon frame. The further abandonment of older framing methods was encouraged by the introduction of the inexpensive wire nail during the 1880s.

Whether the upright or the circular saw was used in their manufacture, boards were used in a rough state, just as they came from the sawmill, when applied as wall or roof sheathing or as subflooring. When used as sheathing, such boards served the dual purpose of roughly enclosing the frame of a house and of providing a substratum for a waterproof covering.

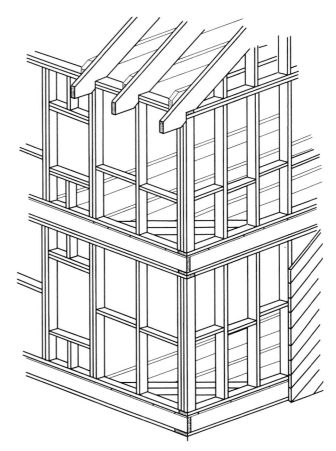

Western, or platform, frame. Introduced in eastern construction during the early twentieth century, the western frame is a variant on the balloon frame. It has an independent floor frame at each story, offering ease of construction, integral firestopping, and uniform shrinkage. Drawing by author.

Characteristic marks of the circular sawmill. Photograph by author.

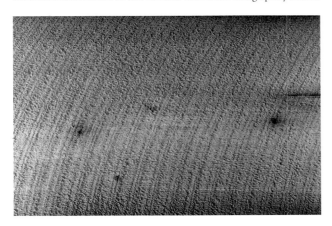

The Western, or Platform, Frame. The early twentieth century saw the introduction into New England carpentry of yet another evolution of the balloon framing technique. Like the classic balloon frame, the western, or platform, frame is built of light, sawn studs, joists, and rafters, all nailed together. But the platform frame, as its name implies, is constructed one story at a time. Each wall has a two-by-four-inch sole at its base, and a plate, usually consisting of doubled two-by-fours, at its top. Each story is built as an independent unit or box. Each floor membrane is fully boarded with its subflooring. This solid floor offers a safe and convenient surface on which to frame the walls that will rest on that floor. Since the walls are framed one story at a time, they can be laid out on the floor, nailed together, and then tipped upright as units. Western framing offered the first method of house construction that did not call for handling and erecting timbers or studs that were two stories high.

The platform frame quickly superseded the balloon frame. Because it has a fully framed and boarded floor membrane at each story, this frame eliminates the long stud spaces that pose a fire danger in the classic balloon frame and thus eliminates the need for inserting firestops at or between the floor levels. Because it uses scantling of shorter lengths, the platform frame takes advantage of standard "mill run" stock, eliminating the custom sawing of long members and offering economies both in materials and labor. Lacking long studs, the platform frame is inherently more rigid than the balloon frame, especially if boarded diagonally or if diagonal board braces are recessed into the faces of its studs and corner posts. Because each floor of the platform frame supports both the external walls and the interior partitions of the story above, the platform frame shrinks evenly, eliminating the differential settlement that was common with both the braced frame and the balloon frame.

Hand-split and shaved pine shingles. *Left to right*: shingle of circa 1715; shingle of circa 1800 with gray paint; shingle of circa 1865. Photograph by Bill Finney.

Roof Coverings: Wooden Shingles. Until well into the twentieth century, the most common waterproof covering for roofs has been the wooden shingle. In northern New England, such shingles have traditionally been nailed directly to the upper face of roof sheathing, using light nails of the type (forged, cut, or wire) most available in a given period.

In the rafter-and-purlin roof frame, which remained the norm in northern New England until the early nineteenth century, roof sheathing boards were applied vertically, running from the ridgepole down across the purlins to the eaves. Such a heavily sheathed roof provides good support against snow loads. But wooden shingles need ventilation of their undersides, so refuse-grade lumber, with its characteristic waney edges and resulting gaps between boards, is often encountered as roof sheathing in eighteenth-century houses. In cases where straight-edged merchantable lumber was used for roof sheathing, carpenters often deliberately left spaces between adjacent boards to afford some ventilation for the wooden shingles. Very rarely, one will find sheets of birch bark applied beneath shingles, evidently as a flashing against water or as a wind stop. Since such an impermeable substance prevents the ventilation of the undersides of shingles, its use was probably counterproductive and therefore is seldom

seen except around openings for chimneys, skylights, or scuttles.

In more southerly locales and in regions where roofs of closely spaced common rafters were traditional, wooden shingles are often nailed directly to wooden strapping or shingle laths that run between rafters, instead of to a substratum of solid roof sheathing. Such a method provides the maximum amount of ventilation for wooden shingles. Recognizing the need for ventilation beneath such shingles, some carpenters in northern New England emulated the southern system by applying horizontal battens to the upper faces of roof-sheathing boards and nailing the shingles to these. This method (sometimes seen in shingling jobs of the late nineteenth and early twentieth centuries) has the advantage of retaining the snow-load-bearing capacity of solid roof sheathing while offering the best possible ventilation of the shingle covering. As common rafter roofs with horizontal sheathing boards became popular in the 1830s and later, these boards could be spaced some distance apart to offer wooden shingles almost the same degree of ventilation as roof battens.

The most common species used for wooden shingles in northern New England was eastern white pine. Oak and cedar were frequently chosen in Massachusetts and southern New England, and cedar was also employed in the

Champlain Valley of western Vermont. But the straight-grained pine of the northern regions, much more plentiful there than cedar, was split into shingles from the earliest days of settlement. Pine shingles became a major item of export as well as of domestic consumption. In the year between the summers of 1718 and 1719, 615,000 shingles were exported from Piscataqua alone; in the five years between 1770 and 1775, almost 42 million shingles left the same port.

Shingles were split with a froe (a cleaving tool driven into the wood with a beetle or mallet) from a bolt of clear, straight-grained pine. After the rough shingle was split off, it was clamped in a device called a shaving horse and was smoothed and tapered with a drawknife. A New Hampshire law of 1760 required that all merchantable shingles be either fifteen or eighteen inches long, at least three inches wide, and half an inch thick at the butt, "well rived and shaved." A finished shingle made by this method has a smooth face and back, showing the natural irregularities of straight-grained wood only in a few areas where the drawknife has not removed all evidence of splitting. When not weathered, such shingles possess a smoother surface than the later sawn shingles.

Occasionally, one will encounter homemade shingles that do not meet this standard and were left rough, especially at the butt, where they were clamped in the jaw of the shaving horse. These are akin to the roughly split "shakes" sold today for rustic effect, although modern shakes are even cruder in appearance. These partially finished split shingles do not represent the normal, carefully shaved quality of the merchantable shingle of the eighteenth or early nineteenth century.

Hand-split shingles, sometimes advertised as "rift" shingles, were marketed as an alternative to sawn shingles at least as late as the 1860s and were undoubtedly made by rural people for their own use into the twentieth century. Various machines were devised during the nineteenth century to split bolts of wood into rough shingles, which were finished with a drawknife. Shingles made on such a machine are usually indistinguishable from those made completely by hand with a froe, and such machines continued in limited use into the twentieth century. It is possible, therefore, to encounter split shingles in utilitarian use even after 1900. Beginning in the early 1900s, architects sometimes specified hand-split shingles for deliberate architectural effect.

Beginning in the 1820s, however, a number of New

England inventors began to devise ways to use the new circular saw as a means of cutting shingles from short bolts of wood. Such machinery offered a great saving in labor and became especially popular as the initial patents expired and users no longer had to pay royalties to use the new technology. Small water-powered shingle mills began to appear on streams throughout rural New England. By 1850, New Hampshire alone had over five hundred water-powered sawmills, which manufactured nearly thirty million shingles each year; by 1874, the number of mills had increased to 762, and the production of sawn shingles had risen to nearly seventy million. Sawn shingles are easily distinguished from split shingles by the curving marks of the circular saw that are visible on their unweathered surfaces.

While most wooden shingles were undoubtedly applied to roofs with no further treatment, many were painted. Areas of roofing from the eighteenth and early nineteenth centuries that have survived beneath later coverings frequently reveal the use of color. The most common pigments found on surviving examples are Spanish brown, red ochre, and various grays. Documents frequently mention the use of red for meetinghouse roofs of the period, and this preference was undoubtedly reflected on the roofs of private houses. Some wood-shingle roofs were covered with a mastic of pine tar as an alternative to paint. In 1773, the town of Rindge, New Hampshire, voted to cover the wooden shingles of their meetinghouse roof with pitch and sand, thereby ensuring better resistance to the sun and weather than paint or tar alone could offer.

The fashion of painting or staining wooden roof shingles persisted to a large extent into the twentieth century. The continuing use of roof colors was fostered by the increasing sophistication of Victorian paint theories and fashions and by the ready availability of inexpensive oil-based stains that allowed shingles to be dipped before laying instead of being painted after they were nailed on. Colored wooden roofs also imitated more costly colored roof coverings like slate.

Composition Roofing. Other roof coverings supplemented wood shingles during the nineteenth century. The development of alternative roofing materials was largely spurred by the fear of fire in the compact cities of New England. Since the 1600s, Boston had adopted laws (largely unenforced) requiring buildings to be roofed with slate. A rash of devastating fires in the years immediately after 1800 in several New England cities renewed interest in fireproof roofing materials. One technique, used only rarely on private dwellings, called for roofs to be built in the form of slightly pitched decks. These were covered with a "composition" of pine tar (the only tar then readily available) and gravel. Composition roofs made with pine tar were not as successful as those made later with bituminous tars. They tended to leak badly within ten to twenty years, after which they were invariably covered with a more traditional roofing material and usually with an entirely new high-pitched roof frame. Traces of composition roofs have occasionally been found beneath these later roofs on New England houses, usually on large and ambitious Federal period dwellings whose original owners were anxious to flaunt an unusual flat-roofed design.

Slate Roofing. Much more common was the old idea of roofing with slate. Slate had been quarried in New England since the 1600s but was only rarely used as a roof covering, except perhaps in Boston. By the late 1700s, slate was being imported from Wales, but because of its weight and difficulty of transportation, it was probably of little use beyond its ports of entry. Nevertheless, the relatively cheap price of Welsh slate tended to discourage the growth of a New England slate industry for many years.

The idea of roofing with slate was widely recommended in the years immediately after 1800 as a result of several great urban fires in New England. These fires had spread out of control largely because wind-borne brands from dry wood-shingled roofs had quickly ignited other such roofs. Yet despite its fireproof nature and resistance to weathering, slate was adopted for roofing houses almost exclusively in seaports and other large cities.

In 1812, however, a slate quarry was opened in Guilford, in Vermont's lower Connecticut River valley. Other quarries were subsequently developed in eastern Vermont, providing roofing slate of good quality to nearby communities in both Vermont and New Hampshire and along the lower stretches of the Connecticut River. The first commercial roofing slate quarries in western Vermont were opened in 1847, and within ten years were producing forty-five thousand squares of roofing, nearly twice the amount imported from abroad. (A square of roofing is enough material to cover one hundred square feet of roof surface.) The quarries of western Vermont and adjoining New York produce slate of several unique colors, including the widely used sea green and highly prized purple and red slates. By about 1850, other quarries were being developed in central Vermont, notably at Northfield. Meanwhile, excellent roofing slates were discovered in Maine, with some quarries opened by the 1830s.

The large-scale growth of the roofing-slate industry in New England, with its strong effect on buildings over a widespread area, was not possible until the development of an extensive railroad network during the midcentury. After long-distance transportation of slate became feasible, Pennsylvania slates were introduced into the New England market, broadening the range of available materials, and roofers began to mix slates in polychrome patterns and to add hitherto unknown colors and patterns to roofs.

Metal Roofing. Metal roofing also was attempted on an increasing scale during the nineteenth century. Sheet lead for flashing and other limited roofing uses had been imported from England since the 1600s, and occasional evidence of its early presence can be found in eighteenth-century houses. Because of its cost, however, lead was seldom used as the principal roof covering for houses in New England, although records tell of some Boston houses roofed entirely with lead in the early 1700s.

Sheet copper was manufactured in the United States in increasing quantities beginning in the 1790s, at first largely for covering ships' hulls to reduce fouling. As it became more readily available and less expensive, sheet copper was used more frequently on buildings. By 1815, New England writers were recommending copper as a roofing material, but the use of copper in the early years of the nineteenth century seems to have been restricted largely to difficult areas such as the domes of public buildings, bell decks in steeples, and the flat roofs of doorway porticos. The use of copper as a roofing material increased in the latter part of the nineteenth century. Due to its expense, however, copper was more used for roofing public buildings than for private houses.

Not long after American-made sheet copper began to be available, a cheaper metal roofing material appeared in the marketplace. This was tin-plated sheet iron. At first imported from Britain in the early nineteenth century, tinned iron became a commonplace roof covering as workmen gained experience in its application and knowledge of its behavior under varying climatic conditions. At first applied as a flat roof membrane with soldered joints, tinplate was eventually joined by using the "standing seam" common today on pitched roofs. Originally made

Advertisements for iron and steel roofing, *Scientific American, Architect's and Builder's Edition*, September 1891.

from sheets of iron dipped in molten tin, the material evolved into tin-coated steel as the cost of steel declined in the late nineteenth century. In the 1930s an electrolytic tin-plating process superseded the dipping of steel into molten tin.

During the first half of the nineteenth century, tinplate roofing was most common on ambitious buildings, both public and private. As the material became cheaper following the Civil War, it began to appear more frequently on smaller homes. It was especially favored in areas of heavy snowfall, since its smooth surface encouraged snow to slide off a roof rather than accumulating to a dangerous weight. During the late nineteenth century, sheets of tinned steel were frequently stamped with ornamental patterns to resemble shingles or tiles and were manufactured with interlocking joints that permitted unsoldered installation, using nails alone. Some of these products were manufactured in strip form, with each strip embossed to look like several shingles; others took the form of interlocking individual shingles.

Because tin is an expensive metal, almost wholly imported from Britain, American manufacturers sought other metallic coatings for sheet iron or steel roofing. Tin

was frequently alloyed with lead as a coating for sheet iron or steel. Called terneplate, this type of metal roofing has a dull finish before painting, in contrast to the bright silver of a pure tin coating. Both tinplate and terneplate roofing require a well-maintained coat of paint for longevity.

Zinc, of which America had an ample domestic supply, was a favored substitute for tin or terne coatings on metal roofing. Zinc-coated iron roofing began to compete with tin by the late 1830s. At first, iron or steel was hot-dipped in a bath of molten zinc, producing a thick and durable protective coating. True galvanizing, in which a coating of zinc is applied to iron or steel by electrolytic action, was developed during the 1840s and eventually became a widely used method of zinc-plating plain, corrugated, and stamped or embossed sheets of iron or steel. Like tin- and terne-plated roofing products, zinc-plated roofing was manufactured both as strips and as individual, interlocking shingles.

Asphalt-Felt Roofing. Wooden shingles, slates, and metal roof coverings were almost the only roofing products available until the late nineteenth century. An important new family of roofing products began to make its appearance in the 1880s. These were the asphalt-impregnated wool felts, which took the form of building papers, roll roofing, and shingles. These products have multiplied and diversified during the past century to become the predominant form of roof covering in the United States.

Asphalt-impregnated felt was first marketed as a roll roofing material, either with a smooth (often mica-covered) surface or with a granular or mineral-faced surface composed of crushed slate or granite pressed into the asphalt. Around 1900, the mineral-faced form of asphalt-impregnated felt began to be marketed as roofing shingles, cut first as individual rectangles and, after about 1915, as strips with notches that simulated the butts of two or three individual shingles. This form of roofing persists today with little change except for a wider variety of colors and butt designs and changes in the felts employed.

Roofing Tiles. Also increasingly available in the late nineteenth century were artificial roofing materials that vied with slate in durability. Roofing tiles, made of clay and baked like bricks to a ceramic hardness, were available in a wide variety of shapes and colors by the turn of the twentieth century. They were costly and so appear mostly on public buildings and on the more expensive private dwellings. Because of their considerable thickness and weight, roofing tiles tend to resist breakage and to offer a very durable roof covering. Like slate, they sometimes outlast the nails with which they were fastened to the roof; thus, a common failure is the slippage of the tile due to corrosion of the nails.

Cement-Asbestos Shingles. A second artificial product that gained widespread favor shortly after 1900 was the cement-asbestos shingle. Formed under great pressure from the newly available mineral fiber asbestos, and from Portland cement, these shingles were first marketed by the

---

Advertisement for Heppes "Giant" asphalt roofing shingles, *The National Builder*, July 1914. Newly introduced to the market at this period, asphalt roofing shingles were made from asphalt-impregnated wool felt, covered with granules of crushed slate. Most early asphalt shingles were individual sheets that approximated the size of wooden shingles.

Keasebey and Mattison Company as "Century" shingles and by the Johns-Manville Company as "Transite" shingles. They were formed with square butts, sometimes clipped at the corners to create a hexagonal pattern, for laying in the "American" method of horizontal courses. They were also made in a diamond shape for laying in the "French" or "Russian" method, which created diagonal courses of shingles and saved on the cost and weight of the shingles. Because of their thinness and gray color, cement-asbestos shingles resemble weathered wood shingles, especially when covered with moss or lichens. They are a very durable roof covering, though they have a tendency to crush or split if roughly treated by roofers.

Exterior Wall Coverings: Clapboards. Until the twentieth century the walls of New England houses were covered with a much narrower range of materials than roofs were. Many records attest to the fact that houses in the seventeenth and eighteenth centuries were often covered only with sheathing boards (undoubtedly with their edges beveled or half-lapped) nailed horizontally to the frame. These were left exposed to the weather, sometimes for generations, and apparently served as an adequate if not ideal type of wall covering. Most of the houses covered with such "weather boards" were modest dwellings owned by poor people and so had a short life. This type of wall treatment therefore appears more often in written nineteenth-century reminiscences than as a physical survival. On rare occasions, however, carefully jointed sheathing bearing the marks of long exposure to the weather is discovered under a later covering of clapboards.

In general, however, the New England climate demanded a better wall covering than mere boards. Driving rain and snow easily penetrate any form of covering that does not have a strong overlap, almost like the covering of a roof. For this reason, the clapboard, known but not widely used in England, was quickly adopted by the first settlers as an appropriate wall treatment for New England houses. With minor changes, the clapboard remains a favored and highly effective wall covering.

In northern New England the eastern white pine was quickly discovered to be the ideal wood for clapboards. As was the case with framing, shingling, and splitting laths, southern New Englanders of the eighteenth century strongly preferred to use oak instead of pine for clapboards during the eighteenth century. The northern pine forests offered an almost inexhaustible supply of clap-

Asbestos "Century" Shingles

The Architectural Possibilities of this Artificial Roofing Slate

THE residence of James Hough, Toledo, Ohio, here shown, is a fine example of a style of architecture where the roof plays an important part. Asbestos "Century" Shingles, because of their variety of shape and different colors make a roof that has architectural character and is not a mere covering for a house.

The Architect, Mr. Wm. Thurstin, and the Contractor, Mr. J. McClintich, both of Toledo, are to be congratulated on its fine appearance.

It is the **patented "Century" process** that makes these Shingles possible. A light-weight, fireproof roofing material—uniform in texture, with a durability never before practical with any artificial or natural roofing material.

If you have not the facts about the Asbestos "Century" Shingles—and there are many owners and prospective owners in your community who will want them—write us today for samples, terms and trade prices.

KEASBEY & MATTISON CO., Factors
Dept. E, Ambler, Pa.
Branch Offices in Principal Cities of the United States

---

board material, and clapboards, like other forest products, became an item of export from New England.

Until the nineteenth century most clapboards were riven or split from bolts of straight-grained wood. The process was similar to that of splitting shingles, except that the greater length of clapboards required correspondingly greater care in controlling the split. Eighteenth-century statutes required that merchantable pine clapboards be five-eighths of an inch thick at the butt, five inches wide, and four and a half feet long, "well Rived, Shaved, & made Strait." Like shingles, clapboards were shaved or planed after being riven. On rare occasions a molding plane was used to bead the butt of eighteenth-century clapboards, and beading was resumed in some machine-made clapboards of the latter nineteenth century.

Given the familiarity of the eighteenth-century carpen-

Advertisement for cement-asbestos "Century" shingles, *Building Age* magazine, June 1915. Introduced into the United States during the first decade of the twentieth century, cement-asbestos shingles immediately gained favor as a roofing material, and later as a wall covering. Keasbey & Mattison Company at first dominated the American market, but the H. W. Johns-Manville Company introduced "Transite" cement-asbestos shingles after 1910.

---

ter with the drawknife, it is not surprising that this tool was used not only to finish clapboards but also to fit them to buildings. It was an almost universal practice of carpenters until well into the nineteenth century to skive and lap the ends of clapboards in order to provide a weatherproof joint. By 1830 or so, this technique was abandoned in favor of simple butt joints at the ends of clapboards, a practice that is universal today except when the more painstaking older method is used in restoration work.

Until the advent of the machine-made cut nail just before 1800, clapboards were attached to the walls with rose-headed nails of forged wrought iron. In northern New England, clapboards were applied over wall sheathing; in southern New England they were often nailed directly to the studs of the frame. Even in the north, where sheathing underlies the clapboards, carpenters usually nailed through the sheathing boards and into the studs behind them. The large heads of wrought iron nails therefore trace the pattern of the underlying studs and posts on the face of the wall, creating a pattern that often remains visible even when the clapboards are covered by many layers of built-up paint.

It became the custom in some parts of New England to grade the exposure of clapboards, providing less exposure

---

Hand-split pine clapboards with skived and lapped ends, Wheelwright House, Portsmouth, New Hampshire, circa 1780. Photograph by Jack E. Boucher, 1961. Library of Congress, Prints and Photographs Division, Historic American Buildings Survey, Reproduction Number 1983 (HABS): 202.

near the bottom of a wall than near the roof. This practice may have been intended to provide greater protection against rain and roof splashback near the foundation, or it may have been ornamental, or both.

The riving and shaving of clapboards was an exacting and time-consuming job. From the 1780s through the 1820s, buildings in western Vermont were frequently covered with a type of sawn clapboard. Typically, these clapboards were cut on an upright saw to a thickness of about half an inch, and their faces were planed smooth. Workers beveled the top edges of the faces and the bottom edges of the backs of these boards with drawknives, creating tight laps of about one inch. Craftsmen in the Shaker communities of New Hampshire sometimes adopted a similar wall covering, very different from the split clapboards used on neighboring homes. Like the anchor-bent framing of the Shaker meetinghouses, this type of wall cladding suggests a borrowing from the Hudson River region.

Experimenters with the circular saw quickly perceived that the speed of the new machine could vastly increase the production of clapboards, which are nothing more than wedge-shaped slices from a log. By the 1820s several American inventors had applied the circular saw to clapboard production, and the technology quickly spread to every area where mill owners had the capital to invest in the new machinery. After the mid-1800s, as sawmills were introduced into the extensive spruce regions of northern New England, clapboards were often sawn from spruce as well as from the long-familiar white pine.

The earliest machines for sawing clapboards passed a log over the blade of a circular saw, rotating the log slightly on each pass so that the saw made a series of radial cuts some five or six inches deep. The slices of wood left between these cuts were split off as individual clapboards. These had the same characteristics of grain as riven clapboards, being cut at right angles to the annual rings of the wood. The inventors of such clapboard mills rightly claimed that their radially sawn product was far better than a sawn clapboard that did not follow the grain in this manner. Radially sawn clapboards are still manufactured by a limited number of mills with machines not dissimilar to those of the 1820s. Most clapboards of today, however, are sawn by band saws or by circular saws that lack the special carriage needed to suspend a log for radial sawing. Modern clapboards therefore have a greater tendency to cup, split, or twist when exposed to the weather than did either riven or radially sawn clapboards.

Wall Shingles. Several new house styles called for the use of wooden shingles as wall covering during the last decades of the nineteenth century. The Queen Anne style, which reveled in changing materials and patterns, frequently included bands of shingles as well as clapboards on walls. Usually painted, such shingles often had fancy butts that were sawn to resemble fish scales or saw teeth or to produce diamond or hexagonal patterns.

The shingle style gained great favor in New England during the late 1800s and early 1900s. Shingles were usually stained brown or dark red rather than painted and sometimes laid in double courses to produce twin shadow lines at each course. The shingle style blended easily with the introduction of the bungalow in the early decades of the twentieth century. In New England the favorite wall covering for the bungalow also was the wooden shingle. Improved railroad transportation had made western red cedar shingles readily available in the Northeast by the turn of the twentieth century, and these soft, enduring shingles

Hand-shaved pine clapboards, Matthew Harvey House, Sutton, New Hampshire, circa 1784. Seen at a distance, these clapboards reveal a slightly irregular texture that reflects the grain of the wood from which they were split. Their graded exposure to the weather is a common eighteenth-century technique. Photograph by author.

were well adapted to the stained finishes that characterized the shingle style and the New England bungalow.

The increasing popularity of cement-asbestos shingles as a roof covering quickly suggested their use on walls. Such shingles were used as wall cladding with increasing frequency during the first half of the twentieth century, especially for inexpensive houses.

Drop Siding. Drop siding is a form of exterior wall sheathing that is nailed horizontally to wall studs and left exposed to the weather with no further covering. To render it weatherproof, drop siding is manufactured with tongue-and-groove or shiplapped joints between adjacent boards. The boards are further shaped in various patterns to emphasize their shadow lines and provide an attractive wall texture. Because drop siding never becomes truly impervious to driving rains, its use is generally restricted to cottages, garages, and other inexpensive buildings.

One of the most common patterns of drop siding is "novelty" siding. Novelty siding was introduced around the time of the Civil War and is sometimes seen on late-nineteenth-century summer cottages as well as on more modern buildings. Because drop siding is usually manufactured with a complex profile, its production became more economical as woodworking machines, especially four-sided shapers, were improved in the late nineteenth century.

Finished Woodwork. Although clapboards and shingles were originally riven from bolts of wood, by far the greatest part of the wood used in finishing a building was the product of the sawmill. Wherever sawn lumber was exposed to view, it had to be finished. When used for the visible finish of rooms or for the exterior trim of a house, rough boards had to be planed and often molded as well. Simple hand tools sufficed for this work until well into the nineteenth century and, to a certain extent, until the beginning of the twentieth.

Hand Planes. The smoothing of lumber for finished woodwork (traditionally called "joiner's work") was accomplished through the use of hand planes, called "bench planes," until the introduction of planing machinery in the 1830s. Originally made with wooden stocks or bodies of various lengths, and with blades or cutting irons ad-

Sawn board partially smoothed by a bench plane, circa 1800. The smoothing of mill-sawn wood was the first step toward using the board for finished joiner's work. This board is the back of a piece of wainscoting. Photograph by author.

justed by simple wooden wedges, such planes evolved during the nineteenth century into steel tools with sensitive screw adjustments for their blades. Both wood and metal bench planes are still manufactured, and both types are used today by those who prefer hand tools for some or all of their work. Since hand planes were used almost exclusively to smooth joiner's work until well into the nineteenth century, they remain essential in duplicating the texture of old finish.

Without going into the precise use of bench planes (the subject of a vast body of nineteenth- and twentieth-century literature), we can say that those that are used to give a smooth finish to the surface of boards have their blades ground and honed to a slightly convex curve. As a result, they impart a slight hollow to the surface of a board as they pass over it. A hand-planed board thus has a slightly rippled surface, sometimes so subtle that it can be detected only under a strong, raking light. This texture can normally be seen on close inspection or even felt with the fingers on all house joinery, including doors and other paneled work, unless paint has built up so thickly as to mask the original surface.

Planing Machinery. Beginning in the 1830s, American inventors began to turn their minds to the planing of lumber by machine. In 1828, William Woodworth of Hudson, New York, patented a rotary planer. Over the next five to ten years, Woodworth was followed by a number of others

Jointer (bench plane) made by George Henry Warren (1829–1900), Hudson, New Hampshire, prior to 1857. Made of beech, this twenty-eight-inch long plane was used to straighten the edges of boards. Photograph by Bill Finney.

who developed high-speed water-powered machinery, not only for planing lumber but also for the laborious joiner's task of mortising and tenoning. The combination of these machines allowed the rapid manufacture of such time-consuming products as doors, blinds, and window sashes. From this period on, those living reasonably close to a woodworking mill found it more economical to use machine-planed lumber than to plane their own boards by hand.

In contrast to the slightly undulating surface of a hand-planed board, a machine-planed board at first appears almost smooth. Careful inspection of such a board (especially if it is not covered thickly with paint) will reveal a multitude of closely spaced indentations running across its width. Usually not more than an eighth of an inch apart, these tiny ripples are the cuts made by rapidly rotating knives on a cylindrical cutting head as the board is fed beneath the head. The sharper the knives and the faster their speed of rotation, the smaller will be the parallel tracks and the smoother will be the board produced by a machine planer.

At first powered by the new high-speed water turbine, planing machines began to proliferate during the 1830s. Beginning in the 1840s, steam-powered planing mills began to appear in cities, where there was typically no water-power available but where there was an extensive demand for finished lumber. Specialized shops began to make use of the new machinery. By 1850 the state of New Hampshire alone had some forty shops devoted to the manufacture of doors, sashes, and blinds and to the mechanical planing of lumber. By 1870 the number of planing mills in this single state had increased to about ninety. It is rare to find a piece of hand-planed lumber in any building constructed after the mid-nineteenth century.

Moldings. Rough boards may also be transformed into moldings. A molding is a curved surface cut from or impressed into a material. While it might seem that an infinite number of such curves could be devised, historically only a limited number of molding profiles have been used in architecture. Most of these have names that denote their general shape, although countless variations of profile are possible within those relatively few named contours. Often, two or more moldings will be combined for increased visual interest. In such cases, a flat band called a fillet usually separates the individual contours, making each of the separate curved profiles more distinct and visually striking.

Architects and sculptors have always recognized that the molding has a visual power out of proportion with its simple nature. The act of impressing a curve into a flat surface immediately evokes a response in the human eye that cannot be explained on rational grounds alone. The play of light and shade across a regularly curved surface is naturally pleasing, and much thought and artistic impulse have been devoted over the centuries to the subtleties of such surfaces.

The use of moldings in the Western tradition first flourished in the classical societies of Greece and Rome. The first Europeans to arrive in New England came at a time of medieval or postmedieval culture and came from a vernacular and a domestic building tradition. Because these settlers had little familiarity with the classical world, the initial use of moldings in New England houses was rudimentary. It remained for a later generation of English immigrants and, through them, a later generation of native-born American joiners to rediscover the molding as an important adjunct of architecture.

During the seventeenth century, moldings were used, if at all, to decorate the actual frame of a house, which was largely exposed to view, or to provide some articulation of the otherwise flat boards used for wall sheathing or door components. Typically, moldings that were used to add interest to framing members were large and bold, in keeping with the heaviness of the elements they decorated. But they were also limited in profile, most frequently being a quarter-round planed into the lower edges, or arrises, of summer beams or the like. Probably more often, such sharp edges were softened by a simple chamfer rather than by a curved molding. A chamfer could be made with a drawknife, a chisel, or a flat plane, whereas a curved molding required a special tool that might not be owned by every carpenter.

Moldings applied to wall sheathing, door stiles and rails, and other planed boards were usually very shallow until the early 1700s. They were cut by the aptly named creasing plane, which produced a weak contour that we now call a shadow molding. Sometimes applied at the center of a board as well as at its edges, shadow moldings were apparently seen as a relief to the monotony of flat surfaces rather than as an expression of the structural unity of the member into which they were planed.

This purely decorative or textural use of moldings began to be supplanted in New England during the early 1700s. Shortly after the turn of the eighteenth century,

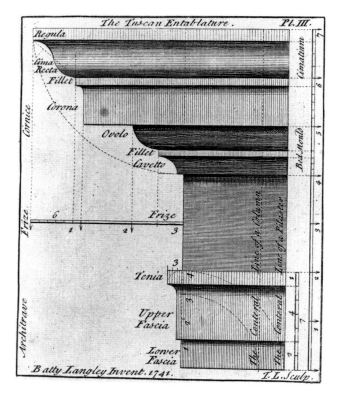

Plate III (1741), showing the moldings and components of the Tuscan entablature, from Batty and Thomas Langley, *The Builder's Jewel; or, the Youth's Instructor and Workman's Remembrancer* (London, 1754). Books like this instructed rural craftsmen in the proper details and proportions of Renaissance architecture and were crucial to the introduction of academic forms to the American colonies during the Georgian period.

New England saw an influx of joiners who had been trained in Britain and who were familiar on a workman's level with the classical tradition. This tradition made extensive, symbolic use of a series of moldings. These contours were derived from Roman prototypes that had been rediscovered and studied by various architects during the Renaissance.

During the early 1700s, as immigrant craftsmen brought new ideas and new molding tools into New England, certain English authors were publishing a number of expensive and elaborate books to explain and justify Renaissance principles of design and to encourage wealthy patrons to build according to these principles. To ensure that craftsmen would be capable of understanding and reproducing details required by these grand designs, other authors began to publish a number of builder's handbooks.

The builder's handbook was frequently a pocket-size manual, richly illustrated with engravings that showed diagrammatically how to assemble moldings and other classical details into proper architectural form. Thanks to

careful measurements made by Renaissance architects and to the translation into English of the Roman writer Vitruvius, builders of the 1700s understood that Roman architecture had followed strict rules. These rules governed the proportioning of buildings, the design of parts of buildings, and the use of the classical orders, which included both columns and moldings. Authors of builder's guidebooks had the task of simplifying these rules into somewhat mechanical formulas that would ensure that even a builder, with his limited tradesman's education, would be capable of fashioning proper classical features.

Many of these small, practical volumes found their way to America. Here they had a profound effect by offering some understanding of classical architecture and by providing both homeowner and builder with a rough idea of what a modern building ought to look like.

The result of this new understanding was the abandonment of old, seventeenth-century building traditions and the substitution of an entirely classical architecture, which we have come to call the Georgian style. The hallmark of the Georgian style was the molding. No longer planed into structural members, the Georgian molding was cut from a separate board and was applied wherever required

Molding tool and molding. Wooden tools fashioned all architectural moldings until the introduction of molding machinery with rotating knives shortly before 1850. Photograph by Bill Finney.

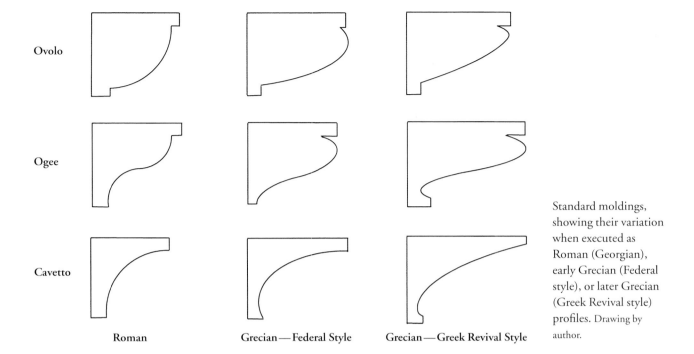

Ovolo		
Ogee		
Cavetto		
Roman	Grecian — Federal Style	Grecian — Greek Revival Style

Standard moldings, showing their variation when executed as Roman (Georgian), early Grecian (Federal style), or later Grecian (Greek Revival style) profiles. Drawing by author.

by the rules of architecture. Various moldings could be assembled to create imposing classical features such as cornices, exterior doorways (then called frontispieces), and mantelpieces.

The molding is fashioned by a molding plane, sometimes called a molding tool by those who insist that a true plane can create only a flat (or plane) surface. Like a bench plane, a molding plane has a wooden body or stock and an iron or blade. Unlike the bench plane, the molding plane has a curved sole and a curved cutting edge to its blade. As it is passed repeatedly along the length of a board, the plane thus cuts the curved profile of a molding.

New England joiners often bought their molding planes from import merchants, from specialized plane makers, or from other joiners. Sometimes, they made their planes themselves, using other planes as a pattern and getting a blacksmith to forge the blade. During the eighteenth century the range of molding profiles needed by a joiner was restricted to the Roman moldings found in builder's guidebooks. These are basically sets of S-curves (called ogees or cymas), quarter-rounds (called ovolos), and coves or hollows (called cavettos and scotias) in various sizes and combinations.

While few people today give moldings a second glance, craftsmen and patrons of architecture in the early 1700s regarded the introduction of Roman moldings to New

England as a momentous development. The application of moldings to the exterior and interior of a building clearly differentiated the structure from the style of the previous century. The proper use of moldings implied classical learning in both patron and craftsman and showed an understanding of the principles that had shaped European architecture since the beginning of the Renaissance.

About a century later the entire vocabulary of moldings changed. Around 1800 the Roman molding was replaced by the Grecian molding, which had already been adopted in England following the first careful archaeological investigations and measurements of Greek buildings. Roman and Greek moldings share the same range of basic shapes and the same names. But the curves of the Roman molding are based on segments of a circle, while those of the Grecian molding are so-called conic sections— ellipses, parabolas, or hyperbolas. The Grecian molding offers a softer profile than the Roman, with a more interesting play of light and shadow. The introduction of Grecian moldings into American architecture gave the Federal style of the early 1800s a pervasive but subtle difference from the Georgian style that had preceded it.

The introduction of the Grecian molding into the United States immediately rendered many joiners' tools obsolete. The need to abandon old tools and old ways caused a wholesale rethinking of architectural decoration —the first of several instances during the nineteenth century when an old style was swept away by a quite different newer style. Federal period doors, windows, and paneling differ from Georgian; and the entire layout and appearance of rooms during the Federal period differs from what was common before 1800.

During the 1830s, when Federal-style moldings were giving way to heavier profiles favored in the Greek Revival style, inventors began to devise machinery to manufacture moldings by water- or steam power. About 1834, George Page, Jerub Amber Fay, and Edward Joslin of Keene, New Hampshire, formed a partnership for the manufacture of woodworking machinery. Eventually incorporated under the name of J. A. Fay and Company, the firm introduced the first powered molding machines manufactured in the United States. In 1847 the firm established branches in Worcester, Massachusetts; Norwich, Connecticut; and Cincinnati, Ohio. In 1848 the company began to produce the first successful molding machine built for general use. Eventually consolidating its business in Cincinnati, the

J. A. Fay and Egan Company became the largest manufacturer of woodworking machinery in the world.

The machine-made molding evolved into extremely complex forms. Hand-planed moldings are limited in size by the friction of the plane against the wood; some of the larger hand molding planes have pins by which an apprentice could help the master pull the blade against the resistance of the wood (see figure, page 157). Powerful molding machinery could produce large moldings without regard to the limitations of human strength. It is rare to find architectural moldings cut from hardwoods like mahogany, chestnut, walnut, or cherry before 1850. With the help of powerful machinery, these woods became useful to the molding manufacturer and available to the architect and joiner. Varnished hardwood often supplanted painted pine in molded work after the Civil War. Before the advent of machinery, moldings tended to be limited to combinations of the simple cymas, ogees, and cavettos described above. After machines were introduced and then refined to cut all four sides of a piece of molding in one pass, contours of greater complexity became available, and

Wood engraving of turner's shop, illustrating the use of a great wheel lathe, from Edward Hazen, *Popular Technology; or, Professions and Trades* (New York, 1846).

moldings could be cut so precisely that they could be assembled into still larger and more complex features.

As molding machinery achieved the capability of producing an almost infinite variety of shapes, architects and woodworkers began to sense a need for standardization, which would make the products of one manufacturer compatible with those of other manufacturers. By the 1870s and 1880s, woodworkers' associations were issuing catalogs of standardized moldings, and millwork manufacturers across the United States and Canada were beginning to produce interchangeable products. Many of these stock profiles continued in use throughout the twentieth century.

Even after the introduction of successful molding machines, many carpenters and joiners continued to make moldings by hand for individual jobs. Most of the molding planes that survive today were made in the mid- to late 1800s. They cut the profiles favored in Greek Revival and Victorian woodwork. A few have been traced to the ownership of sash, blind, and door manufacturers, suggesting that hand planing continued to be useful for some jobs even in mechanized woodworking shops. In the construction of private homes, especially those with pine (rather than hardwood) detailing, some carpenters probably used handmade moldings throughout the nineteenth century. Old molding planes are again being used in restoration, where they can provide an economical alternative to the time-consuming process of cutting molder or shaper blades to a historical profile.

Turnings. Until the late nineteenth century, lathe work, or turning, was largely restricted in American architecture to the production of balusters for staircases. Most eighteenth- and early-nineteenth-century turners earned their living primarily through the manufacture of furniture, especially chairs, table legs, and bedsteads.

Yet the balustrade, especially in a dwelling with a broad central entry or stair hall, is one of the most dramatic single features of a house. For this reason, the skill of the turner has always been important in architecture—and never more so than in the great Georgian mansions of the mid-1700s.

Before the advent of powered lathes in the nineteenth century, the trade of the turner was strictly a handicraft, relying on the skill and muscular strength of the turner, sometimes with the help of an apprentice, to spin the wood against the cutting edge of a hand-held chisel. The

Newel post and balusters, Governor John Langdon Mansion, Portsmouth, New Hampshire, 1786. The triple pattern of balusters is characteristic of the work of Bristol-trained turner John Mills, who immigrated to Portsmouth about 1725, and his son, Richard. Open newel posts are found only in the most costly houses of the Piscataqua region. Photograph by author.

most primitive of lathes was the spring-pole lathe, in which a cord extended from the end of an elastic sapling fixed to the ceiling, around the work (the piece to be shaped), and down to a treadle. With such a tool, the work was alternately spun toward and away from the cutting edge of the chisel, allowing the turner only an intermittent cutting action. More sophisticated was the flywheel lathe, with which the craftsman turned a heavy flywheel attached by a crank to his treadle, thereby gaining continuous cutting action. Best of all was the great wheel lathe, in which the chuck of the lathe was driven by a cord that ran around a large wheel that stood a few feet from the

lathe and was turned by an apprentice or a laborer. By permitting the turner to concentrate on his work and to guide his chisel without driving the lathe with his leg, the great wheel lathe allowed precise work. This was undoubtedly the type of lathe used whenever possible by the professional turner.

Turning had already developed into a complex trade in England by the seventeenth century. While the trade found limited expression in New England houses of the 1600s, it was given far greater importance in the increasingly grand houses of the 1700s. At this time, too, a few English-trained turners arrived in New England to supplement the native craftsmen and to introduce many local variations in the design of the classical, vase-shaped baluster. Georgian balusters often made use of such sophisticated embellishments as fluting, which produces a

Foundation wall in a brick house, with the stones bedded in lime-sand mortar. The bricks above the stonemasonry serve as backing for split-stone underpinning placed at grade level on the exterior of the building. William Jones House, Claremont Plains, Claremont, New Hampshire, 1847–1850. Photograph by David S. Putnam.

Typical dry-laid stone foundation walls, John Cram House, Hampton Falls, New Hampshire, circa 1700. Photograph by L. C. Durette, circa 1937. Library of Congress, Prints and Photographs Division, Historic American Buildings Survey, Reproduction Number HABS, NH, 8 – HAMTOF, 1.

columnar effect, or revived the seventeenth-century technique of swash turning, which produces a baroque spiral.

Masonry

The woodworking trades were essential in the construction of the New England house. It was usually the joiner who was recognized as the superintendent of a building's construction and who served as the architect if the building required a formal plan. New Englanders long preferred wooden houses to those of masonry. When George Washington toured New England in 1789 and wondered at the scarcity of brick houses in a land so full of clay, he was told that local people were convinced that wooden houses were more wholesome than masonry dwellings in a damp, foggy climate.

Nevertheless, the skills of the mason were essential even in the construction of a wooden house and became still more critical as brick houses became more popular after 1800.

Stonemasonry. Virtually every permanent dwelling needed at least a partial cellar for storage of root vegetables, and here the skills of the stonemason were called into

play. Cellars were dug by hand or with the aid of draft animals, which were employed to break the earth with plows and to pull it out of the excavation with drag scoops. Cellar walls were laid in local stone. The simpler and cheaper the dwelling or the closer it lay to the frontier, the greater the likelihood that its cellar walls will be found to be unworked rocks. In those areas where glacially rounded fieldstones abound, these were used for cellar walls despite their inherent instability; in areas where flatter or more faceted stones occur, these were preferred.

Wherever possible, of course, stonemasons attempted to build cellar walls of rocks with a flat bed or bottom and with other flat surfaces. Stones used in well-built cellar walls were often broken to provide a more stable shape, especially if the native fieldstone is rounded. Masons usually broke stones by striking them with a stone axe or other sharp edge. Split fieldstone was commonly laid with one of its flat surfaces facing inward to provide a plumb wall surface.

Both physical and documentary evidence suggest that the below-grade portions of cellar walls were laid dry during the 1700s and early 1800s, except in the wealthiest homes, and were backfilled with earth for support as they were laid. After laying, such walls were sometimes pointed with lime mortar, as a means of reducing the infiltration of dirt and the entry of vermin, and sometimes left unpointed. In such construction a certain amount of leakage of both water and soil from outside is to be expected and can hardly be prevented. The above-ground portions of such walls, being exposed to the weather and to the splashing of rainwater from the eaves of the house, were laid with full beds of lime mortar.

The cellars of early houses were intended to perform specific functions in food storage and processing. Cellars were an asset to the domestic economy of the house, more related to the kitchen than to any other upstairs room.

Split-granite underpinning, Heald House, Wilton, New Hampshire, circa 1830. The technique of splitting granite with flat wedges, introduced to New England around 1767, resulted in the common use of split-stone underpinning for frame and brick houses by the early 1800s. In rural areas, underpinning stones were often used with a split face and not finished further. Photograph by author.

Hammered-granite underpinning, Portsmouth, New Hampshire, circa 1810. In urban areas or on more costly buildings, split-granite underpinning stones were usually hammered to a "true" or flat face. Photograph by author.

Cellars needed to be cool, damp, and dark for the better storage of vegetables or the processing of dairy products. The floor of the basement was nothing more than the bottom of the cellar excavation, except where sand was brought in to cover and protect root crops from winter cold. Such cellars are often difficult to adapt to such modern uses as furnace room or workshop space.

By the late eighteenth century, the technique of splitting granite with wedges was becoming widespread in New England and quickly led to a dramatic improvement in building foundations. The Scottish stonemason John Park, who immigrated to Groton, Massachusetts, in 1767, is said to have introduced this technique to New England. Workers first applied the splitting technique mostly to the erratic boulders that had been spread by glaciers across the New England landscape. By 1850, quarries were being cut into the ledges of many parts of New England, and "dimension stone" was being extracted in almost any shape and size.

Split granite, showing evidence of the use of flat wedges, Concord, New Hampshire, circa 1820. The use of flat wedges inserted in chiseled slots leaves shallow indentations like those seen along the bottom of this stone. Photograph by author.

During the late 1700s, "wrought" or "hewn" granite underpinning began to become a favored foundation material for both frame and brick houses. Large, rectangular blocks of granite, hammered on their edges and their outer faces to provide a flat and lightly textured surface, were mounted atop the rougher fieldstone cellar walls to provide the visible support for the house above grade. Often split to a thickness of only six inches or so, these slabs were usually backed with a tier of bricks to thicken the wall enough to support the sills of a frame house or the wall masonry of a brick one.

It will often be found that older houses, built before hammered or dressed granite was available, were underpinned with split and hammered stone, when it was later introduced. In such buildings the original foundation walls were constructed of local fieldstone, thoroughly mortared where exposed to the elements above grade. The somewhat irregular above-ground walls of such foundations were often covered with a strongly projecting wooden "water table" that was affixed to the wall of the house at the sill level and provided a base for the first course of clapboards. The old foundation stonework was sometimes replaced with dressed granite—often restricted, for economy's sake, to the public sides of the house. Replacement of the underpinning was often accompanied by the removal of the old sloping water table that had covered the rough original stones. The old shelflike water table then gave way to a simple skirt board nailed flat against the lower wall of the house.

By about 1800, stonecutters in many parts of New England had perfected the basic techniques of finishing and shaping granite. These craftsmen were not only able to split large slabs and posts from boulders or ledges but had also learned to use hammers and chisels to shape the stone to a wide variety of forms, including steps, thresholds, curbs, lintels, columns, and rainwater troughs and basins.

In the years just before 1830, at the same period that new techniques were being applied to the framing of buildings, a new granite splitting method was introduced. Prior to that time the procedure for splitting granite entailed the cutting of a line of shallow slots in the face of the stone, using a sharpened bar or coarse chisel struck with a heavy hammer. Flat steel wedges were placed between shims of sheet iron and driven into these slots, splitting the stone.

The new splitting method used a "plug drill," which had a V-shaped point and was rotated slightly between each blow of the hammer, thus creating a round hole two or three inches deep. Into this hole were placed a pair of half-round steel shims, or "feathers," and between these was driven a wedge, or "plug," that exerted outward pressure and split the stone. The advantage of the "plug-and-feathers" method of splitting was the greater depth within the stone at which the wedges exerted their pressure, thus allowing larger pieces to be split more accurately.

The new splitting technology seems to have spread rather rapidly through the granite-quarrying centers of New England, although one is likely to find evidence of both old and new methods being used concurrently in stonework of the 1830s. The technique employed on a given stone is easily seen on the split face and provides some aid in dating granite masonry. The old flat-wedge method is marked by a series of slotlike depressions, which extend inward an inch or so from the edges. The plug-and-feathers method leaves a row of rounded holes, two or three inches deep and usually about six inches apart.

The latter part of the nineteenth century saw the development of far more sophisticated methods of quarrying and cutting granite. The most revolutionary changes occurred because of the introduction of compressed air as a source of power for quarrying tools, permitting a vast expansion of the quantities of stone that could be quarried and processed.

This same period witnessed the increasing use of split stones, bedded in mortar, for all parts of a building's foundation. It is rare to find a large, expensive, post–Civil War house with foundation walls made from natural fieldstone, laid dry. Rather, foundations of this period tend increasingly to be built of rough ashlar, well cemented. Cellars of the latter 1800s also often tend to be deeper than those of the early nineteenth century, especially where a house was intended from the beginning to be heated by a furnace or boiler placed in the basement and fed by fuel stored in a wood or coal room.

Concrete and Concrete Blocks. Building foundations were for the most part made of unit masonry—individually laid stones or bricks—until well into the twentieth century. Although Portland cement became commonplace in the United States after the 1890s, it was only rarely used to create poured monolithic concrete foundations. Portable cement mixers, often powered by gasoline engines, were increasingly used by contractors after about 1910, but these machines produced only small batches.

Granite ledge, showing evidence of splitting with flat wedges (*lower left*) and plugs and feathers (*vertical lines*), Hooksett, New Hampshire, circa 1830. Evidence of the simultaneous use of the older and newer techniques is commonplace around 1830, as older tools wore out and were replaced with newer ones. Photograph by author.

Concrete made in these small machines is usually recognizable by its layered structure, having been poured one batch at a time. Truly uniform concrete foundations became possible only with the establishment of a multitude of local batching plants and with the availability of trucks equipped to mix concrete in transit to the job. In many areas, such equipment did not appear until after World War II.

The increasing availability and cheapness of Portland cement after the turn of the twentieth century helped builders to become more familiar with the material. This familiarity inspired expanded use of Portland cement concrete, especially as motor-driven concrete mixers became a standard part of contractors' equipment. Introduction of the new material and the new machinery brought wide-

spread adoption of the concrete block as a building material during the first decade of the twentieth century.

The majority of concrete blocks used during the early years of the century were hollow-core blocks with a textured face that was intended to be exposed to view. These blocks were made in small, portable, metal machines that usually made a single block at a time. Block manufacture entailed tamping a mixture of stiff concrete into a mold or flask and then releasing the green block onto a pallet that was carried away for curing. Widely advertised in the early

---

(*Opposite*) Doorway with a split-granite lintel, showing evidence of the use of plugs and feathers, circa 1850. The technique of using a rotated plug drill to create a round hole leaves semi-cylindrical marks on the edges of the stone. This technique superseded the use of flat wedges in slots around 1830. William Jones House, Claremont Plains, Claremont, New Hampshire, 1847–1850. Photograph by David S. Putnam.

(*Right*) Comparison of granite splitting with flat wedges in chiseled slots (circa 1770 to about 1830) and with plugs and feathers in a round hole made by a plug drill (after 1830). Drawing by author.

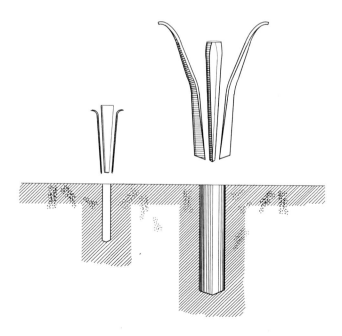

1900s, these machines were sometimes used by individuals to make blocks for a prospective home for themselves. Contractors bought many machines to provide materials for their business. Homeowners sometimes used the machines to generate supplementary income on a part-time basis.

Most of the blocks made by these machines had an ornamented face, and many machines had interchangeable face molds that created blocks resembling pitch-faced or hammered ashlar. Since the surface details of such blocks needed to be well defined, users of the machines often employed a fine concrete, sometimes with artificial coloring or an aggregate of stone dust as a surface material, with a

———————————————————

Advertisement for concrete block machine, *American Carpenter and Builder* magazine, March 1908. The widespread availability of Portland cement after 1900 resulted in the increasing popularity of concrete blocks as a fireproof building material. Early blocks were manufactured locally in simple molds or "machines" that typically imparted the appearance of rough or hammered stone to the blocks.

coarser mix for the rest of the block. Such special surface treatments were eased by the introduction, early in the century, of "face-down" machines, which had the face mold at the bottom of the flask. These machines received the refined concrete first, against the mold, with the ordinary concrete tamped on top of the face veneer.

House foundations of the early 1900s tend to be laid up in local stone below grade. This stone is often set in mortar made with Portland cement, which bonds the wall into a strong, rigid fabric. Above grade, fashion often dictated the use of hard brick. The early twentieth century also saw an enthusiasm for cobblestone masonry. Where rounded stone was available, it was often used above grade to achieve the rustic effect that was so favored at that period. Cobblestone masonry was almost always laid in a hard mortar that had a high proportion of Portland cement.

Brick Manufacture. Like stonemasonry, bricklaying quickly attained new stature after 1800. Brick buildings had been rare in eighteenth-century New England, being found mostly in Boston and in a few outlying centers, like

Medford, Massachusetts, where brickmaking evolved into a local specialty.

Although a few centers like Medford became noted for brick manufacture, bricks were also made throughout the settled portions of New England from the early 1600s. Brickmaking was possible wherever beds of clay existed and where someone with skill in the trade was available. The first houses in any newly settled region might have chimneys built of wood or rough stone; a wood-framed chimney, plastered with clay, survived in Andover, New Hampshire, as late as 1845. But settlers were eager to substitute brick chimneys as soon as possible. Thus, chimneys consumed most of the bricks manufactured in New England throughout the 1600s and 1700s.

Brickmaking is a two-stage process. First, the natural clay must be prepared and molded. Second, the molded bricks must be fired or baked until they become a ceramic. Clay as taken directly from the ground is not suitable for molding. If pure, it is extremely stiff, sticky, and almost unworkable. Such clay must be tempered, or rendered more plastic. Traditionally, this was accomplished by digging the clay from the claybank in the fall and allowing it to freeze and thaw, with repeated turnings, over the winter.

Weathering of the clay was followed by re-wetting and

Pug mill, Henry Simpson brickyard, Pembroke, New Hampshire, circa 1890. Placed in front of a bank of clay, this mill was turned by the horse at the right rear to mix clay, sand, and water into a workable mortar. The man at the left is holding a brick mold. Hacked (stacked) green bricks are drying on the far left. Photograph courtesy of the New Hampshire Historical Society.

---

mechanical kneading, accomplished by driving cattle or horses over the lumps of clay, by pressing the clay under a heavy wheel attached to a rotating boom, or by feeding the clay through a horse- or ox-driven pug mill. A pug mill is a box or cylinder enclosing a rotating armature with projecting lugs. These wooden knives slice through the mass of clay and loosen the compacted, minuscule particles or flakes that constitute natural clay deposits. Most clays have to have sand added during tempering in order to make the material more plastic and workable.

Once it is brought to the consistency of a stiff mortar, clay can be molded. This was accomplished by taking a lump of clay and throwing it into a rectangular wood or metal mold, then striking off the surplus with a straightedge. A brick mold is simply a rectangular frame, often subdivided so as to shape several bricks at once, that is placed on a table during the molding process. If the mold had a bottom, the bricks had to be carefully tipped out onto the ground to begin drying. If the mold was made without a bottom, it was placed on a board or pallet and lifted off the blocks of clay, which were carried off and carefully stacked under cover to dry and stiffen for some days or weeks. The blocks of clay had then become "green" bricks, ready for the firing or baking process that would transform them into a ceramic.

To enable the sticky clay block to drop out of the brick mold, the mold was usually lubricated with water or dusted with dry sand. A brick formed in a wetted mold is called a water-struck brick. Water-struck bricks are characterized by a slick surface that remains after firing. A brick cast from a sanded mold is called a sand-struck brick. The sides of sand-struck bricks retain the abrasive grittiness of sand after firing and therefore do not possess the shiny surface usually seen in water-struck bricks. Modern manufacturers also sell what they *call* water-struck bricks. With few exceptions, these are an extruded product finished and fired to resemble handmade bricks, but they are not truly an equivalent of early hand-molded, water-struck bricks.

Special methods were sometimes employed to mold face bricks (bricks exposed on the outer surface of a wall) of high quality. Even in the eighteenth century, wooden molds were commonly lined with iron or other metal to provide smoother faces to the bricks as well as to prolong the life of the mold. By the early nineteenth century, such metal-shod molds were often wiped with animal oil instead of being dipped in water, producing a brick with a smoother face than that of a common water-struck brick.

Bricks with even smoother faces and sharper edges became available in the second decade of the nineteenth century with the introduction of re-pressing machines. These devices, usually hand-operated, forced a green brick into a metal mold under great pressure, compressing the rough product into a perfect rectangular prism. The first brick-making machines were introduced at about the same period, doing away with much of the labor of hand molding. The principles of the two types of machinery were combined in the 1830s and later, making machine-manufactured pressed bricks an economical alternative to the hand-molded product. But until steam power and, later, electricity were introduced in brickyards, the machinery used in brickmaking was largely hand- or animal-powered.

Laws regulated brick sizes from the seventeenth century. The dimensions of brick molds were carefully specified, so that the finished product would be uniform. Before the Revolution, laws in both Massachusetts and New Hampshire specified that molds should be sized so that the finished bricks, after firing, would measure nine inches long, four and a quarter inches deep, and two and a half inches high. These dimensions are close to those of the English "statute" or common brick, and the New England brick laws were clearly based on earlier British regulations. The discovery of seal-marked bricks in the walls of the Macpheadris-Warner House (1716–1719) in Portsmouth, New Hampshire, suggests that brick molds were inspected and that green bricks were occasionally impressed with the inspector's seal to certify their conformity with the statute.

In fact, however, the size of the finished brick depended on more than the size of the mold. All clays shrink during the firing process, some clays more than others. Those bricks closest to the fires in the kiln shrink more than those away from the heat, so that the bricks from a single firing can vary considerably in size even though all may have been dropped from a single mold.

It was important that bricks be uniform, because eighteenth-century bricklayers (like other tradesmen) were frequently not paid on the basis of their own claims for work done. Rather, if their contract was "by measure," their work was measured or "surveyed" by an independent third party, who placed a fair value on the quantity of work

Brick seal, circa 1715; diameter, about five-eighths inch. Found in a few bricks in the walls of the Macpheadris-Warner House, Portsmouth, New Hampshire (1716–1719), these marks indicate that a provincial inspector approved the size of the mold from which the bricks were made and sealed the bricks while they were still soft. Drawing by author.

performed. The surveyor calculated the number of bricks in a job by measuring the finished wall or structure. Accuracy in surveying and pricing the completed work demanded that the bricks conform to standard dimensions.

Once molded and air-dried, green bricks were ready for firing, or "burning." Until well into the nineteenth century, and indeed until after the mid-twentieth century in some small New England brickyards, bricks were fired or vitrified with the same method that had been used since the 1600s. The green bricks were carefully stacked by hand in a "clamp" or "scove kiln"—a large, rectangular structure with corbeled arches running at intervals through its base and with innumerable gaps or interstices throughout the entire construction. A clamp or kiln of this nature might typically contain from fifteen to thirty thousand bricks. Brickmakers "scoved," or covered the outer faces of the pile, with an unmortared veneer of hardened bricks from earlier firings and carefully pargeted, or plastered, these bricks with clay so that fires built in the arches would suffuse their heat through the entire mass. Hot gases exited through the top of the pile, which was also loosely covered with refuse bricks.

Brickyard, Pembroke, New Hampshire, circa 1890. A kiln of bricks is being fired at the right, with steam rising from the kiln and wooden shutters placed against the shed to break the wind and control the draft. Photograph courtesy of the Pembroke Historical Society, Pembroke, N.H.

The burning, or vitrifying, of bricks in such a kiln was a skilled art. Building the clamp from green bricks might take several weeks. Firing and cooling a clamp of bricks could require a week or more, and during that time the brickmaker had to exercise judgment and vigilance. With wood as a fuel, the temperature of the fires could vary depending on the dryness and species used. The draft in the kiln could be affected by prevailing winds, and brickmakers controlled the fires by making or closing openings in the clay covering of the clamp. The kiln could heat unevenly, resulting in overburned or underburned bricks, and this too had to be compensated for by adjusting the draft. The entire clamp shrank as the bricks were vitrified, and the brickmaker had to keep the subsidence of the pile as even as possible. The final color of the bricks depended on both the character of the local clay and the amount of

oxygen fed to the fire, so the brickmaker also had to learn to gauge the reaction of the clay to varying conditions of draft at different stages of the burning.

The process of burning a clamp of bricks began with a gentle fire, which drove off the moisture in the green bricks and warmed the entire clamp. This step was necessary to prevent the bricks from exploding because of steam generated within them during the later stages of firing. As the smoke issuing from the top of the pile turned from white water vapor to a darker hue, the brickmaker knew that the water had been driven out of the clay and that he could safely intensify the heat by adding fast-burning fuel and adjusting the draft at the arches. The temperature was gradually raised to a point between 1500 and 2000 degrees

Henry Abbott brickyard, Sturgeon Creek, Eliot, Maine, circa 1885. In the foreground is a field of plowed clay, waiting to be tempered in the pug mill at the center of the picture. At the rear, left, and center, are two scove kilns, the one in the center being dismantled after firing. Robert Whitehouse photograph, courtesy of John P. Adams.

Fahrenheit, bringing the bricks in the lower part of the kiln to an incandescent state. Typically, the fire was alternately fed and slackened and the drafts adjusted, so that the uppermost bricks would gradually heat as much as possible. Eventually, flames would appear in the flues at the top of the kiln.

After the firing was complete and the kiln was slowly

cooled over a period of several days, the entire pile was taken apart by hand and the bricks sorted for various uses. Despite the best skill of the brickmaker, the bricks near the fire would inevitably be more vitrified than those at the top of the kiln. The bricks that made up the corbels of the arches would normally be burned black and often would be twisted and even fused together by the intense heat of the fire. These were called "arch" or "clinker" bricks. Other bricks from the lower kiln would normally retain their true shape yet would be found to have acquired a green or black glaze because of potassium salts found in the clay and the wood fuel. The bricks in the mid-region of the kiln would be the characteristic bricks of the burning, taking on a color that reflected their clay and their method of firing. Even here, however, individual bricks would normally display a range of hues resulting from their direct exposure to hot gases or from their protection by adjacent bricks in the stack. The bricks at the top of the kiln, the coolest region, would normally be underburned, light in color, soft, and very susceptible to crumbling under damp conditions. These were called "samel" or "salmon" bricks. When made from common New England clays, they are indeed of a pink or salmon color.

Clays from various regions burn to different colors. The clays of the coastal plain and of some of the major river valleys (most of which had been the beds of ancient glacial lakes) normally range from gray to a striking blue in color when dug from the earth. These clays contain a sufficient amount of iron to vitrify to a strong, deep red. The clays of some inland locales burn to a much paler pink even when fully vitrified, resembling the underburned, or salmon, bricks of the coastal regions. Generally, the darker-burning clays were favored as New England brickmaking grew from a craft to an industry in the later nineteenth century, so major commercial brickyards tended to become concentrated in locales that yielded bricks of deep red.

Isolated brick houses are sometimes found in country locations in which an entire kiln of bricks, clearly burned on the spot, has been consumed in construction. Such houses contain everything from clinkers to salmon bricks; they illustrate the different uses to which bricklayers put the varying grades of brick. The twisted clinkers, too misshapen to be laid in a wall but highly resistant to dampness, were sometimes used for a pavement in the cellar. The hard-burned, glazed bricks, occasionally used as or-

namental headers in certain brick bonds, are more often found in chimney bases and other foundation work where their resistance to dampness is a valuable quality. The bricks of moderate hardness and good color will be found as face bricks in the exterior walls of such a house. Softer bricks will be found as backing behind the face bricks, where they will not be exposed to the weather. Bricks with good hardness and sharp edges will be found as lining in fireplaces; but chimney stacks that are well protected within the building will often be found to have been built with salmon bricks. The very softest of such bricks were probably discarded immediately and will long ago have crumbled to red dust in the weather.

Occasionally, one will find salmon bricks used, as they had often been in seventeenth-century Massachusetts, as wall filling in framed houses. In such cases, the frame of the dwelling was erected and sheathed, and the spaces between the posts and studs were then filled with soft brick "nogging" laid dry or in clay or lime mortar. Hidden within the wall cavities, this infilling served as a windbreak and as insulation. It is encountered occasionally in eighteenth-century houses (the three-story Moffatt-Ladd House in Portsmouth, New Hampshire, being an example) and may sometimes be found in dwellings (even isolated farmhouses) built throughout the nineteenth century. Representing an added expense in both labor and materials, such brick nogging is encountered in only a small percentage of houses.

Brick nogging laid in clay mortar, Laundry Building, Shaker Village, Canterbury, New Hampshire, 1816. Soft, "salmon" bricks were often used as wall filling during the seventeenth through mid-nineteenth centuries, providing some resistance to air infiltration through wall cavities. Photograph by author.

Lime. While glacial clay provided ample raw material for brickmaking, the lime necessary to lay weatherproof brick walls was at first hard to obtain in the Northeast. Accounts suggest that until the early 1700s, when stone lime began to be generally accessible along the New England coast, lime was frequently obtained by calcining (heating) oyster shells. Crushed shells also were added to stone lime to extend this valuable product.

Limestone was discovered in Rhode Island about 1660, in northern Massachusetts in 1697, and in Thomaston, Maine, about 1730. Following each discovery, lime kilns (furnaces for "burning" the stone to transform it into lime) were immediately constructed to meet the needs of the region. Despite its availability, however, lime was largely used in making plaster and in building the exposed portions of chimneys, not in constructing brick dwellings. These remained rare until after 1800.

When burned or calcined in a kiln, limestone is brought to a red or yellow heat at temperatures ranging from 800 to 1700 degrees Fahrenheit. The resulting product is a lumpy, crumbly substance called quicklime. In order to be used in mortar or plaster, quicklime has to be slaked, or hydrated, by the addition of water. The slaking process

Lime kilns, Rockport, Maine, nineteenth century. Built of granite or limestone with a fire-resistant lining, wood-fired kilns were used to heat limestone (carbonate of lime) to about 800 degrees Fahrenheit, converting it to chemically active quicklime (calcium oxide), used in making mortar and plaster. Photograph by author.

creates a powerful chemical reaction, during which great quantities of heat are generated. The lime expands its volume two or three times, and the lumps of quicklime crumble into a powder. Water added during the slaking process is partially or wholly driven off as steam by the heat of the reaction. Depending on the amount of water added, slaking can leave a dry white powder that can be passed through a sieve to break up any remaining lumps or can result in a plastic paste called putty. Whether powder or putty, this slaked lime is ready for use in making mortar. Powdered slaked lime, in bags, can be purchased for masonry work, and lime putty is available in air-tight containers.

Clay Mortar. Lime was not the only material used in bricklaying. Until 1800 or later, most chimneys in New

England were partly laid in clay mortar for reasons of economy, custom, or both. Clay mortar is quickly recognizable by its softness, its blue-green color, and its tendency to run down the exposed faces of the chimney stack. In such chimneys, lime was reserved for the foundations and for the portion of the stack above the roof, both of which were exposed to dampness that would quickly have destroyed construction laid in clay. Clay-built chimneys have proved durable and stable, more than justifying the original bricklayers' trust in them. Houses with such stacks have often been moved, sometimes roughly, with little or no damage to the chimneys. The practice of laying chimneys in clay was generally restricted to framed dwellings. Brick houses often have the chimneys bonded with an exterior wall, and therefore use lime mortar throughout.

Chimney Construction. Chimney construction varied somewhat from period to period, but retained certain underlying principles as long as fireplaces continued in use. Brickmasons prefer to work from a plumb line, so one face of a chimney is frequently a flat vertical surface. In houses with a center chimney, this plumb face is normally oriented toward the front of the house, where it forms the back wall of the entry and where a triple-run or winding staircase may rise against it. In "double" houses, which have a central stair hall and two chimneys, the plumb

Detail, central chimney of the Benjamin Hubbard Weeks House, Concord, New Hampshire, circa 1790. Except in brick houses, a mortar made of clay and sand was the usual cement for chimney construction from the 1600s through the early 1800s. Soft-burned bricks were often used in those parts of chimneys that were not exposed to dampness. Photograph by author.

sides of the chimneys may face the center of the house or the outer walls, depending on the preference of the mason or the need for closets or passageways beside the stacks. In brick houses where chimneys are bonded to the outer walls, stacks may sometimes be found to step back on both sides; but the preference for building from a plumb line usually persists even in the chimneys of brick dwellings.

While chimneys in northern New England are almost invariably built of bricks above the first floor of a house, their foundations may vary considerably in materials and construction. Many houses have only a partial cellar. In these buildings, the chimney may rest on footings set on unexcavated ground, with its base, sustained by a retaining wall of stone, forming one of the cellar walls of the dwelling. In somewhat more ambitious houses, the basement may extend around two or three sides of a chimney base, but the base itself may remain an unexcavated projection supported on its sides by stone foundation walls.

In many central-chimney dwellings the chimney stack will be found to have been built on an artificial foundation rather than on unexcavated ground. Such foundations can vary widely in size and construction. Some eighteenth-century houses have chimney bases consisting of twin stone piers spanned by heavy split logs. The brick portion of the chimney is constructed atop the log platform, the first-floor hearths being well insulated from the underlying wood by layers of brick, clay, or rock salt. In many houses built after the turn of the nineteenth century, split stone, or large, flat stone slabs, are used instead of logs to support the chimney stack.

Brick vaults are one of the most common types of chimney bases. Particularly popular after 1800, these imposing arched foundations occasionally occur throughout the eighteenth century as well. Such vaults are built on piers that rest on stone footings beneath the level of the cellar floor. The bricks chosen for vault construction are typically hard-burned, many of them naturally glazed by the heat of the kiln so as to resist the damp conditions of the cellar. Brick vaults are often found to have a brick wall at one end and wooden doors at the other, thus creating a room beneath the chimney for the storage of foodstuffs.

Chimney stacks are often ingeniously contrived to serve their dual purposes of heating the house and cooking foods. Before the introduction of the cookstove in the early nineteenth century, the first essential of cooking was a large fireplace with a crane. Many old houses have more

Smoke chamber in a chimney of the Robert Wallace ("Ocean-Born Mary") House, Henniker, New Hampshire, late eighteenth century. Smoke chambers were sometimes built within the cavities between fireplaces in large chimneys. These chambers may be accessible through doors opening from stair landings part of the way up the side of the chimney. Photograph by Gerda Peterich, circa 1964. Library of Congress, Prints and Photographs Division, Historic American Buildings Survey, Reproduction Number 1984 (HABS): 60.

thickness (often no more than half an inch) might not be able to support the weight of the bricks above. In such cases, a stout wooden beam was often placed in the brickwork a few courses above the iron lintel, well insulated from the heat of the flue. A vertical iron rod or bolt connecting the two members allowed the wooden beam to support the center of the weaker (but fireproof) iron bar.

Many central chimneys were built so that the backs of opposite fireplaces are separated by a void in the center of the stack. This cavity often provides room for the swelling back of the brick oven, which is typically built within, or beside, the kitchen fireplace. But the same cavity is often given a second use. Sometimes it is made accessible through a door in the front of the chimney (often, below

than one such hearth, but one of these fireplaces is usually the largest, is associated with a brick oven, and is in a room that clearly served as the primary kitchen. Boiling, broiling, roasting, and frying were all possible on such hearths, either by direct exposure to the heat of the flames of a wood fire or within a vessel placed over the coals.

The bricks above fireplace openings were supported by a variety of means. During the seventeenth and early eighteenth centuries the lintel was usually wooden. Once wrought iron became available through import or local manufacture, iron bars were preferred for fireplace lintels because they could not burn. In very wide fireplaces, especially in kitchen fireplaces, an iron lintel of the available

Attic smoke chamber attached to a chimney in the Captain Keyran Walsh House, Portsmouth, New Hampshire, circa 1800. Some smoke chambers, like this one, were built adjacent to the flue of the kitchen fireplace and received smoke from the frequent kitchen fires though holes in the side of the chimney. Photograph by Douglas Armsden, circa 1970, courtesy of Strawbery Banke Museum.

Kitchen fireplace, Parish House ("Old Parsonage"), Newington, New Hampshire, circa 1765. The oven in this fireplace is at the left rear corner. Smoke from heating the oven emerges from the mouth and passes up the main chimney flue. Photograph by L. C. Durette, circa 1937. Library of Congress, Prints and Photographs Division, Historic American Buildings Survey, Reproduction Number HABS, NH, 8 – NEWI, 2.

the stairs that ascend to the second floor) and serves as a warm storage closet. In other cases the cavity is sealed off, except for a small port that opens on the front entry of the house. The chamber is fitted with iron cross-bars that allow meat to be hung within it and smoked over smoldering fires built on its floor.

Another form of smoke chamber was built against the side of a chimney rather than within its center. Typically, this type of chamber was placed in an upper story or in the attic, adjacent to the flue of the kitchen fireplace, where a nearly constant fire was kept burning. Two holes in the flue, one at the bottom of the chamber and one at the top, permitted the constant circulation of smoke in the brick chamber.

The brick oven, favored for baking from the seventeenth century until well into the nineteenth, was almost always associated with the kitchen fireplace. In some houses, secondary ovens were built in conjunction with other fireplaces or were placed in a summer kitchen and provided with their own chimney. In houses built before the end of the eighteenth century, ovens were usually placed so that their doors opened at the backs or on one of the cheeks of the kitchen fireplace. Such ovens were

heated by building fires within them, with the smoke issuing from the door and exiting up the flue of the fireplace. Once the oven was hot, the coals and ashes were removed and the door was covered with an iron or wooden "stopper" to retain the heat for baking.

By the late 1700s the position of the oven had typically moved to the face of the chimney, at the right or left of the kitchen fireplace. Such an oven must have a separate flue, which is built just inside its door and rises to merge with the adjacent kitchen fireplace flue, thereby exhausting the smoke of the oven fire. The earliest of these flanking ovens, like their predecessors within the fireplace, were fitted with sheet iron stoppers. These could be placed at the front of the oven opening so as to allow the smoke to exit up the flue or, when heating was completed, could be pushed back snugly against an inner door of the oven to seal in its heat.

Beginning in the early nineteenth century, many New England foundries were casting oven door units that represented the final refinement of the brick oven. These units have a hinged iron door with a movable vent that controls the air draft to the oven fire. Above the door is a sliding damper that is opened while the oven is heating

Kitchen fireplace, Robert Wallace ("Ocean-Born Mary") House, Henniker, New Hampshire, late eighteenth century. Ovens of the late 1700s are often found beside the kitchen fireplace rather than within the rear wall of the fireplace. Such ovens usually have a separate flue to carry off the smoke during heating of the oven. Photograph by Gerda Peterich, circa 1964. Library of Congress, Prints and Photographs Division, Historic American Buildings Survey, Reproduction Number 1984 (HABS): 60.

and is closed during cooking. By manipulating the vent and the damper, the cook could regulate the heat of the oven fire, obtaining a fierce or a gentle blaze as desired.

Most flanking ovens are built at a height of about thirty-two inches above the forehearth of the fireplace. Below them, these ovens typically have a cavity, often with its own separate hinged iron door. In some cases these cavities have ash chutes that empty into a vault or a brick box in the cellar, allowing the easy removal and storage of fireplace and oven ashes. In other cases the cavities have no exit and are roofed with combustible wooden planks, suggesting that they were used for storing fuel rather than hot ashes.

By the early nineteenth century many houses were also equipped with a means of boiling water in large quantities. Constructed in kitchens or summer kitchens, caldrons, or "set kettles," were large, cast-iron vessels supported by a brick arch, or firebox, with its own separate flue. Much more elaborate were "Rumford works" — roasting ovens and cooking pots set into massive brick stoves with small, separate fire chambers that conserved fuel and reduced heat in the kitchen. Because of the cost of buying the cast-

iron components of such a cooking system and of building the elaborate brickwork, Rumford kitchens were restricted to the homes of the wealthy. The introduction of cast-iron kitchen ranges by the 1830s ended the building of elaborate Rumford works.

Oven, Bailey Parker House, Pembroke, New Hampshire, circa 1830. By the 1820s, various foundries were manufacturing cast iron oven doors to supplant the sheet iron stoppers that had sealed oven mouths. These doors have sliding vents to admit air during heating, and top dampers to close the flue after the oven is hot. Photograph by author.

Brick Masonry. While bricks enjoyed extensive use in chimney construction from the seventeenth century, entire brick houses were rare in New England until the early 1800s. At that period a change in architectural style, combined with the effects of major urban fires, overcame the long-standing prejudice that New Englanders had harbored against brick dwellings. Once that prejudice was swept away in cities, brick houses began to appear even in the country.

The early 1800s saw the advent of the Federal style in architecture, the American equivalent of the Adam style in England. This style favored the placement of chimneys against the outside walls in both wooden and brick buildings. In brick structures, placement of chimneys against the exterior walls invited the use of the outer walls of the building as one of the three sides of the chimney. Sometimes, when creosote-producing stoves have been used in such chimneys for many decades, the pathway of the chimney flue is traceable on the outside of the structure by a creosote stain that has leached through the brickwork.

When "laying up" exterior walls, bricklayers employ a variety of bonds, or arrangements of bricks. As seen in the face of a wall, bricks are laid either as "stretchers," where the length of the brick is exposed to view, or as "headers," where the end is seen. The arrangement or sequence of headers and stretchers creates the bond, and the bonding of a wall provides both a regular and attractive pattern and

Oven and ash pit doors made by Ellis and Company, South Carver, Massachusetts, and dated 1850. Although cast-iron kitchen ranges began to gain popularity in the 1830s, many cooks continued to prefer to bake in brick ovens. With cast ornamentation comparable to that of a contemporary stove, this oven door has sliding dampers to control firing and to retain heat. It was installed in a late-eighteenth-century house in Portsmouth, New Hampshire, sometime after 1850. Photograph by Bill Finney.

---

a means of locking the face bricks and the backing bricks into a solid mass that will not crack apart.

Until the 1830s almost all brick buildings in northern New England were laid up in Flemish bond or in a combination of Flemish bond with what later became known as "common" or American bond. In Flemish bond, each course is composed of alternating stretchers and headers, laid in such a way that the headers of one course lie directly above the stretchers of the course below. The result is a richly patterned wall, giving the impression of interlocking brick crosses over the entire surface. It is also a strong wall, in which every other brick extends into the backing course and locks the inner and outer tiers of brickwork firmly together.

The few surviving eighteenth-century brick buildings in northern New England employ the Flemish bond and often make a deliberate use of dark-burned headers laid as a contrast to the redder stretchers. This creates a checkered

Flemish bond with dark headers, Weeks House, Greenland, New Hampshire, circa 1710. As seen on the sides of some of the stretchers in this wall, the ends of bricks exposed to intense heat may darken. Masons often used such bricks as headers to emphasize the regular, alternating pattern of the Flemish bond. Photograph by author.

Brick bond with dark headers in a diaper pattern, reflective of Dutch traditions in the Hudson River valley and seen in some late-eighteenth- and early-nineteenth-century buildings in western Vermont. This pattern is seen in the end walls of the John Strong House (1797) in Addison, Vermont. Drawing by author.

pattern on the face of the wall. The use of such colored patterning is seen in both British and Low Country bricklaying traditions. Still more complex contrasting colors and patterns appear in eighteenth-century brick buildings beyond New England, notably in houses built by English Quakers in southern and western New Jersey and in buildings in the Dutch tradition in the Hudson River valley of New York. In both areas the end walls of houses are sometimes decorated in dark diaper or zigzag patterns and occasionally with letters and numerals picked out in dark headers.

Under the influence of the Hudson Valley tradition, western Vermont became the only area of northern New England where strongly patterned brickwork retained fa-

vor as late as the early 1800s. In contrast with other areas, where all the bricks employed in the Flemish bond were generally uniform in color, masons in western Vermont reverted to the eighteenth-century practice of employing dark headers as a counterpoint to the remainder of the bricks in the wall. To achieve the diaper pattern that is sometimes seen in western Vermont, bricklayers used a complex bond that makes careful use of closers, or bricks that are cut to special sizes, to maintain the diagonal lines of dark headers.

Even the earliest brick houses in northern New England exhibit common bond on their lesser walls. In this bond several courses of the face bricks are laid up as stretchers only, having no mechanical connection with the

backing tiers in the wall. Every few courses, however, there is a course composed of headers only, bonding the face bricks to the backing bricks. This bond can be laid much more quickly than Flemish bond, though it lacks some of the strength and the attractiveness of the latter. At first, common bond was used only for side or rear walls of important buildings. The MacPheadris-Warner House in Portsmouth, New Hampshire, built in 1716, uses a common bond on all but its front wall, and in this early example of the bond every fourth course is a header course.

For most buildings of the early 1800s, when brick houses first became truly popular in city and country,

Flemish bond remained universal for the principal walls, with common bond, if used at all, hidden on the sides or rear. By the 1830s, however, brick houses increasingly displayed common bond on all walls. Later in the nineteenth century this bond was used very widely, perhaps lending credibility to its popular name of American bond—a name that ignored the fact that, like Flemish bond, it was also widely known and used in England.

At the same period that common bond began to be accepted for the principal walls of brick houses, a new fashion in brickwork also emerged. This was the use of running, or "plumb," bond, in which the face bricks were all stretchers, attached to the backing tiers by some hidden means. Running bond almost invariably used hard-burned pressed bricks as its outer veneer. Laid with extremely narrow mortar joints that were made possible by the precise molding of the bricks, running bond imparted an appearance of solidity and a uniformity of color not seen in other bonds. The face bricks in a wall of running bond were normally attached to the backing tiers through the use of iron ties placed in the mortar joints every few courses and invisible from the exterior of the building.

The use of a veneer of brick in this manner eventually led to a similar covering for framed structures. Popular by the second half of the nineteenth century, brick veneering over wooden framing was normally composed, as it is today, of a single tier or thickness of brick attached to the

Flemish bond (*right*) and common bond (*left*), 1824. Flemish bond was usually employed on the fronts of buildings before 1830. As seen here, the less exacting common bond might be employed on the sides and rear of a structure. Photograph by author.

Dwelling, brick veneer, Concord, New Hampshire, circa 1880. Granite underpinning and window sills and lintels give this house the appearance of a building with load-bearing brick walls. Photograph by author.

framed wall behind it by metal ties. In early veneered houses these ties might simply be spikes driven into the frame and imbedded in the mortar joints of the brick veneer.

Except in unusual circumstances the brickwork of exterior walls was laid up in lime mortar until Portland cement became readily available in the early twentieth century. As noted earlier, lime for mortar was obtained from limestone except at the earliest period of settlement, when seashells, often taken from huge middens left by the Indians over centuries of occupation, were burned for their lime.

Until the introduction of Portland cement as an alternative binder for mortar, mortar for bricklaying consisted of nothing but slaked lime and sand. Such a mortar is normally white, though its hue can vary according to the color of the sand used as an aggregate. The color of the sand becomes more apparent over time as weather erodes the lime from the surface of the mortar.

Lime mortar hardens by a chemical reaction that takes place as it is exposed to the carbon dioxide in the air, rather than from an internal reaction caused by the water. For this reason, lime putty can be prepared, or lime mortar can be mixed, and then stored under cover for weeks or even months in board-lined pits or other receptacles. Such long-term storage was often done, when circumstances permitted, to ensure the complete slaking of all the lime in the mixture. Because it is air-hardened, lime mortar buried within thick masonry walls may take years to cure or set fully.

Lime-sand mortar is easily worked by the mason and can be retempered or made more plastic by the simple ad-

Repair of a section of the brick wall reveals that it is a four-inch-thick veneer outside a braced wooden frame. Many brick-veneered houses have sheathing boards on the frame, with the bricks attached to these boards by metal ties or spikes cemented into the brick joints. Photograph by author.

dition of water. In setting, such a mortar never hardens to the rocklike consistency of a mortar made with Portland cement. For this reason, it remains weaker than the bricks in a wall, permitting some movement or settlement of the wall without cracking of the bricks. Lime-sand mortar is the preferred mortar for laying and repointing older clamp-burned bricks, which tend to be weaker than bricks burned in modern kilns. The use of Portland cement mortars with such bricks often creates a situation in which the mortar is harder than the bricks; in such cases, various conditions may cause the mortar to damage the bricks rather than allowing the wall to adjust to its normal internal stresses.

As a trade, bricklaying has changed little over the centuries in tools or techniques. Mechanical advances have made the mixing of mortar and the delivery of bricks and mortar to the work site much easier for the bricklayer's tender or helper, who formerly had to carry all materials up ladders and across staging planks in a hod on his shoulder. But once the materials are placed at the elbow of the bricklayer, the job becomes as much of a handicraft as it was in Roman times.

Whether in the early nineteenth century or today, a well-tended bricklayer (that is, one kept supplied with bricks and mortar by a tender or helper) building a plain wall will lay a thousand or more bricks in a day, using a common triangular mason's trowel made of tempered steel with a wooden handle. To maintain this productivity, bricklayers in every generation tend to develop a rhythm that is reflected in the bonding and jointing of the wall. The noticeable difference between early and modern bricklaying is that face bricks in early walls tend to have much finer joints than those in more recent work.

In any era a bricklayer laying up backing tiers or rear walls on a building might gain speed by using a mortar joint of three-eighths or even one-half inch. In nineteenth-century brickwork, however, especially with pressed bricks, bricklayers usually adhered to mortar joints of only one-eighth to one-quarter inch on the principal walls of a building. Such fine joints required well-molded and carefully selected bricks and mortar made from finely screened sand. Such a mortar is difficult to work with, and therefore bricks with fine mortar joints require more time and effort in their laying.

By contrast, twentieth-century brickwork often had mortar joints of one-half inch. With such wide joints, the color and character of the mortar became significant fac-

tors in the aesthetic effect of a wall, whereas in earlier brickwork the bricks themselves provide the dominant color and character of the wall.

Despite the relatively insignificant proportion of wall surface occupied by mortar joints in early brickwork, the joints were often tooled in a decorative manner. Such jointing is accomplished by running a shaped metal tool between the bricks while the mortar is still soft. The most popular joint profile at all periods is a simple groove made by a narrow convex tool. In early-nineteenth-century brickwork, with its typically narrow mortar joints, this groove is often only one-eighth inch wide. The erosion of lime mortar by sun and rain often obliterates the original jointing on many parts of a wall, but evidence of the intended treatment can sometimes be found on sheltered wall surfaces or underneath additions to the structure.

In later-nineteenth-century masonry, particularly stonemasonry, more complex joints are often encountered. The most common of these is a molded bead. Later-nineteenth-century brickwork and stonework also frequently display colored mortar, achieved through the addition of various mineral pigments to the mortar mix. Colored mortar is seldom used throughout a wall; rather, it is applied as "pointing." In pointing, a portion of the mortar joint in

Brick jointing, Bailey Parker House, Pembroke, New Hampshire, circa 1830. A narrow, rounded groove was the most common form of early-nineteenth-century joint detailing. The vertical lines on the faces of the bricks were formed when the mold was lifted off the soft clay prisms. Indentations show how the "green" bricks were stacked upon one another in the kiln. Photograph by author.

which bricks or stones are laid is raked out while still wet. After the mortar has dried, the raked joints are filled with colored mortar and tooled to whatever ornamental profile is desired.

All old brickwork eventually requires repointing, often called tuck pointing by masons. Lime mortar, especially, is relatively soft and is slightly water soluble, so that rain washing down the face of a wall and the effects of heat and cold will eventually erode the mortar joints. When this process has proceeded sufficiently far, the joints must be repointed to prevent serious water penetration and damage to the wall. In exposed masonry, as in chimney stacks laid in a sand-lime mortar, pointing may be advisable as often as every ten years.

In repointing, the deteriorated mortar in the outer zone of the joints is cut out and replaced with fresh mortar, well pressed into the joints and tooled to match the original technique. While there are a number of electric or pneumatic tools used to rake out old mortar joints, these tend to chip or cut the edges of the bricks even in professional hands. In most cases, hand tools should therefore be used for cutting out joints in old brickwork. These consist of narrow chisels and hammers, and their use requires strength, skill, and time. Once the joints are cleaned out and flushed with water, fresh mortar is applied with a narrow pointing trowel and, when somewhat stiff, is then tooled with an appropriate jointer.

One of the most common problems encountered in old brickwork is modern pointing done with hard mortar. A universal ingredient in all commercially prepared mortar mixes, bought by the bag and requiring only the addition of water, is Portland cement. As mentioned earlier, Portland cement is an extremely hard-setting material, producing a mortar that is likely to be stronger than that used originally on old brickwork. The general rule in repointing is that the new mortar should be no harder than the original mortar. Thus, the addition of Portland cement in significant proportions to a repointing mortar is seldom recommended.

Portland cement may be hazardous when improperly used in masonry that predates its introduction, yet this material is of crucial importance to more modern buildings and may be very appropriately used in their restoration. Both Portland cement and lime are adhesives that are capable of binding aggregates into a solid mass having many of the qualities of stone. Lime and Portland cement differ in that lime hardens or sets upon exposure to carbon dioxide in the air—returning, in effect, to the chemical composition of the limestone from which it was originally manufactured.

Portland cement, by contrast, sets upon exposure to water and does not require air to complete the chemical reaction that results in its hardening. It is thus classed as a hydraulic cement, and it is capable of setting under water—an invaluable quality when it is used in concrete foundations for bridges or piers.

"Gravel," or Concrete, Walls. A few New England houses built after 1850 have walls built of a concrete that uses lime (or occasionally clay) as a cement and sand and stones as an aggregate. Although few in number, these houses are a response to one of the most unusual books on house construction to have been published in the mid-nineteenth century, an era that was filled with persuasive treatises on various aspects of house building. That book was Orson S. Fowler's *A Home for All; or the Gravel Wall and Octagon Mode of Building New, Cheap, Convenient, Superior, and Adapted to Rich and Poor.*

Before writing his book, Fowler had been a successful practitioner of phrenology, a nineteenth-century method of assessing human character by analyzing the shape of the skull. With his own thriving publishing house, Fowler published the first edition of *A Home for All* in 1848. In that edition, he concentrated on "board wall" construction, not on concrete. By 1853 when he published a second edition, Fowler had become convinced that lime-based concrete was "nature's building material" and that the octagonal floor plan was superior to all others, not only for dwellings but also for schoolhouses and church buildings.

Given the radical nature of Fowler's suggestions, it is striking that his advice was followed at all. Yet, octagonal houses are to be found in most of the then-settled parts of the United States. These buildings are few in number, and many are built of standard framed construction or of brick, but it is a testament to Fowler's persuasiveness that people who had never known any but rectangular houses and rooms should have been convinced to adopt his ideas.

Those who fully subscribed to Fowler's plan built their houses of concrete, not wood or brick. In the absence of Portland cement, Fowler recommended lime as a cement, hand-mixed in various proportions with sand and stones and shoveled into forms that were raised up the walls when each shallow layer of concrete had hardened sufficiently to permit the next layer to be deposited. As an alter-

Riven (hand-split) laths, Captain John Sherburne House, Portsmouth, New Hampshire, circa 1703. Riven lath is split along the grain of the wood and is therefore slightly irregular, with a ribbed surface. This lath is attached with hand-wrought nails. Photograph by author.

native to lime, Fowler suggested a clay-stone concrete, to be protected from the weather by an impervious cladding, and a few houses of this material were actually built in northern New England. Whatever the formula employed, most gravel-wall houses were either clapboarded or rendered with lime stucco to protect their walls from rain and frost.

Plastering. Masons in the eighteenth and early nineteenth centuries spent much of their time doing plastering, which had not yet become a separate trade. Plastering has always been the single most effective method of sealing the walls of a house against the infiltration of air and of providing an attractive and permanent finish for interior partitions and ceilings. For this reason, plaster was applied to the inner walls of all but the crudest dwellings from the 1600s and to the ceilings of most houses from the very early 1700s. Plastering undoubtedly consumed most of the lime produced in New England even after the fashion for brick construction appeared in the early 1800s.

Until recently, most plaster has been a mortar made from lime and sand, differing only slightly from the mortar used in bricklaying. Because plaster must be given a smooth finish, greater care is taken in selecting and preparing its ingredients than in making mortar for bricklaying. Lime for plaster, for example, was slaked as far in advance of use as possible, the putty being kept in plank-lined pits for as long as a year or more in a process called souring. The putty was passed through a sieve to break up

any particles of unslaked lime, which caused "popping," pitting, and disintegration of the plaster if they hydrated after application. The sand, likewise, was screened to remove any large particles that would interfere with the smooth application of the mortar.

Lime plaster is applied with a trowel to a perforated or textured surface to which the mortar will bind by mechanical adhesion. Such a surface may be offered by rough brickwork, rough-sawn lumber, or smooth boards that have been hacked or roughened by a hatchet, and plaster will often be found to have been applied to such surfaces in old houses. Technically, plastering on rough masonry is called rendering, to distinguish it from plastering on lath.

The universally preferred substratum of lime plaster was wooden lath. Wooden lath can take several forms, each form being predominant at a given period. The earliest type generally encountered in New England is riven or split lath. Riven laths are individual strips of wood, traditionally four feet in length or slightly more, skillfully split from bolts or blocks of pine or hemlock in northern New England and from oak in southern New England. Such laths are immediately recognizable by their slightly undulating surfaces (the lath having been split along the natural lines of cleavage in the wood) and by their ribbed texture, which reveals the grain of the annual rings of the wood. Riven lath is normally found in houses ranging from the 1600s to the late 1700s. Because this is the same period when the hand-forged nail was universal, most riven lath will be found to be nailed to its supporting studs or joists

Split-board lath (back of lath, showing plaster keys), David Allison House, Concord, New Hampshire, circa 1830. This type of lath is made from mill-sawn boards, split at both ends and nailed with the splits wedged open. The horizontal board near the bottom is the back of a chair rail. The wall studs were split from wide planks. Photograph by author, courtesy of Richard and Barbara Lemieux.

with fairly short (1¼- to 1½-inch) hand-forged nails having somewhat irregular heads. Machine-made cut nails began to come into use in the 1790s.

Riven lath is probably the best form of wooden lath ever devised. It offers many voids through which the plaster can squeeze and harden into "keys," which mechanically lock the sheets of mortar to the wooden foundation. Its striated surface offers a further bond with the plaster. Although riven lath was still used as late as 1900 in limited quantities, its high cost of production had made it a rarity even a hundred years earlier.

Beginning around 1800 the use of individual riven laths was generally superseded by split-board lath. Split-board lath is composed of rough-sawn boards of refuse quality, almost always sawn on an upright or reciprocating sawmill and eight or more feet in length. These boards were cloven at several places at each end so as to produce splits

that run partway down the length of the board. They were then nailed to the wall studs or ceiling joists with their splits wedged open, thus creating a number of fissures through which the plaster could be pressed. Because this type of lath has a far higher proportion of wood and a far lower proportion of voids than riven lath, it offers a poorer opportunity for the plaster to form keys. This is therefore the poorest type of wooden lath, especially for use on ceilings. It is not uncommon to find large areas of ceiling plaster that have broken loose and are sagging from such lath or to see evidence of areas where the plaster has fallen in former years and has been redone.

Because the introduction of split-board lath coincided with the development of the machine-made cut nail, most lath of this type will be found to be nailed to the underlying framing with cut nails.

Despite its relatively poor quality, split-board lath en-

Circular sawn lath, circa 1900. Carpenters used a piece of lath as a spacer in nailing this plaster foundation. Photograph by author.

---

joyed almost universal popularity until the mid-1800s, when the introduction of the circular saw made possible the production of individually sawn laths. Yet the preference for individual laths was not universal, and one sometimes finds sawn board lath that evidently dates from the mid- to late 1800s and is made from rough boards bearing the marks of the circular saw rather than the older upright saw.

The last type of wooden lath was the individual sawn lath. These are four-foot strips of wood very similar in dimensions to riven lath. They are distinguishable from riven laths in having a sawn rather than a split texture, and they were generally sawn in such a way as to raise the fibers of the wood and to produce a slightly fuzzy texture that would bond well with the plaster. They were nailed to the underlying framing with cut or wire nails (depending on the period), using a piece of lath as a spacer. This produced a gap of about one-quarter inch between adjacent laths and offered an opportunity for the plaster to form

strong keys. This type of lath remained common until after World War II.

It is frequently possible to detect the type of lath used in a building by simply looking at the face of an exposed plaster wall or ceiling. Unless repainting has been frequent, each type of lath will eventually reveal its image on plaster, especially on uninsulated ceilings. The slow passage of air through the fissures between the laths results in a deposit of dirt on the surface of the plaster. This migration of warm air will eventually turn part of the plaster gray, with the laths and their supporting framing standing out as whiter areas than the gaps between them. The adhesion of dirt may also be partly due to condensation of water vapor on colder areas of plaster. Such condensation may occur at the cold plaster keys but not in areas where the insulating qualities of wooden laths or joists keep the plaster a bit warmer. In one-coat plastering, too, the plaster is often applied thinly enough to register the undulations of the underlying lath, often making it possible to tell at a glance whether a ceiling has riven, split-board, or sawn lath.

The early twentieth century saw the introduction of several types of nonwooden lath. Even before 1900 a variety of patterns of expanded metal lath were on the market. Made from sheets of steel that were rolled to create ribs, perforated, and stretched to expand the perforations, the several brands of metal lath were touted as fireproof. Plaster easily penetrated their plentiful voids, forming very effective keys. At first used more in commercial buildings than in homes, expanded metal lath became more common in domestic use during the early 1900s. A form of wire cloth was frequently used during the same period as a base for exterior stucco.

Three types of metal lath in widespread use in the early twentieth century. The woven wire lath at the left was intended for exterior stucco. The other two, expanded metal lath (*center*) and ribbed metal lath (*right*), and patterns similar to them were mostly used in interior plastering. Drawing by author.

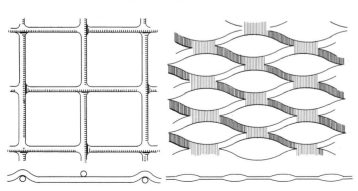
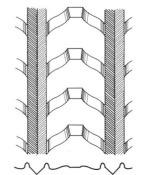

Whatever the type of lath employed, lime plaster was applied with a plasterer's trowel, well pressed onto the lath in order to squeeze some of the plaster through the gaps. The trowel used by plasterers in the eighteenth and nineteenth centuries was a flat sheet of polished iron or steel, rounded at one end, with a wooden handle riveted to its back. It was narrower than the common plastering trowel of today, measuring about ten inches long by two and a half inches wide, and was used in laying and smoothing most flat plaster work. Because early plaster was applied and finished with such a tool, it retains a slightly rippled or undulating surface, quite noticeable, for example, under the raking light cast by a window on a ceiling. This hand-troweled surface is in contrast to the perfectly flat surface achieved by later plaster, which was smoothed by long straightedges.

Depending on the period and the quality of the work, plaster could be applied in one, two, or three coats. The lime mortar was prepared differently for each of these applications.

One-coat plastering is commonly found in houses of the 1700s and early 1800s. Mortar for this kind of work was prepared from lime putty and screened sand, to which was added a considerable quantity of cattle hair obtained from tanneries. This hair was thoroughly mixed with the mortar, using a two-pronged iron rake, and provided a fibrous binder that locked the entire sheet of plaster into a single mass even when cracks developed in it over time. When one-coat plaster is damaged, the binding hair (which bleaches to a yellow or pale red from the action of the lime) will be seen at or near the troweled surface of the mortar. This surface may be left somewhat rough (as on walls intended for wallpapering), or may be finished quite smoothly (as on ceilings) by hard, incessant troweling as the plaster sets. One will occasionally encounter bits of charcoal at or near the surface of coarsely finished one-coat plaster. These are a residue of the burning or calcining process and are evidence that the lime was not carefully screened before being mixed with the sand.

One-coat plastering began to be superseded by two- or three-coat work as the nineteenth century progressed, yet remained common for roughly finished areas in basements, attics, storage areas, and outbuildings.

Plaster applied by the one-coat method was also used in hidden areas as soundproofing and insulation. When the exterior walls of old houses are opened, one-coat plaster is sometimes found applied to the inner face of wall sheathing, between the studs, where it serves as a windbreak and as thermal insulation. Such "back plastering" is usually applied to laths that were nailed directly to the sheathing or, in better work, to furring strips nailed to the sides of the wall studs. In less exacting work, the plaster was simply rendered or troweled onto the rough-sawn inner surface of the wall sheathing. Occasionally, the sheathing will have been further roughened by chopping with a hatchet. Similarly, lath may be applied beneath floorboards and plaster may be applied between the joists before the ceiling is finished off. This type of double plastering served as "deadening," or soundproofing, and deadening was also used in interior partitions to cut down on sound transmission between rooms. Since this type of plastering nearly doubled the work of the plasterer, it is most frequently found in expensive houses, though it is occasionally found in simple dwellings where the builder was especially concerned about heat loss.

Increasingly common for finish plastering during the early to mid-nineteenth century was two-coat work, which

Applying the scratch coat of plaster over sawn wooden lath. The first, or scratch, coat is composed of lime, sand, and animal hair as a binder. The plasterer at the left is scratching the still-soft plaster to prepare its surface for the brown coat. The boards at the bottom of the walls are the grounds for a baseboard to be applied later. From William S. Lowndes and D. Knickerbacker Boyd, *Plastering*, 1923.

Applying the second, or brown, coat of plaster. The vertical and horizontal strips are screeds, or bands of plaster that are applied to the walls, carefully plumbed, and used as guides to obtain a perfect plane in the wall surface. The plasterer is using a two-handed float, or derby, to level the brown coat between the screeds. From Lowndes and Boyd, *Plastering*, 1923.

produced a smoother, more even surface. With this technique, the mortar for the first coat was exactly like that used in one-coat work: a mixture of lime, sand, and cattle hair. When this coat had dried sufficiently, a thin second coat, consisting of plain lime putty or lime putty with some finely screened sand was troweled over the base coat. This was often brought to a smooth finish by being wetted by a bristle brush that the plasterer held in his left hand while he worked the trowel with his right hand. Because pure lime putty is very white, this type of surface was occasionally left exposed to view, without either whitewash or wallpaper, as the finish of a wall or ceiling.

The most finished type of plaster work, and the technique that became the standard for good craftsmanship in the latter half of the nineteenth century and the first half of the twentieth, was three-coat plastering. In this work, again, the base coat was composed of lime, sand, and hair. Since this coat was to serve as the base for two subsequent coats, it was not left with a troweled surface. Rather, it was allowed to stiffen somewhat, and was then scarified with a

comb, usually made from pointed laths. Because it was roughened in this way, the first coat in three-coat plastering was referred to as the scratch coat.

The second coat in the three-coat job was the key to the perfectly flat or plane surface that characterizes this technique. Like the scratch coat, the second coat was composed of lime, sand, and hair. The mortar contained relatively less hair and more sand than the scratch coat and, because of the color imparted by the sand, was called the brown coat. Before this coat was applied to the full wall surface, the plasterer applied carefully leveled bands of brown coat mortar at intervals over the wall or ceiling, either as vertical strips on walls or as a grid on ceilings. Called screeds, these strips were carefully brought to a true plane through the use of long straightedges. Once they were laid and partially set, screeds became guides that ensured a perfectly true surface for an infilling of brown coat material, which was applied over the entire wall or ceiling. This infilling was leveled with a two-handed float, or "derby," and for this reason the brown coat in a three-coat job was sometimes referred to as the floated coat.

Applying the finishing, or skim, coat of plaster. The plasterer on the right is applying the finishing coat to a thickness of about an eighth of an inch. The plasterer on the left is wetting the surface of the plaster and polishing it with a steel trowel, one of several options used to impart a desired texture to the finished surface. From Lowndes and Boyd, *Plastering*, 1923.

The third or final coat in three-coat plastering created a well-finished surface over the perfectly leveled base provided by the brown coat. Because it served as a well-finished veneer of plaster, the third coat was very thin—usually not more than one-eighth of an inch in thickness. Called the skim, white, or finishing coat, this mortar usually consisted of lime putty and a very fine, white sand, sometimes with the addition of plaster of Paris (a gypsum product) to hasten its setting or of marble dust to provide a shiny surface. After application, the white coat was sometimes moistened with a bristle brush while being polished with a steel trowel.

During the eighteenth and early nineteenth centuries, it was customary for the joiners to install most or all of their room finishes before the lathing and plastering were begun. In most cases, the finish woodwork was probably given its priming coat of paint so that it would not take up too much moisture and swell excessively as the plaster dried. The plasterers then came to the job and finished all the rooms before the painters applied the final colors to the woodwork.

This method of working resulted in a different relationship between wall and ceiling plaster and joiner's work than is seen in more modern houses. Because the joiner's work was installed before plastering, the masons had to trowel their plaster against the edges of the finish woodwork, using these edges to gauge the thickness of the plaster as they applied it. The plaster was not normally applied to a thickness that totally buried the edges of casings and baseboards; rather, a small projection of the woodwork, or "reveal," was left exposed above the plane of the plaster. Nevertheless, much of the depth of the woodwork was buried below the surface of the plaster, resulting in much less relief of the woodwork above the wall or ceiling surfaces than was normal at a later time.

Beginning with the advent of the Federal style in the 1790s, plastered walls began to assume a new importance as paneling and wainscoting diminished in popularity for room finishes. At the same time, changes in joinery and molding profiles resulted in a tendency for door and window casings and baseboards to be placed in higher relief above the plastered surfaces of walls. As time went on, it became increasingly commonplace for joiners to apply "grounds," or strips of wood equal in thickness to the plaster, to wall or ceiling framing in locations where finish woodwork was to be applied. Plasterers stopped their work against these grounds, and then the joiners returned to apply the finished woodwork over the grounds, thereby covering both the grounds and the borders of the plastered surfaces.

This method of finishing rooms became increasingly popular during the first half of the nineteenth century and almost universal during the latter half. It had the advantages of allowing the finished woodwork, which was especially susceptible to the dampness of fresh plaster, to be applied after the house had dried and of giving the woodwork a strong projection above plastered surfaces. More important from the plasterer's standpoint, the application of grounds provided a border around the room, offering a perfect guide for the straightedges and derbies used in three-coat work. For this reason, the use of plaster grounds became universal as three-coat work eventually became the standard technique of the plasterer's craft.

Beginning in the early twentieth century, gypsum plasters were manufactured in greater quantity than before and were often substituted for lime plasters. One drawback of lime plaster is its slow setting time. Lime plaster often requires many days or even several weeks to harden after the application of each coat, with the windows kept open to exhaust great quantities of evaporating water and to keep a free circulation of the air necessary for its hardening. Because finished woodwork tends to swell and warp in damp conditions, it is impossible to install the trim in a building that has been plastered with lime until the structure has dried thoroughly.

Gypsum plaster, by contrast, hardens like Portland cement, through an internal chemical reaction that begins as soon as water is added to the powdered cement. For this reason, gypsum plaster sets much more quickly than lime, in hours rather than days or weeks, and may be fully hardened before the water in the mix has evaporated. This permits one coat to be applied over another in rapid succession, with the undercoats still remaining moist (though fully hardened) and thereby aiding the adhesion of overlying coats.

Because of its quick setting time, gypsum plaster was used with increasing frequency as the twentieth century progressed. It was first used in the manner of lime plaster, for three-coat work, with fibers of coconut, asbestos, wood, or (later) nylon increasingly substituted for animal hair in the scratch and brown coats.

The first decades of the twentieth century also saw the introduction of the two forms of gypsum wallboard that have since dominated the market. The first, gypsum lath, is composed of a core of rigid gypsum plaster that was covered with gypsum-impregnated cardboard or fiberboard (later changed to a special form of paper). Formed into sheets, this material can be cut or sawn to any shape and nailed to the studding of the building. A skim coat of gypsum plaster is then applied over the entire wall, producing a surface of unbroken gypsum plaster. Early forms of gypsum lath were marketed under trade names like Rocklath and Roman Wall Plaster Board.

The second form of gypsum wallboard was meant to be applied to the framing as a finished surface, suitable for paint or wallpaper. The joints between the sheets were either covered with wooden battens, if the style of finish called for a paneled appearance, or were sealed with a gypsum compound. The remainder of the surface was not plastered. By 1916 the Aladdin Company, well-known manufacturer of pre-cut houses, was offering Aladdin Plaster Board and standard lath and plaster as alternative interior finishes but was praising the wallboard as generally superior to traditional plaster and as "the single greatest achievement in the builder's craft in the last generation." Marketed under such other trade names as Sheetrock and MasterRock, this form of gypsum sheet became the dominant type of wall covering after World War II. It eventually came to be known under the generic name "drywall."

In comparison to drywall construction, it is evident that traditional plaster is a true handicraft. Plastered walls and ceilings in a house represent a large investment of labor and money on the part of the original builders. Like hand-planed woodwork or narrow-jointed brickwork, old plaster imparts a subtle texture and a general feeling of hand workmanship. The loss of this texture can greatly diminish the integrity of a room. Regrettably, old plaster is usually the portion of a building's fabric that is least understood and valued by homeowner and contractor alike and often seems to stand in the way of procedures like insulating and wiring. Because of its soft nature and its exposure to casual damage, old plaster is often found in an unattractive condition.

Many homeowners also subscribe to the old myth that ceilings were left unplastered in the 1700s and even the 1800s, and countless plastered ceilings have succumbed to the once-pervasive craze for "exposed beams." For these reasons, much of the workmanship inherent in early plastering has been lost to ill-considered and unnecessary removal. A house that retains a high percentage of its orig-

"Running" a plaster cornice. The plasterer is guiding a template along horizontal strips of plaster or wood to create an approximate profile of the cornice in plaster made from lime, sand, and animal hair. After this has hardened, he will apply a mixture of lime putty and plaster of Paris and then run the template along this coating to obtain the final profile of the cornice. From Lowndes and Boyd, *Plastering*, 1923.

inal plastering is therefore one that offers a special responsibility and opportunity to its owner. There are many techniques for saving damaged plaster, almost all of them less expensive than the too-common procedure of tearing out the original work and substituting drywall or other forms of gypsum board.

Ornamental Plaster. Gypsum plaster had become important in some aspects of plastering long before its introduction for general use in wall and ceiling work. Gypsum, especially in the familiar form of plaster of Paris (so named because it was mined and processed in great quantities in the vicinity of Paris), was much used during the nineteenth century for both plaster moldings and plaster ornaments.

Beginning generally in the 1830s, in the more elaborate houses of the Greek Revival style, molded plaster cornices began to make their appearance. The "running," or casting, of these cornices became an increasingly important aspect of the plasterer's trade during the nineteenth century. The cornices themselves evolved from simple, unadorned moldings to elaborate features with bands or

ornaments of cast plaster detailing that were added after the basic moldings had been run.

A plaster cornice was molded from a band of wet plaster that was applied at the juncture of the walls and ceiling of a room. Straightedges were usually attached to the wall below this wet plaster to provide rails to guide a mold or template. Held to a true line by these rails, the template was run horizontally through the bed of soft mortar at the cornice level, shaping the mortar into the finished profile of the desired moldings.

The mold was a simple frame with guides to follow the straightedges and with a silhouette or profile of the cornice cut from wood or sheet metal and held within the frame. The mortar used for a plaster cornice was "gauged stuff," a mixture of lime (with or without sand) and plaster of Paris. The addition of the gypsum cement to the mixture caused the mortar to set quickly, usually within thirty minutes or less, and to hold the profile given to it by the moving template.

During the later nineteenth century and in the twentieth, such molded cornices were often decorated with additional features, such as dentils, modillions, and brackets, which could not be molded in place by a moving template. These were cast separately from plaster of Paris that had been poured into molds and were then attached to the molded cornice by liquid plaster of Paris.

Another form of cast plaster ornamentation that became popular during the nineteenth century was the ceiling "centerpiece" or "center flower." This was a rosette of leaves or flowers placed at the center of a room's ceiling. After the advent of illuminating gas in some cities after 1850, these medallions often supported a chandelier. At other times or in rural homes, the rosettes were sometimes applied simply for ornamental effect. In church auditoriums or other halls, centerpieces sometimes disguised a ceiling ventilator that carried off stale air.

This technique of applied plaster ornament reached its greatest elaboration in buildings of the early twentieth century. The origins of this form of ornament in New

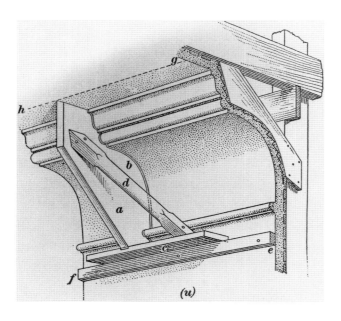

Cross section of a plaster cornice on metal lath, showing the template, *a-d-b*, used to obtain the final profile. From Lowndes and Boyd, *Plastering*, 1923.

Ceiling centerpiece, Portsmouth, New Hampshire, circa 1804. Requiring skills that were not yet widespread, stucco ceiling ornamentation was rare in northern New England during the first decades of the nineteenth century. Photograph by author.

England buildings, however, extend back to the fashion for "stucco work," which coincided with the introduction of the Federal style in the 1790s. The grander houses and public buildings of the late 1700s and early 1800s occasionally contained some cast and applied plaster of Paris features, executed by English-trained stucco workers. These details echoed delicate molded ornaments of "composition," which were often applied at the same period to wooden features, especially mantelpieces, to simulate carving. Together, molded plaster and composition detailing during the early 1800s set the stage for ever increasing use of these techniques over a period of more than a century.

Wallboards. The early twentieth century, which saw the increasing use of gypsum plaster and gypsum wallboards, also witnessed the advent of nonmineral wallboards that were meant to replace traditional plaster altogether. These boards were light enough to be installed by a

Designs for ceiling centerpieces from Asher Benjamin, *The Practice of Architecture* (Boston, 1833). By the 1830s the production of centerpieces, usually made as a single circular unit, had become widespread. The ornaments were sold by dealers as embellishments to rooms in the Greek Revival style. Photograph courtesy of the New Hampshire Historical Society.

single carpenter. The joints between boards were normally covered by battens, creating a paneled wall and ceiling effect that was compatible with the interiors of bungalows and other homes in the Arts and Crafts style. Some boards were suitable for painting; others had a white or wood-grained factory finish. Many were made of compressed wood pulp, but others employed other vegetable fibers or reconstituted newsprint.

Among the wallboards that were popular by the 1920s were Sterling (made from wood fiber), Fibro-Wallboard (made from wood fiber), Peerless and Utility (both made from layers of heavy cardboard or fiberboard cemented with asphalt), Fiberlic (made from root fibers), Homasote (made from repulped newspaper), Celotex (made from bagasse—sugar cane waste), and Beaver Board (made from wood pulp). Many of these products, including Neponset Wall Board, Utility Wall Board, Peerless Wall Board, Quality Wall Board, Ceil-Board, and Rockboard, could be had with a wood-grain finish.

Hardware

Wrought Nails. Few dwellings in the European or American tradition can be built without hardware. A log house with a dirt floor and a roof of bark might be constructed without nails, and that fact was probably one of the main attractions of the log hut to settlers in the eighteenth century. Anything more elaborate than this would require nails of several types and probably hinges, hooks, latches, and assorted fireplace hardware.

Many town histories tell of settlers, about to move on to new frontiers, burning their old houses in order to salvage the nails. Most of these tales may be apocryphal and at best can apply only to dwellings in which the labor invested in making the nails exceeded the labor invested in building the house. They do, however, remind us of the value placed on the work of the blacksmith.

The nail was, and still is, the most humble yet the most important of all forms of hardware. From the time of first settlement until the late 1700s, all nails in New England were made as they had been since ancient times. Each nail was hand-forged from strips or rods of wrought iron by a general blacksmith or by a specialized nailmaker. The latter was sometimes a convict in a prison forge shop.

The process involved bringing the rod to a red or yellow heat in the forge and drawing it to a point by blows of

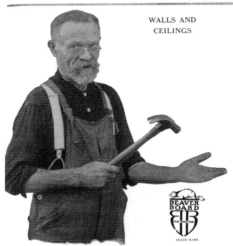

BEAVER BOARD

WALLS AND
CEILINGS

There's Real Satisfaction in Jobs Like This

"When Mrs. Thatcher down here on Pearl Street suggested that I use BEAVER BOARD for remodeling her living room, I was almost afraid to tackle it. You see, I had never used the stuff and was a little bit leery of how the job would look.

"But she persuaded me to try it, and now I'm glad I did. The board was easy to put up, nice to work with, and the room's a beauty. Everybody admires it, and it's been the means of getting me more BEAVER BOARD jobs.

"That's been five years now, and the old lady has never had a cent's worth of repairs. You see, BEAVER BOARD can't crack, and that's more than you can say about plaster when a job settles.

"Take it from me, there's good money in BEAVER BOARD jobs. I'd advise you to write to the company—they'll tell you all about it, without putting you under obligation. Just send 'em your name and address."

The Beaver Board Companies
United States: 190 Beaver Road, Buffalo, N. Y.
Canada: 190 Wall St., Beaverdale, Ottawa
Great Britain: 4 Southampton Row, London, W.C.
Branches in sixteen cities
Please quote BUILDING AGE when writing to advertisers

Advertisement for Beaver Board, *Building Age* magazine, January 1915. By the early twentieth century, a wide range of wall boards and plaster boards had begun to supplant three-coat plastering. Wall boards like Beaver Board were usually nailed to studs, with their joints covered by wooden battens, creating a paneled effect that was especially compatible with the "craftsman" style.

a hammer on an anvil. The nailmaker then cut the tapered section from the rod, inserted it in a die or tool that exposed the cut end, and flattened the projecting end into a nail head with further blows of the hammer. A skilled nailmaker, working with malleable wrought iron, could accomplish all this in less than a minute, without reheating the rod in the process.

Hand-forged nails were made in a wide range of sizes. These sizes were originally described in two ways. Nails bought in bulk were sized according to their weight, usually specified as so many pounds per thousand nails. In medieval times, nails were also described according to their price per hundred, expressed in English pence or shillings (abbreviated "d" or "s"). Carpenters came to recognize nails of given lengths as "ten penny" or "twenty penny" nails and to use the price as a description of nail sizes. This nomenclature was retained even after nail prices changed over time, so even before the settlement of North America the term "penny" bore no relationship to nail prices and was strictly a designation of nail length. The terminology persisted after cut and wire nails superseded forged nails, and the designation "penny" ("d") is still used, as it has been for hundreds of years, to denote nail length.

Despite the intermittent establishment of ironworks from the early seventeenth century through the mid-nineteenth, New England never achieved self-sufficiency in the manufacture of iron. Much iron continued to be imported from England, Sweden, and Russia until a time when supplies from elsewhere in the United States could be brought economically to the New England market. A major problem was the state in which iron is usually found in New England. Except in a few small deposits of "magnetic" iron ore, or magnetite (most of them not found or exploited until the early nineteenth century), iron in New England is encountered in the form of limonite, or bog ore. This is a crust or bed of ore that accumulated in water and may remain on the bottom of a pond or stream or may be found in the earth where a body of water formerly stood. Limonite usually occurs in relatively small deposits, and the scattered and limited distribution of this ore worked against the development of a vigorous iron industry in New England.

New England nailmakers, then, often worked from imported iron, and this undoubtedly added to the expense of their product. In any case, the process of making a hand-forged nail was a time-consuming one yet was one that provided a very wide range of nail sizes and types, much greater than the varieties later available in machine-made nails. By varying the point, shank, and head of a hand-forged nail, the blacksmith could achieve many special characteristics that were closely suited to many different jobs. Because the hand-made nail was forged from wrought iron, a highly malleable metal, it also clenched easily and without breaking.

The most commonly encountered type of forged nail is the rose-headed nail, named for the faceted shape of its head. This nail was used in various sizes and weights for a variety of jobs where the holding power of its large head was important. It is frequently seen as a clapboard, lath, and sheathing nail. In one of its smallest forms, the rose-headed nail was used as a shingle nail.

The second most commonly seen nail is the clasp nail, which has a head that is flattened on the anvil on opposite sides. This creates an elongated T-head, which can be driven below the surface of woodwork and puttied over. The clasp nail served as the common finish nail for work that required a fastener of some size and strength, such as the nailing of floor boards or paneled walls. For very fine finish work, brads or sprigs, tiny slivers of iron with or without small L-shaped heads, were commonly used.

Less frequently seen are clout nails, which have a disk-shaped head, flat on top and often countersunk beneath. These were forged in a die that gave their heads a very regular form, and were used mostly in attaching hardware to wood. These were sometimes used in attaching H or HL hinges, as (more commonly) were ordinary rose-headed nails or dog nails, which had a higher and more faceted head. Any nail that was used to attach a hinge might also be "botched" by the addition of a small leather washer under the head of the nail. The compression of the leather during the clenching of the nail would protect the head of the nail from splitting off and would prevent any loosening and rattling of the nail over time, keeping the hinge firm virtually forever.

Hand-forged nails of any type might be drawn to a fine, needle-like point, left relatively blunt, or given a flattened, shovel-like point, depending on the nature of the wood to be nailed.

It is not uncommon to find hand-forged nails in limited use as late as 1900 or later. Always prized for their malleability and strength when clenched, such nails continued to be made for constructing batten doors, for attaching strap hinges, for boat building, and for horseshoeing. For country carpentry, forged nails continued to be made entirely by hand by local blacksmiths; but during the nineteenth century, machines were devised to speed up the forging process.

Cut Nails. Meanwhile, however, a different type of machine, making a different type of nail, was being introduced. A number of American inventors began experimenting, by the 1780s, with devices to manufacture nails —Nathan Read and Jacob Perkins of Massachusetts emerging as dominant figures in the early years of experi-

Making hand-forged nails entails heating the nail rod and hammering it to a point, partially cutting the end of the rod, inserting the end in a heading tool, and forging the head of the nail with a few blows of the hammer. Photographs by author.

mentation. The simplest and most feasible idea called for nails to be sliced cold from a sheet or bar of wrought iron, rather than being forged by hammer blows from heated iron. Machines to slice such nails and eventually to head them as part of one continuous manufacturing process were developed by several inventors. Available in large quantities and at reasonable prices, these "cut" nails were widely used by 1800 in building projects in coastal towns

and in inland communities where local merchants could supply them. Within a few years, cut nails dominated the market for such common uses as nailing sheathing, flooring, clapboards, and shingles.

The cut nail has both strengths and weaknesses as a fas-

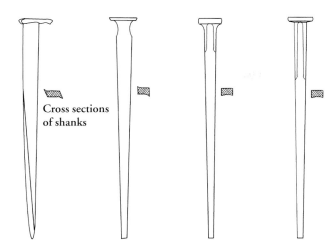

Cross sections of shanks

Cut nails displayed evolutionary changes as machines were developed, during the early 1800s, to cut and head the nails with increasing efficiency. *Left to right:* post-1790 to c. 1820, hand headed; post-1790 to c. 1820, machine headed, two-operation machine; post-1810 to c. 1840, machine headed, one-operation machine; c. 1835 to c. 1890, modern. Drawing by author, after Maureen Phillips.

tener. Because it is sliced cold from an iron bar, the cut nail is very strong and stiff when driven straight into wood. On the other hand, wrought iron is a fibrous material with microscopic strands of glasslike slag interwoven with strands of nearly pure iron. The rolling of the iron straps that were used in nail making caused the fibers of the metal to run parallel to the length of the strap. When a nail was sheared off the end of such a strap, the iron fibers ran across the shank of the nail rather than along the shank. For these reasons, early cut nails often broke when bent for clenching and sometimes when simply being driven into the wood. Perhaps for this reason it has been noted that clapboards or laths attached with cut nails were sometimes fastened with a larger hand-forged nail at their center.

To overcome this tendency toward brittleness, some nail manufacturers obtained very wide iron straps, sheared strips off these straps, and inserted the strips into the machines with the grain of the iron running parallel to the shanks of the nails.

Some of the earliest cut nails were slivers of iron, headed by hand after being sheared off the strap. A few early machines were developed to head cut nails in a second, separate operation. Sometime after 1810, more sophisticated machines became capable of clamping the

sheared sliver of iron and heading it in a single sequence of operations. This technology improved after about 1835, and advancements in the machinery were reflected in visible differences in the nails. Cut nails can thus be roughly separated into different evolutionary stages, with date ranges assigned to each phase.

Because they are formed from cold metal, the heads of cut nails tend to be small, like those of a finish nail. For this reason, when used for finished joinery during the first part of the nineteenth century, cut nails were often simply driven flush with the surface of the wood and painted without being set and puttied. While well adapted to such finish use, the small head of the cut nail lacks the bearing of the expansive head of a hand-forged rose-headed nail. Thus, the cut nail was not fitted to every use. But where appropriate (and this included the majority of nailing processes), the cut nail offered a cheap substitute for the handmade nail and greatly aided the building trades.

Wire Nails. The cut nail remained dominant for most of the nineteenth century. Beginning in the 1880s, however, a new form of machine-made nail began to appear in the American market. This was the wire nail, at first called the *pointe de Paris* or the French nail. As its various names imply, this new product was made from round steel wire of varying gauges or diameters and was a French invention. Unlike the cut nail, the wire nail is round rather than square or rectangular in cross-section, and its shank does not taper except at the extreme point.

Probably due to the softness of the stock from which it was manufactured, the wire nail was initially confined to such light uses as the fastening of boxes and crates. In time, however, wire nail machines were adapted to varying grades and gauges of steel wire, and the wire nail began to overtake the cut nail as the dominant fastener in Amer-

Wire nails were introduced during the late 1800s and became increasingly dominant during the twentieth century. *Top,* common; *bottom,* finish. Drawing by author.

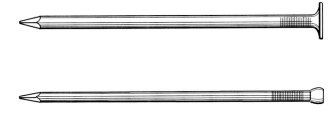

ican building. Because of the malleability of the low-carbon steel wire from which this type of nail is made, wire nails accept a wider range of heads than do cut nails. The machine-made wire nails of the twentieth century began to offer as much variety as the hand-forged nails of the eighteenth. The shanks of wire nails vary more than those of any other type. They may be smooth, fluted, twisted, or threaded; they may be uncoated, resin-coated or etched for greater holding power, or coated with a non-corroding metal like zinc.

Wood Screws. Perhaps the second most basic hardware product, after the nail, is the screw. This was not always so, because until the mid-nineteenth century the screw was an expensive handmade product and was far less effective as a fastener than the modern screw. During the eighteenth century, the screw was used mostly by cabinet-makers as a means of securely fastening the small hinges and catches used in their work. Occasionally, screws were used to fasten H and HL hinges to doors, and screws were used universally with the butt hinges that became increasingly common after 1800 or so.

A handmade screw is easily distinguished from its modern counterpart by several features. Its head tends to be slightly irregular and to have a hand-cut groove, sometimes accidentally placed a bit off-center. If a screw is not encrusted with paint, these features will often be noticeable without withdrawing the screw. When a handmade screw is backed out of the wood, its difference from the modern screw is much more striking. The shank does not taper, but is of uniform cross-section from the head to the end. Its threads tend to be closer together, flat-edged rather than sharp, and to have less angle than those of a modern screw. More important, the screw has no point, unless one has been cut by hand.

The gimlet-pointed, self-tapping screw of today is one of the more recent developments in basic hardware. Two New York inventors, Thomas J. Sloan and Thomas W. Harvey, patented improved machinery for manufacturing such screws in 1846. Wood screws made after the mid-nineteenth century thus became cheaper and more uniform than earlier screws, which were difficult to work with and required various makeshifts on the part of carpenters.

Although it is always good practice to pre-drill a hole for a wood screw, this was absolutely essential for flat-ended screws, and the hole had to be comparatively large. Because the thread of such a screw ended at the blunt end,

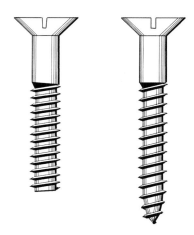

Machinery to manufacture the modern gimlet-pointed screw (*right*) was patented in 1846. Earlier screws (*left*) had threads and slots of lesser regularity and required the careful drilling of pilot holes before they were driven. Drawing by author.

it often twisted and tore the wood fibers of the hole, preventing the following thread from obtaining a good grip in the hole. To overcome this problem, carpenters sometimes filed blunt-ended screws to a conical point or to a threaded point like that of a modern screw. As an alternative, they sometimes fashioned a single screw into a tap to cut threads into the walls of the holes that had been drilled for the permanent screws. They did this by filing off part of the thread of the pilot screw on four sides, leaving sharp-edged remnants. When screwed into and out of the hole, this tap prepared the wood for the permanent screw to follow.

By ensuring a solid grip between the hole and the thread, these techniques also aided in the removal of screws. Withdrawal of a handmade screw is often difficult because of damage that occurred to the walls of the hole in driving the screw. When such damage has occurred, it is often nearly impossible to back the screw out of the wood when removing hardware because the screw merely turns in the hole. Laborious filing of the screws or tapping of the drilled holes reduced this difficulty, but the problem was not overcome until Sloan's and Harvey's patents made possible the cheap manufacture of the modern pointed screw. The development of the modern screw, in turn, had a strong effect on the flowering of the entire hardware trade after the mid-nineteenth century.

Hinges. While the nail and the screw were the indispensable units of hardware, convenience demanded many other iron and brass products. These were widely manufactured in eighteenth-century New England by local blacksmiths and founders, but many hinges, latches, catches, and similar products were manufactured for export in the great ironworking centers of England. The cost of manufacturing standard hardware products in these cities was kept low through factory production and specialization, and English hardware was imported into America in large quantities both before and after the Revolution.

Foremost among the more complex products of the ironworker was the hinge. For interior doors and hinged interior window shutters, the so-called H or HL hinge remained the standard type of hinge until the late 1700s or later. Made of iron and sold in pairs, these hinges derived their names from their shapes, and they were nailed to the face of a door and its casing. The long leaves of the H or the L of these hinges permitted a number of nails to be used in attaching the hardware without the risk of splitting the door or its casing.

Because of the nearly insatiable demand for H and HL hinges throughout the British Empire, great numbers of them were manufactured in specialized shops in England. The scale of operation in these shops and the specialized, repetitive nature of the work made the hinges less expensive than they would have been if made on order by local blacksmiths. Despite the fact that American smiths could and did make H and HL hinges, we often see such hinges offered by hardware dealers who probably acquired their stock through importation rather than through local manufacture. For this reason, it is usually difficult to tell

whether the hinges in an eighteenth-century New England house were made locally or in an English shop.

Hinges evolved over time. H and HL hinges of the 1600s and early 1700s frequently had the ends of their leaves cut and filed to ornamental, foliated forms. This extra chisel and file work, though highly attractive, added to the cost of what was essentially a utilitarian item. The practice tended to disappear during the eighteenth century, and the leaves of later H and HL hinges are commonly square-ended. Some H hinges, probably intended more for cabinetwork than for buildings, were coated with tin, which gave them a silvered finish.

Most H and HL hinges have welded joints or knuckles, with pins that are sweated into the wrapped iron of the joint and often flattened or riveted at their ends. Doors or interior shutters hung on such hinges are permanently fixed and can be removed only by prying the nails of the hinge from the door or casing. This makes it difficult to adjust a door to the normal settlement of the house, and the usual expedient is simply to plane or saw off parts of the door that may begin to rub on the frame or on the threshold.

H and HL hinges are usually made of fairly thin iron. Over time, with constant use, the joints of such hinges wear and loosen so that the door slowly drops and may drag on the threshold or floor. It is therefore not uncommon to find that old doors have been sawed at the bottom to stop this rubbing and fitted with a strip of wood at the top to fill the gap that develops above the door. It is also not unusual to find old doors that were later re-hung with butts; in such cases, it is often possible to find a depression or "shadow" in the paint where the leaf of the H or HL hinge was removed from the door.

Toward the end of the eighteenth century, as butts became available in some areas, it became fashionable to camouflage H and HL hinges so that they resembled the newer hardware. This was often accomplished by nailing the fixed leaf of the hinge to the door frame and then applying the door casing over that part of the hinge or by recessing the movable leaf flush with the surface of the door. The result was that only the knuckle of the hinge was noticeable, as with a butt.

Until the late 1700s, H hinges were usually attached with nails. When fastened by this method, the hinge needed only punched holes in its leaves, made by the blacksmith when the iron was hot. Small nails were driven through these holes, with or without botching (the use of

H and HL hinges. The style with foliated ends (*left*) was most common during the first half of the eighteenth century. Most H and HL hinges used in New England were probably imported products from English factories. Photograph by author.

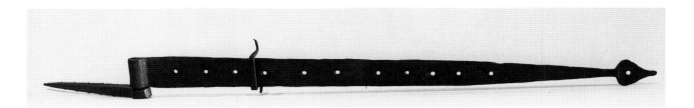

leather patches under the nail heads), and the nails that passed through the door or shutter were clenched or doubled over flush with the wood on the back of the stile.

In the late 1700s it became more common to attach hinges with wood screws, which were becoming more readily available. Hinges intended for use with screws have countersunk holes in their leaves, allowing the flat head of the screw to lie flush with the surface of the leaf. The use of screws also offered the possibility of demounting the door or window shutter from the wall without damaging it.

Heavy exterior doors in many houses were hung on another type of hinge throughout the eighteenth century. This was the strap hinge. As its name implies, this was a long, heavy, forged strap of iron, usually having an eye at one end and a decorative round or arrow-shaped terminal at the other. Strap hinges were occasionally forged with a knuckle that was attached to a leaf like that of an H hinge. Such hinges are called cross garnet hinges and were most common in the seventeenth and early eighteenth centuries, becoming less favored over time. They were used for both interior and exterior doors.

Forged strap hinge and pintle, New Hampshire, nineteenth century. Long strap hinges were often used to hang barn and shed doors, as well as heavy exterior doors of dwelling houses. Barbs kept the shafts of the pintles fixed in the building frame. Clenched iron staples were sometimes driven down over the straps to supplement the heavy nails that held the hinges to the door. Photograph by Bill Finney.

More commonly, however, the strap hinge has a forge-welded (sometimes merely a wrapped) eye at its end, and this eye is slipped down over the vertical pin of a "hook" or pintle. At right angles to its pin, the pintle normally has a long, tapered shaft, often square in section and given a series of chiseled barbs at its sharp edges. The shaft of the pintle is driven into the door frame or stud, and the barbs prevent its working loose over time. The eye of the hinge slips over the pin, allowing the door to swing freely and to be lifted off its supports when necessary. The strap of the hinge is normally attached to the top and bottom rails of the door with clenched nails, often botched with leather, and occasionally with rivets or handmade bolts in one or two of the punched holes of the strap.

Branched strap hinge, Chase House, Portsmouth, New Hampshire, 1762. Branched hinges were sometimes employed in hanging the principal doors of eighteenth-century houses. This hinge appears to be attached with nails that have been "botched" with leather washers. Photograph by Jack E. Boucher, 1961. Library of Congress, Prints and Photographs Division, Historic American Buildings Survey, Reproduction Number 1984 (HABS): 60.

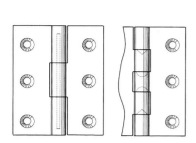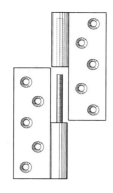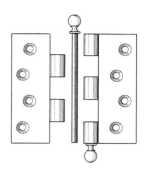

Butt hinges, various patterns and manufacturing techniques from the nineteenth and twentieth centuries. *Left to right*: cast-iron butt, fixed pin; cast-iron butt, cast socket joint; cast-iron loose-joint butt; slip pin butt. Drawing by author.

Strap hinges are normally quite long and help to reinforce the wooden structure of the door to which they are fixed. For especially heavy doors, as well as for decorative effect, strap hinges are sometimes branched, with an arm that extends vertically along a door's stile, at right angles to the principal strap. Unlike many forms of hardware, strap hinges were commonly made by local blacksmiths. Because they could be forged in any length and thereby adapted to doors of any size or weight, strap hinges remained popular for some uses well after newer products superseded them in house construction. They continued to be hand-forged until the twentieth century for use on large barn and warehouse doors or for heavy fireproof window shutters and were only slowly replaced by the machine-made steel strap hinges still sold today for such uses. At the same time, however, factory-made strap hinges with screw-pointed pintles, similar to those sold today, became available after the mid-1800s and gradually supplanted hand-forged hinges in all but rural areas.

Beginning around 1800, a new form of hinge began to be readily available from New England hardware dealers and to replace H, HL, and strap hinges. This is the butt, the type most common today. In form, the butt is like a small book, swiveling on its knuckle or joint and pierced through its leaves for screws. Instead of being fixed to the face of a door like its predecessors, the butt is mortised into the edge of the door or shutter and the corresponding points on the door or window frame. In its usual installation, the butt is nearly invisible, with only the knuckle exposed to view.

The earliest butts were manufactured in England and were made of cast iron. It is unclear when British manufacturers began to produce this type of hinge; one English patent was registered in 1775, but this does not necessarily represent the earliest date of manufacture. Cabinetmakers had long used iron, steel, and brass butt hinges in their trade, but these hinges were normally attached to the face of the work, in the manner of hand-forged H hinges or dovetail ("butterfly") hinges.

Whatever the date of their origin, butts do not generally appear on doors in New England houses until about 1800; in some regions, H and HL hinges were used for some years after this date. Many of the cast-iron butts found in old houses were made in the United States. Some are marked N[EW] ENGLAND BUTT Cº, and others BALDWIN PATENT, both denoting New England manufacture.

In any case, the cast-iron butts found in use beginning around 1800 represent an important economy of manufacture. Being cast rather than hand-forged, they were standardized in size (and therefore interchangeable) and were made by a much more rapid process than hand assembly. The earliest butts had fixed, or "fast," pins or cast joints, and their two leaves cannot be separated. These butts therefore suffered, in comparison with later types, from the need to unscrew the hinge in order to demount the door from its frame.

Later in the nineteenth century, probably around 1850, a new type of cast-iron hinge, the loose-joint butt, was introduced to the New England market. Rather than having a fixed joint, this type of butt is made in two parts. The half that attaches to the door frame has a pin of heavy wrought-iron wire, and the half that was mortised to the edge of the door has a socket to receive the pin. This allows the door to be lifted off its frame after being opened at right angles to the wall. The only disadvantage with this very convenient type of butt is that each is either a right-hand or a left-hand hinge; the butt cannot be reversed without mounting the pin upside down and thereby making the hinge useless.

The modern type of butt, with a loose, or "slip," pin

THE CLARK MFG. CO.,

MANUFACTURERS OF

Builders' Hardware,

418 to 428 NIAGARA STREET,

BUFFALO, N. Y.

DOOR LOCKS, DOOR KNOBS (With Patented Improvements), BLIND HINGES, GATE HINGES, PULLEYS, &c.

The illustration represents our latest design for **Loose Pin and Loose Joint Door Butts,** Genuine Bronze, Bronze Plated and Roman Bronze.

that can be removed to disconnect the two halves of the joint, became increasingly common after the Civil War. This type of butt has the advantage of permitting easy demounting of the door yet allowing each hinge to be used for either right-hand or left-hand swing. Butts with slip pins have generally been made of steel, brass, or bronze instead of cast iron. During the latter half of the nineteenth century, many of these butts were cast or stamped with bas-relief designs in their leaves and with ornamental finials on their pins, thus drawing attention to a form of hinge that had originally been noted for its inconspicuousness.

Latches and Locks. Just as the American manufacture of hinges reflected earlier British developments, so did the American manufacture of latches and locks. During the eighteenth century, the common type of inexpensive latch was the Suffolk style of thumb latch, a hand-forged iron latch with two separate cusps connected by a bowed grasp or handle. Extending through the top cusp (or the handle just below it) is a thumb piece connected to a swiveling lever that projects through the door and raises the latch bar from a catch on the opposite side. The latch bar is usu-

ally attached to the middle rail of the door by a simple nail or screw, and the catch is usually merely driven into the door casing.

Suffolk latches were widely used until the early nineteenth century. Like H and HL hinges, these latches were so much in demand that they were produced in large quantities in specialized British shops and regularly imported by merchants in coastal New England. In general, the more elaborate or unusual a hand-forged thumb latch is, the greater the likelihood that it is a local product; the more generic its appearance, the greater the likelihood that it is the product of a hardware manufactory.

By the early nineteenth century the Suffolk latch was widely superseded by a new type of thumb latch that tended to be the product of standardized production in large hardware manufactories. This is the so-called Norfolk latch, popular from about 1800 to about 1840. Norfolk latches have a sheet-iron plate, usually cut to an ornamental outline at its top and bottom, that is screwed to the door. Attached to this plate is a curved or rectilinear grip or handle of cast or wrought iron. Grips of Norfolk latches were often turned or cast to a symmetrical baluster profile, or had a boss of pewter cast around their midsection, or were cast into a mold, or were hammered while hot into a swage that gave them a ribbed or patterned swelling at their midpoint. Above the grip and penetrating the plate and the door is a thumbpiece with a lever, much like the same part of a Suffolk latch. On the opposite side of the door is a lift bar, often loosely riveted to its own small iron plate, which in turn is screwed to the rail of the door. The bar may have an iron lifting knob at its midpoint. The catch into which the lift bar falls is usually riveted to an iron plate that is screwed to the door casing instead of being driven into the casing.

Altogether, the Norfolk latch is a much more complex

Hand-forged thumb latch of the Suffolk pattern. Suffolk latches were widely made in New England but were also imported from England in large numbers during the eighteenth century. Photograph by Bill Finney.

(*Left*) Norfolk latch, circa 1830, showing its several components and the dozen screws needed to mount it on the door. Thumb latches of this type, hand-forged but made in large factories, tended to replace Suffolk latches during the early years of the nineteenth century. Photograph by Bill Finney.

(*Left, below*) Three patterns of Norfolk latch, showing a variety of back plates and swaged iron grasps. Many Norfolk latches were made in England and imported, but American factories also produced large numbers in various styles and sizes. Photograph by author.

piece of hardware than the Suffolk latch and requires many more screws (often up to twelve) to attach its parts to both sides of the door and to the door casing. Yet, due to its use of standardized parts of cast iron, swaged wrought iron, and sheared sheet iron, the Norfolk latch was relatively inexpensive and survives in large numbers.

Beginning in the 1840s, several American patents were issued for cast-iron thumb latches in the Suffolk (double cusp) pattern, although British hardware manufacturers had long offered cast-iron versions of the Norfolk latch. Used mostly in utilitarian locations like cellar and shed doors, cast-iron thumb latches were popular well into the twentieth century and have now been superseded by comparable latches forged from steel.

Rim lock, Carpenter's patent, English. Patented in 1830 and identified by a round brass seal, Carpenter's lock became a popular import into the United States and was widely used on both inside and exterior doors. Its striker lifts up and drops into a receptacle instead of retracting into the case. Photograph by author.

From the eighteenth century to the present, latches operating with a knob were considered more elegant than thumb latches. Long confined to the homes of the wealthy, such latches began to be less expensive and thus more common by 1800. By 1830 or so, even houses that had thumb latches on their inside doors often had a knob latch on the front door.

The most common type of knob latch was probably the rim lock. Rim locks have their mechanisms enclosed in metal boxes that are screwed to the face of the door. During the eighteenth century, most rim locks used in North America were handmade in England. The manufacture of these complex mechanisms required great skill in forging the fixed and moving parts of the lock and in hand-filing each moving piece to the close tolerances required for smooth and faultless operation. Eighteenth-century English locksmiths built their locks to fit previously made keys, rather than vice versa, and made each part to suit its purpose. These devices have no ready-made or interchangeable parts; however similar their iron or brass covers or their visible trimmings may be, each lock is a work of individual craftsmanship.

The innovations of several British patents were reflected in the types of rim latches that were sold in the colonies or, later, in the United States. One of the most important of the patented British rim locks was Carpenter's patent, made in England largely for the export trade. Patented in 1830, this iron-cased lock has round brass knobs and an embossed circular brass seal applied to the case. The Carpenter lock has a distinctive lever-type

Advertisement for a mortise lock, Sargent and Company, New Haven, Connecticut, 1896. By the 1850s, Sargent had become a leading American manufacturer of builder's hardware. Mortise locks became increasingly popular after the Civil War, especially in new construction, where heavier doors readily accommodated the thickness of their cases. *Scientific American, Building Edition*, May 1896.

Architects who specify

Sargent's Locks know that they are the best made—that they give satisfaction in every way—that the Easy Spring permits the Latch-Bolt to act promptly so that the door may be closed gently, while the Knob action is firm—that this principle prolongs the life of the Lock for many years. ∴ ∴ ∴ ∴ ∴ ∴ ∴
Sargent's Fine Locks and Artisic Hardware Trimmings are made by

SARGENT & COMPANY,

New York ; and New Haven, Conn.

Harmonious proportions, beautiful finishes and the utility of each piece make SARGENT'S ARTISTIC HARDWARE desirable for first-class dwellings everywhere. ∴ ∴ ∴

striker that rides up a diagonal incline on the keeper and drops into the latched position rather than withdrawing into the case as in most rim locks. Due to its imposing appearance and relative cheapness, the Carpenter lock is often found on the front doors of houses built in the 1830s and 1840s. Later versions of the Carpenter lock, still bearing the characteristic brass seal on their iron cases, were still being made and sold by British and American manufacturers as late as 1865.

By the mid-nineteenth century, some American manufacturers were producing rim locks with cast-iron cases and cast- or wrought-iron mechanisms. These locks often had ceramic knobs in simulated white porcelain or in "mineral" material that resembled brown marble. Some of these locks were made with the traditional horizontal case to be attached to the latch rails of doors; others were made with vertical cases for doors of the Greek Revival style, with low middle rails.

At the same time, mortise latches and locks of various patterns were becoming available at reasonable cost. Formerly made by hand like rim locks and quite rare, these devices have narrow boxes that are inserted in a mortise cut into a stile of the door, hiding the entire mechanism except for the projecting beveled end of the latch and the two door knobs. Mortise latches became very popular when small, cheap sets with all-cast-iron parts, some of them as thin as three-eighths inch, were placed on the market for interior doors. The tops and bottoms of the cases of many such latches are rounded, allowing the necessary mortise to be prepared by drilling an overlapping series of holes with a bit, with little chisel work required. Easily inserted even in delicate Federal-style doors, these latches, with white, black, or marbled ceramic knobs, often replaced thumb latches in older houses that had been equipped with the latter.

During the 1830s, Connecticut emerged as the leading producer of metal wares, ranging from brass clock movements and firearms to builder's hardware, in New England. Connecticut companies made a specialty of door latches and locks, dramatically reducing the traditional American reliance on imported British hardware. In 1846 the Russell and Erwin Company was formed in New Britain, Connecticut, from the merger of earlier hardware manufacturers. In 1865, Russell and Erwin published a richly illustrated catalog of over four hundred pages, showing their own products and those of other manufacturers. Reproduced in facsimile in 1980, this encyclopedic

Wood engraving of a painter's and glazier's shop, showing a window sash being glazed (*center*) and an apprentice grinding paint pigments with a stone slab and muller (*right*); from Edward Hazen, *Popular Technology; or, Professions and Trades* (New York, 1846).

publication reveals that, by the end of the Civil War, Americans had access to as broad an array of hardware products as are available today. The catalog includes a wider variety of standard products, like hinges, rim locks, and sash locks, than are now available, as well as scores of specialty items that are no longer obtainable.

Paint

From time immemorial, human beings have been captivated by pigments. An object of ordinary interest is often transformed by the simple act of coating it with color. Paint, a colored pigment in liquid form, is an especially powerful ally of architecture. Not only can paint protect the wood or masonry to which it is applied, but it changes and beautifies the entire aspect of a building or an architectural element. Paint draws the eye to a building. It heightens the interest of a flat surface like a planed board or of a textured surface like a clapboarded wall. Paint has a special ability to enhance and strengthen the beautiful curves and flat fillets of a molding or to add crispness and sharp shadows to a carving.

Given the fascination with which the human eye regards the painted surface, it is not surprising that early American buildings were painted whenever possible. Many people could not afford to paint the exterior of their houses, at least not with an expensive pigment like white lead, which had to be renewed every twenty years or so. But few failed to paint their interiors, where a good coat of paint was an investment that might last a generation or longer. In pre-Victorian New England we seldom find an interior that has always been left unpainted. Many a room that has been laboriously stripped of its paint in a twentieth-century restoration has thus been transformed in a way that would have been distasteful to the original owners, who laid out some of their treasure to color the chambers in which they lived.

Applied plain, paint transforms the appearance of a material by interposing a coating of pigment between the material and the viewer's eye. But paint may be applied in other ways. It may be coated with a semitransparent glaze or varnish to increase the apparent depth of the pigmented film, thus emphasizing both the optical quality of the paint and, through varied deposits of the glaze, the curves and boundaries of the features beneath the paint. It

Graining a door, Keyran Walsh House, Portsmouth, New Hampshire, 1970. The late Walter Ketzler is shown reproducing original graining of about 1800 on a six-panel door. Federal period architectural graining often imitated the veneering and stringing seen on furniture of the same period. Photograph by Peter E. Randall, courtesy of Strawbery Banke Museum.

may be applied in layers, with the upper coats varicolored and combed, thus assuming the appearance of marble or exotic wood. It is perhaps paradoxical that New Englanders, who were so averse to exposing native pine to view, were often more than willing to pay for the extra labor necessary to give that pine the appearance of cedar or mahogany.

Even in the eighteenth century, when many private houses went unpainted on the exterior, New England harbored a latent love of startling color combinations. This taste found expression on the outsides of a few private homes but more often was seen on the one building that all householders owned in common. Research has disclosed that eighteenth-century meetinghouses, used for both religious and civic purposes, were often colored brilliantly. The 1790 meetinghouse at Keene, New Hampshire, was painted light yellow with green doors, while that at neighboring Rindge, built in 1796, had yellow clapboards and a red roof. Other meetinghouses were painted pea green or blue. The surviving interiors of several eighteenth-century meetinghouses show similar love of color. While box pews were often left unpainted to save the cost of coloring so much woodwork, the pine pulpits were grained to resemble cedar, pine columns and pilasters were painted to resemble variegated marble, and the paneled breastwork, or front, of the galleries was sometimes transformed by paint into a combination of exotic wood and marble.

When an owner could afford it, similar treatments were seen in private homes. Evidence of glazing is sometimes found. Polychrome treatments of paneling, pilasters, and the interiors of *beaufaits* or corner cupboards are occasionally discovered, usually buried under later paints. One New Hampshire ship's cabin in 1722 had "the Mouldings done with vermilion, the sides or margins [of the panels] with green, and the columns with blue." Similar color schemes undoubtedly occurred in household parlors of the period. Marbling and graining were not uncommon. By the early nineteenth century, when veneered and inlaid furniture was fashionable, door panels were sometimes grained to resemble flitches of mahogany, set off by stripes that simulate the light stringing seen on cabinetwork of the time.

Paint is made of microscopic particles, either white or colored, that are suspended in a liquid that will dry and harden either by its own action or in combination with other substances in the mixture. The particles are called pigments, and the liquid is called the vehicle of the paint. The pigment can be a powder as inexpensive as lime or as expensive as ground gemstone; the vehicle can be as common as water or milk or as complex as a synthetically produced oil.

Throughout most of American history, interior woodwork has been painted. While evidence suggests that the rooms of seventeenth-century houses were often brightened with whitewash (lime, glue, and water) applied both to plaster and framing members, oil-based paints were preferred during the eighteenth and nineteenth centuries. Occasionally, one finds evidence of wooden paneling having been left unpainted for a long time and sometimes never painted at all. Sometimes, too, Federal-period houses had features such as staircase handrails or mantelpiece inserts made from varnished hardwoods. But in general the universal preference was for painted interior woodwork until the advent of hardwood joinery in the mid-nineteenth century. Thereafter, down to the twentieth century, both hardwoods and the harder conifers were often employed for interior finish, protected and enhanced by varnish.

Over the centuries, countless recipes for paint have been employed. Often, cheap paints have been used for some jobs, while at the same period expensive or even rare materials were being lavished on the buildings of the wealthy. In the eighteenth century, for example, rooms in many houses were periodically freshened with coats of whitewash, composed largely of lime and water. At the same time, the chambers of the rich were covered in expensive paints made of white lead mixed in linseed oil and further embellished with pigments to add brilliant colors or to allow the paint to be patterned to resemble rare woods or marbles. Often, buildings that were initially covered with inexpensive paints or not painted at all were later painted with enduring white lead as that pigment became less expensive. Most old buildings therefore embody a complex and interesting history of painted finishes. If investigated, this history can tell us much about the taste, budget, and cultural contacts of earlier owners.

For centuries, the best paint for interior and exterior use has been white lead mixed in linseed oil. White lead (basic lead carbonate) is a fine powder. Traditionally, the pigment was made by exposing sheets of metallic lead to the acidic fumes of grape skins or vinegar and to gentle warmth in specially fashioned clay vessels stacked within sealed chambers for a period of several months. Because the production of this white pigment depended on a slow chemical reaction, the pigment remained expensive until more rapid methods of production were devised in the late nineteenth century; but even in the first half of the twentieth century, manufacturers had trouble meeting the demand for the pigment.

To prepare it for use by traditional methods, basic lead carbonate powder was finely ground and mixed with linseed oil by means of a stone slab and a stone muller. The work was done by hand and was often consigned to apprentices. The result was a smooth, heavy, creamy paste, which could be further thinned for application with brushes and could be tinted to virtually any color through the addition of other pigments. White lead paint is noted for its pure whiteness and its opacity or hiding power. White lead and linseed oil have an affinity for one another, allowing an especially large amount of pigment to be suspended in a given volume of oil. Lead has a drying

effect on the oil, helping the paint to harden, yet pure white lead paint never becomes as brittle and as subject to cracking or crazing as do paints made with zinc, another traditional metallic pigment.

After the advent of ready-made paints in the late nineteenth century, a mixture of white lead and oil was often sold by the can. Then as now, however, ready-made paints were sometimes cheapened by the addition of extenders like chalk. To obtain the highest quality in their paints, the best painters bought their pigment in the form of paste white lead, which is pure basic lead carbonate mixed with enough linseed oil to make it into a thick paste suitable for thinning with more linseed oil. American manufacturers sold paste white lead in tins ranging in weight from one to a hundred pounds. Using this material and pure oil and adding tinting colors and driers as necessary, painters were able to control and guarantee the quality of the product they used.

As an exterior paint, white lead has no equal. It is easy to apply, offering no drag to the brush, and having a chemical tendency to repel water, it endures the weather well. All paints eventually deteriorate, but white lead paint does so in a way that leaves the surface ready for repainting with relatively little preparation. Instead of cracking or peeling, white lead slowly erodes from the surface, thinning until the wood beneath it is exposed. Called chalking, this form of deterioration leaves a surface that merely needs to be cleaned of powdered residue and repainted. The failure of a good paint job in white lead is slow, with the paint often enduring for twenty years or more before repainting is necessary.

White lead has one drawback as an exterior paint. In the presence of some forms of air pollution, notably sulfur compounds, white lead may turn brown or black, disfiguring the building. Of no consequence in rural areas, this shortcoming became noticeable during the nineteenth century as high-sulfur coal became a more common fuel in cities and prompted the search for another white pigment that could be substituted for lead.

As an interior paint, white lead has two shortcomings that were not considered of importance when no other metallic pigments were available but have been noticed since. First, lead in oil dries with a ropy or stringy texture, retaining the marks of the brush. This means that the painter must use tools of good quality in applying lead and must follow the grain of the wood in joined elements like doors and paneling. Because the paint does not level itself in drying, lead paint demands a higher level of craft in the painter than do other metallic pigments.

Second, lead paint is poisonous. This was long recognized and accommodated in the painter's trade, but both apprentice and master painters who hand-mixed dry lead pigment (and potters, who used the material as a glaze) nevertheless sometimes fell victim to "painter's colic," a painful abdominal ache that signaled the ingestion of lead particles. Despite the widespread use of lead as an interior pigment, lead poisoning appears to have been uncommon among occupants of houses until house painting and restoration became the hobby of homeowners rather than the domain of the professional painter.

By the mid-nineteenth century the search for a white pigment that was not affected by sulfur fumes led chemists to zinc. Already finding favor for roofing purposes in the mid-1800s, zinc was becoming an important industrial product. Patents for the production of zinc oxide as a white pigment were registered in France and England in the 1840s and in the United States in 1850. While zinc oxide paint is pure white, nonpoisonous, and unaffected by air pollution, it has two defects as a pigment. First, zinc creates a harder paint film than lead does and therefore has a tendency to scale off the wood in outside work. Second, lacking white lead's affinity for oil, zinc oxide cannot be sufficiently concentrated in a given volume of oil to attain the density or covering power of lead. As many as four coats of zinc white were required on new wood, and for this reason painters normally mixed zinc and lead together, with zinc composing only one-third or one-quarter of the mixed pigment. Lead-zinc paint had a reduced tendency to chalk in exterior work.

White lead and zinc remained the only commercially viable white metallic paint pigments until well into the twentieth century. By the late 1920s, experiments were beginning to prove the worth of a third metallic white pigment, titanium dioxide. Like zinc oxide, titanium dioxide is pure white, nonpoisonous, and unaffected by sulfur fumes. Titanium has great hiding power but is inclined to chalk excessively when used alone. For this reason, early titanium paints were usually hardened by the addition of a proportion of zinc oxide.

Today, titanium dioxide is the dominant metallic white pigment in the United States, used in most paints for interior and exterior work. As white lead production has been curtailed and finally stopped in this country, titanium has almost completely taken its place. When ground properly and used with a vehicle of high quality, titanium paint can offer most of the benefits of lead without its drawbacks. Titanium dioxide has a higher refractive index than does lead or zinc; hence, it has greater opacity or hiding power than do the older pigments.

Titanium dioxide is also expensive. For these reasons, titanium is seldom used as the sole ingredient in paint pigment. It is normally extended through the addition of inert materials (usually silica or calcium carbonate) that add to the solid content of the paint without contributing to its pigmentation. While such extenders were also added to lead paint, they were regarded as anathema by good painters, who therefore usually preferred to mix their own paint from pure paste white lead and linseed oil, avoiding the adulterants that were sometimes added to the cheaper grades of factory-mixed lead paints. By contrast, extenders are considered normal in all but the most expensive titanium paints. The great opacity of titanium dioxide permits good surface coverage even with a moderate use of extenders, and the addition of extenders allows the paint to sell within reasonable price ranges. In general, of course, the better paints have the least proportion of extenders.

Titanium dioxide interior paints are self-leveling and thus do not retain the marks of the brush. Those who are interested in preserving evidence of the painter's craft in existing lead paint will usually find that, when applied over lead paint in interior work, titanium paints will not mask the texture of older paint. The new paint will thus reflect the texture of underlying craftsmanship until many coats of newer paint have accumulated on the woodwork.

While many substances can serve as the vehicle, or liquid portion, of paint, the overwhelming favorite for paints intended to cover wood has historically been linseed oil. Linseed oil is an organic oil made by pressing the seeds of the flax plant. The resulting liquid is slightly yellow in color. It has the ability to hold all commonly used pigments in suspension, and it dries rapidly when exposed to the air—all the more quickly if the oil has been boiled or has undergone a chemical treatment to produce a molecular structure similar to that created by boiling. Certain additives are also mixed with linseed oil paints to hasten drying.

Linseed oil paints flow smoothly from the brush and are long-lived on the surface. One peculiarity of linseed oil, however, is its tendency to turn a deeper yellow when not exposed to the ultraviolet radiation of sunlight. This

Eighteenth-century clapboard painted in yellow ochre and linseed oil, showing the effect of ultraviolet light on the oil. The clapboard was sheltered from light after the mid-1700s and the linseed oil darkened. The right-hand end has been exposed to sunlight, bleaching the oil and exposing the natural color of the pigment. Photograph by author.

causes linseed oil paints to change color when shielded from natural light, as in closets or in parts of a room far away from windows. In those rare rooms that retain undisturbed decades-old paint, the woodwork near the windows will often be observed to have a lighter coloration than woodwork away from the light, or at the top of the room where no direct sunlight can fall. The yellowing of linseed oil quickly fades when the paint film is exposed to stronger light, and recurs when the light level is again reduced.

Just as basic lead carbonate remained dominant as a white pigment until well into the twentieth century, linseed oil went unchallenged as a vehicle until after World War II. Alkyd resins, the first synthetic resins, were introduced in the late 1920s, during the same period when experiments were proving the value of titanium dioxide as a paint pigment. By the 1950s, various synthetic resins were being used as paint vehicles; these include phenolic resins, alkyds, vinyls, chlorinated rubber, and hydrocarbon polymers like polystyrene. Today, most "oil-based" paints employ alkyd resins as the vehicle rather than linseed oil or other natural drying oils, or they may include a proportion of the latter.

From time immemorial, water also has been used as a vehicle for inexpensive paints intended for plaster or for rough wooden surfaces. Whitewash is lime suspended in water, with a bit of glue as a binder; traditionally, it was made from freshly slaked quicklime. Calcimine is chalk suspended in water, also with a glue binder. By the late 1800s calcimine had largely superseded whitewash as a whitener for ceilings and walls, although whitewash,

which was thought to have antiseptic qualities, was often employed in freshening barns and cellars well into the twentieth century. Both whitewash and calcimine can be tinted with various pigments, and both are water-soluble to varying degrees. A third water-based paint is casein paint, which employs a substance found in milk or a synthetic chemical equivalent to milk as a binder for chalk and for colored pigments. Casein paint is sold in powdered form, requiring only the addition of water, followed by straining, to make a product ready for application. Unlike whitewash and calcimine, casein paints are often used on finished woodwork as well as plaster.

Color in paint is achieved through colored pigments, either added as tinting colors to white paint or mixed directly in a vehicle to make an inexpensive paint. Traditional painter's colors were naturally occurring mineral or vegetable substances. With the development of synthetic pigments such as Prussian blue and chrome green and yellow during the eighteenth and early nineteenth centuries, a wider palette became available. Late-nineteenth-century advances in chemistry, especially in German laboratories, produced an extensive array of synthetic pigments, often formulated from coal tars. Combined with one another, these pigments offered a virtually limitless range of possible colors.

Just as naturally occurring lime and chalk have always been the cheapest white pigments, certain naturally occurring minerals have always been the cheapest colored pigments. Of these, the iron oxides are predominant. Often referred to as earth colors, iron oxides can occur in reds, yellows, and browns, and often can be changed in hue by heating them to incandescence. Among the iron oxide reds are the pigments called Indian red and Venetian red; among the iron oxide yellows are yellow ochre and raw sienna; among the iron oxide browns are raw and burnt umber, burnt sienna, and Spanish brown, a red-brown ochre.

Evidence indicates that the exteriors of many rural houses, as well as some in towns and cities, were left unpainted during the eighteenth century. When painted, houses were often covered with inexpensive yellow and red paints made by mixing dry, pulverized earth colors with linseed oil. Such buildings sometimes had their exterior trim picked out in white lead paint. Not infrequently, the facades of houses were wholly painted in white lead, but the sides and backs were covered with cheaper red or yellow. In other cases, rare enough in the eighteenth century to excite comment, houses were entirely painted in expensive white lead, either pure or tinted by the addition of a colored pigment.

Mixed alone with oil, earth colors offer a limited palette of rather dull but pleasant hues. Despite their cheapness, however, such paints are extremely long-lived on wood, much more so than white paints. Acting almost as a stain, the red and yellow ochres penetrate and persist on the wood even as the surface ages and erodes under the effects of sun and weather. Mixed with a white metallic pigment, these same colors produce a wide range of hues that are highly appropriate for older houses. When used as tinting pigments, earth colors assume the body and opacity of the metallic pigments to which they are added. Instead of eroding slowly from the surface of the building, as they do when simply mixed with linseed oil, earth colors used as tinting pigments fail, as do the white pigments to which they are added, either by chalking or peeling as the overall paint film breaks down.

An entirely new family of water-based paints appeared after World War II for both interior and exterior use. These are the latex paints. Latex paints are composed of a chemical emulsion (usually an acrylic or a vinyl) suspended in water, forming a vehicle that carries a pigment (usually titanium dioxide with extenders). These paints harden quickly as the water evaporates and the emulsion consolidates. Latex paints have gained great favor because of their ease of application, rapid drying, freedom from the solvent odors associated with oil and alkyd paints, and quick cleanup with soap and water. When first marketed during the late 1940s, latex paints were formulated for interior use only. Today, they are made for interior and exterior use and have developed a longevity equivalent to that of alkyd paints of comparable cost.

Clear finishes were not employed in American buildings during the eighteenth century. Except in those rare occasions when hardwoods like mahogany were employed for joiner's work, clear finishes were used almost exclusively by cabinetmakers. Nor were such finishes common during the first half of the nineteenth century. By the period following the Civil War, however, woods like black walnut and mahogany began to take their place alongside the traditional softwoods in interiors, especially for staircases and other architectural focal points. By the late 1800s, walnut and mahogany were often supplemented by interior features made from a host of other native hardwoods, including chestnut, ash, oak, birch, maple, cherry,

sweetgum, sycamore, and beech, sometimes joined by a few tropical hardwoods.

By the end of the nineteenth century and well into the twentieth, one of the most popular species for interior woodwork was southern yellow pine. Like the hardwoods, this "hard," resinous pine was prized for its grain and so was protected with clear finishes.

By the early twentieth century, rotary lathes for cutting veneers cylindrically from large logs had been developed to the point that a log could be converted to a thin veneer in a process analogous to drawing paper off a paper roll. Rotary lathes not only can produce sheets of far greater continuous length than any other method of obtaining veneers but can do so at far greater speed. Moreover, the grain that is revealed in such veneers is one not seen in normal methods of cutting a log along its length. In most species, these tangential veneers display an endlessly varied figure akin to that of watered silk, producing an attractive appearance (albeit one not seen in traditional woodworking) at low cost. Veneers of this type were commonly used in door panels beginning in the early twentieth century. Because of their strong figure when cut from southern yellow pine, Douglas fir, or birch, such veneers were usually given a clear finish.

Two traditional clear finishes were used almost exclusively in buildings until after the mid-twentieth century. The first is oil-resin (oleo-resinous) varnish. Oil-resin varnish is composed of a natural resin suspended through heating or "cooking" in a drying oil like linseed oil, with the addition of turpentine. The most common varnish resins are the copals, the crystallized juices of certain tropical trees. Varnishes formulated with relatively little oil in proportion to the resin are called short-oil varnishes. They are hard and relatively brittle, suitable mostly for finishing cabinetwork or interior trim. Varnishes with relatively more oil in proportion to the resin are medium- or long-oil finishes. They are more flexible and resistant to the effects of ultraviolet light. Spar varnish, the classic varnish for marine and outdoor uses, is a long-oil varnish. Traditional varnishes dry relatively slowly and in the best work are applied in three or four coats, with a week between coats and light sanding between applications.

The second traditional clear finish is shellac varnish, usually called simply shellac. It is composed of flakes of lac, a resinous incrustation found on the twigs of various Indian and Asian trees, dissolved in wood (denatured) alcohol. Lac is not a direct product of the tree but is formed

Wood engraving of glass-blowers at work, showing an early-nineteenth-century glasshouse with its furnace at the left and a crown of glass being spun at the right; from Edward Hazen, *Popular Technology; or, Professions and Trades* (New York, 1846).

from the sap by the female lac insect, which punctures the bark, imbibes the sap, and exudes a resin in which it lays its eggs. Shellac is the most common of the spirit varnishes, in which a resin is dissolved in volatile spirits that quickly evaporate, leaving the resin as a transparent coating on the wood. After hardening, spirit varnishes remain soluble in their original solvent and are easily removed by rubbing with alcohol. Natural shellac has an orange color and is often used in that form. The varnish can be bleached when used to cover a light wood, in which case it is referred to as white shellac.

Unlike oil varnishes, shellac varnish dries quickly, usually in about ten minutes. This has long made shellac a favorite finish for floors, where the long hardening time of oil varnishes can prevent quick occupancy of a room. Worn or damaged areas of shellacked surfaces can also be touched up easily, without the repair being too evident.

As with pigmented paints, new clear finishes appeared in the marketplace following World War II. Among these, the dominant products are the polyurethanes. Producing very tough finishes, polyurethanes have replaced traditional varnishes in most new construction and are sometimes appropriate for use in house restoration.

Polyurethanes are available for household use in three formulations. Oil-modified polyurethanes harden through the action of oxygen on drying oils within the formula, much as do oil-resin varnishes. Moisture-cured polyurethanes harden through a chemical reaction with water vapor in the atmosphere. Water-borne polyurethanes are based on emulsions suspended in water. Like water-based paints, these finishes have gained favor because of ease of application, lack of chemical solvents, and ease of cleanup with soap and water.

Glass

Glass is largely made from silica sand, to which additives like lime and soda ash impart beneficial qualities. The materials are heated to temperatures as high as 3000 degrees Fahrenheit in a crucible that is placed within a furnace. Depending on its temperature, glass may be a liquid that can be stirred, ladled, poured, and cast or a viscous mass that can be blown into a large bubble with a metal pipe or cut with shears.

Until after World War II, common window glass was

made by four methods. Two of those methods depended on the skill of glassblowers, who made their product entirely by hand. A third method, introduced around 1900, was the first to manufacture window glass partly by machine. A fourth method, introduced around 1915, made glass entirely by machine except for final cutting to marketable sizes. Thus, all window glass made before the turn of the twentieth century is a handmade product, virtually irreplaceable except at considerable cost.

The first hand manufacturing technique, most common in the eighteenth and early nineteenth centuries, was the crown method. In this type of manufacture the blower gathered a mass of molten glass from the furnace on the end of his blowpipe. Blowing the glass into a large sphere, the craftsman attached the bubble to an iron rod (the "pontil") and removed the blowpipe, creating a hole at the point where the pipe had been attached. By repeatedly reheating and spinning the sphere, the blower used centrifugal force to cause the glass to open up into a large disk called a table or crown. When finished and cooled, a crown normally had a diameter of from four to six feet. Panes, or lights, of glass of varying sizes, depending on need, could be cut from this crown. The center of the crown was thickened at the point where the pontil had been attached. Called the bull's-eye, this central boss was normally thrown back into the furnace and re-melted. Occasionally, glass bull's-eyes were used to glaze a transom sash over a door or were substituted for the upper panels

in the door, introducing a bit of daylight into a stair hall or entry.

Because of its method of manufacture, a pane of crown glass is often slightly convex instead of flat. Glaziers normally set such glass with the curve or crown facing outdoors, carefully setting the pane in a bed of putty that compensated for the contour of the glass. Seen from the outside under the right conditions, windows glazed with crown glass often reveal a visible bulge in each pane, as if the glass were swelling outward from air pressure in the building.

The crown method of manufacture produces glass without contact with any solid surface, resulting in panes that are often exceedingly brilliant and reflective. Crown glass remained the favorite type for fine window glazing well into the nineteenth century.

An alternative method of making window glass, called the cylinder method, was practiced throughout the eighteenth and nineteenth centuries alongside the crown method. As its name implies, cylinder glass was fashioned from a cylinder instead of a disk. Like crown glass, cylinder glass started with a heavy "gather" of molten glass—

Diagram showing sheets of various sizes to be cut from forty-eight (*right*) and forty-nine-inch (*left*) glass crowns. Adapted from William Cooper, *Crown Glass Cutter and Glazier's Manual* (Edinburgh, 1835). Drawing by author.

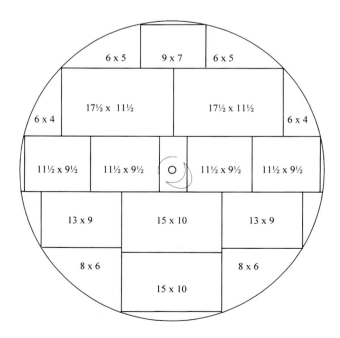

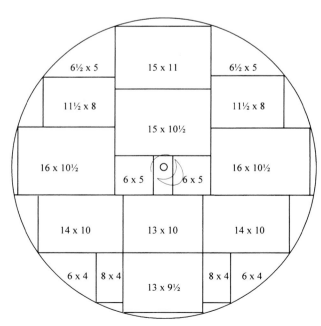

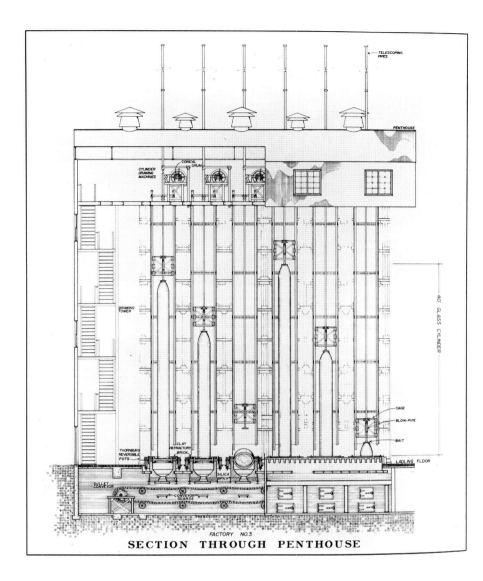

SECTION THROUGH PENTHOUSE

Section through the penthouse of American Window Glass Company Factory No. 3 at Jeannette, Pennsylvania, showing four glass cylinders in the process of being drawn to their full height of forty feet by the patented Lubbers process. Drawing by Victoria Flemming (1991) and J. Shannon Barras (1992). Library of Congress, Prints and Photographs Division, Historic American Engineering Record, Reproduction Number HAER, DLC/PP-1995: PA-4, drawing 12 of 21.

sometimes as much as thirty-five pounds—on a blow-pipe. The mass of glass was blown into a sphere, and the sphere was elongated into a cylinder through repeated heating, blowing, and swinging of the blowpipe. Eventually, the glassblower would produce a cylinder about ten inches in diameter and from four to five feet long. Other craftsmen would then snap off the constricted end where the blowpipe had been attached to the cylinder, would slit the cylinder along its length, and would flatten the glass into a rectangular sheet on a hot table.

The cylinder method produced a larger single sheet of glass than did the crown method. Being rectangular rather than circular, this sheet had less waste after being cut into panes. Yet, because it was flattened against a surface, cylinder glass lacks the brilliant finish of air-cooled crown

glass and may show wrinkles or inclusions. Even though it was flattened on a hot table, cylinder glass usually retains a slight curve in each pane, just as crown glass retains a slight bulge.

The technique of making cylinder glass improved over time. Yet the size of a cylinder was limited by the strength of the glassblower. A blower had to possess enormous strength, endurance, tolerance of heat, and lung capacity to fashion a cylinder, especially a cylinder of double-thick window glass. For this reason, hand-blown cylinders never attained a length of more than five feet nor a diameter greater than a foot.

By about 1900, machines began to be developed that could produce glass cylinders of immense size. These machines employed vertical blowpipes with large flared ends that attached themselves to pools of molten glass. Compressed air was fed through these pipes as motors slowly raised their ends from the bath. A huge cylinder of glass was slowly drawn upward, cooling as it rose.

In its final development, the mechanical cylinder process could produce a glass tube up to thirty inches in diameter and forty feet tall. The improvement of this process between 1900 and 1928 marked the end of hand-blown window glass as a commercial product in the United States. Old glass, so easily overlooked and so easily broken, is the most fragile architectural legacy we have from the eighteenth and nineteenth centuries.

The mechanical cylinder process was itself short-lived. Flat or drawn glass was introduced around 1915. This method involved lowering a metal bar, called the bait, into a tank of molten glass for a few seconds. After the glass had attached itself to the bait, motors raised the bar and the glass was drawn upward in a flat sheet that passed between asbestos rollers. Upon reaching an annealing chamber at the top of the machine, the glass was cut off into sheets of the desired length. Drawn glass eliminated the cutting and flattening processes required in the production of cylinder glass but did not produce an optically perfect product. Drawn glass exhibits some of the wrinkles and variations in thickness that are seen in cylinder glass. Drawn glass technology did, however, eliminate all hand craftsmanship in glass making except for cutting the sheets to the desired sizes.

During the 1950s, drawn glass was itself superseded by a method that extrudes molten glass upon the surface of a bath of molten tin. This "float glass" is more optically perfect than any other product except polished plate glass. While float glass is flawless and inexpensive, it is also characterless. Substitution of float glass for original glazing introduces a subtle disharmony in any but a modern building.

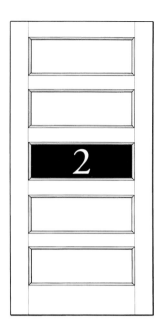

Why a Building Looks the Way It Does: The Evolution of Style

No human tendency, it appears, is more innate than a craving for novelty in the objects we make. The style of things changes constantly—sometimes slowly and imperceptibly, sometimes almost overnight. When style has changed, objects fashioned in a previous style immediately appear outdated and old-fashioned to some degree. After enough time passes, our perception of the outdated appearance of old things is often transformed to a sense of intriguing antiquity in those same things, or to outright and uncritical admiration for the good taste of our predecessors. This admiration, in turn, sometimes engenders a revival of the old style, never fully the same as the original but recognizable as an attempt to pay homage to a previous fashion and to recapture some of its characteristics.

This revivalist impulse is seen in many artifacts but perhaps above all in clothing and in buildings. In buildings, the impulse to turn away from and then embrace old styles is seen again and again. In the latter nineteenth century, for example, several American books illustrated schemes for transforming old "colonial" houses into stylish Queen Anne residences, complete with towers and verandas. By the end of the century, with the advent of the full-blown colonial revival style, fashionable householders were building what they thought were replicas of colonial houses and were turning away from the picturesque tur-

rets and the asymmetry of the Queen Anne style. Shortly thereafter, the polychrome paint schemes of many Queen Anne houses were overpainted in "colonial" white in an attempt to minimize the now-unfashionable idiosyncrasies of the older style.

Similarly, the twentieth-century revulsion against all things Victorian, which probably reached its height in the 1950s and 1960s, has been replaced by an admiration for the self-assured picturesqueness of the buildings of the latter nineteenth century. Not only are houses of that period being restored with great zeal, but reproduced "Victorian" houses are now being designed and their construction plans marketed in magazines, exactly as were the plans of the original houses a century ago. The colonial white paint that disguised a myriad of Queen Anne houses has given way to polychrome color schemes, some of them far more brilliant and complex than would have been considered tasteful in the 1880s. A large and growing industry has sprung up around the public's hunger for woodwork, hardware, plumbing fixtures, textiles, and wallpapers that duplicate those in use a hundred or more years ago.

The ceaseless transformation of style in American architecture probably began during the seventeenth century. As young immigrant carpenters of the "Great Migration" of the 1630s aged, died, and were replaced by second- or

third-generation native-born craftsmen, New England houses underwent noticeable elaboration. The scholar Abbott Lowell Cummings has noted, for example, that in the Massachusetts Bay region dwellings began to display framed overhangs, broad roof gables, and decorative embellishments that had been rare thirty years earlier. These enrichments did not technically represent the advent of a new style but rather reflected a new and striking use of old ideas that had been latent in the work of the immigrant builders. Nevertheless, the adoption of these more elaborate forms served to differentiate the appearance of New

Dow House, Pittsfield, New Hampshire, a three-room, square-frame dwelling dating from the late eighteenth century. This vernacular house type, unrecognized as a distinct form until the 1980s, appears occasionally across much of New England. It is often enlarged by a wing (as here, on the left) or by expansion into a hall and parlor house. Photograph by Delwood J. Garvin, 1965.

England houses of the late 1600s from those built before the midcentury, and the difference would have been strikingly apparent to New Englanders of the period.

By around 1700, however, a truly new style made its appearance in New England and began to signal the eclipse of the postmedieval dwellings of the late 1600s. This new style remained dominant throughout nearly the whole of the eighteenth century and so is generally called the Georgian style in recognition of the English kings who dominated that century. Despite its prevalence in New England for nearly a century, the Georgian style also underwent evolutionary changes over the years. These would probably have been more obvious to people of the time than they are to us.

The great difference between houses of the seventeenth century and those of the Georgian style is that the older houses derived their interior character from the geometry

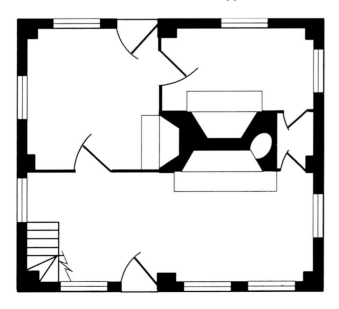

Floor plan, three-room or square-frame house. This house form is characterized by a nearly square plan, an off-center chimney with three fireplaces, and a corner staircase. Drawing by author.

The Parish House ("Old Parsonage"), Newington, New Hampshire, circa 1765, a two-story, hall and parlor house with a central chimney. This common house form, built one room in depth, was sometimes enlarged by the addition of a lean-to at the rear. Photograph by L. C. Durette, circa 1937. Library of Congress, Prints and Photographs Division, Historic American Buildings Survey, Reproduction Number HABS, NH, 8 – NEWI, 2.

and decoration of the building frame, whereas Georgian houses derived their interior character from moldings and paneling that hid the frame. On the exterior, houses of both centuries were usually covered with wooden shingles on the roof and with clapboards on the walls. Despite this similarity in cladding, however, the Georgian house differed from its predecessor in having greater symmetry, a roof of lower pitch, and sliding window sashes, with square panes, or lights, of glass instead of hinged casement windows with diamond-shaped panes, or "quarrels," set in lead. When the owner could afford it, a Georgian house might display a "frontispiece," or classical doorway, of some elaborateness, especially after the first quarter of the eighteenth century.

Symmetry has often been cited as the characteristic that differentiates the Georgian facade from that of the seventeenth century. While it is true that the eighteenth-century ideal was a symmetrical facade, a great many asymmetrical houses were built and still survive that are Georgian in every other respect. Similarly, a Georgian house may be one, two, or three stories in height. It may have a central chimney, two chimneys placed on either side of a central entry or stair hall (called a double house in the eighteenth century), chimneys placed against the outer walls, or any other chimney arrangement that suited the builders.

It may seem confusing that a building can express a style without adhering to a particular floor plan, chimney

Floor plan, hall and parlor house. This floor plan may be one story (the Cape Cod house) or two. Two-story hall and parlor houses were sometimes enlarged by the addition of a lean-to at the rear, usually accompanied by an extension or rebuilding of the chimney to provide a new kitchen fireplace. Drawing by author.

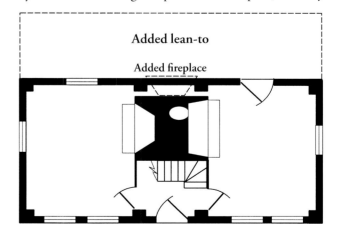

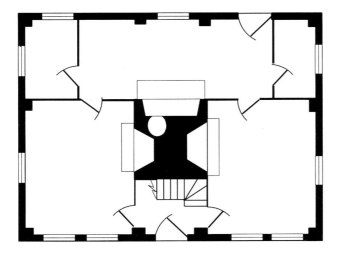

(*Above*) The John Cram House, Hampton Falls, New Hampshire, a two-room-deep house. This form of house might be covered by a gable, gambrel, or hipped roof as the owner wished, with the gable roof by far the most common. Photograph by L. C. Durette, circa 1937. Library of Congress, Prints and Photographs Division, Historic American Buildings SurveyReproduction Number HABS, NH, 8 – HAMTOF, 1.

(*Left*) Floor plan, two-room-deep house. Houses of a full two stories and two-room depth began to appear in the coastal areas of New Hampshire and Maine shortly after 1700. Their frames have posts in line with the rear face of the chimney to provide intermediate supports for floor framing. While the front bedchambers have fireplaces, the chamber over the kitchen is not always heated. Drawing by author.

placement, or fenestration (door and window arrangement). In fact, however, the style of a building is read as much in the way in which its components are designed as in the way in which the entire building is composed. This is true of buildings of all periods; the style that character-

izes the building is expressed in the preponderance of details seen in that structure as much as in the overall design or layout of the building. Each style carried with it general preferences for floor plans and facades, but these preferences varied from one part of the country to another. Each style also carried with it an accepted understanding of how to fashion a door, a window sash, or a molding.

While a structure that adheres to every hallmark of a style may be a better textbook example of that style, every building whose details follow a given style is a representative of that style. Some buildings are "academic" or "high-

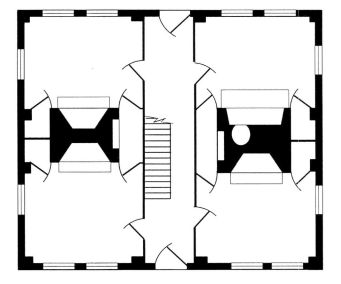

(*Left*) Floor plan of a double house. Drawing by author.

(*Below*) Robert Wallace ("Ocean-Born Mary") House, Henniker, New Hampshire, a double house of the late 1700s. The double house has two chimneys and a central entry or stair hall. It may be covered by a gable, gambrel, or (as here) a hipped roof. Photograph by Gerda Peterich, circa 1964. Library of Congress, Prints and Photographs Division, Historic American Buildings Survey, Reproduction Number 1984 (HABS): 60.

style" examples; others are more commonplace or vernacular examples; still others may have been built at a period of changing taste and therefore express the transition from one style to another.

The fact that the details of a structure proclaim a style and hence a period of construction makes a study of details essential in dating and understanding a building. Together with technological attributes, described in chapter 1, the stylistic features of a building express the assumptions or aspirations of the builder and first owner. Other features frequently express the aspirations of later owners who had different views of what looked right.

The Georgian Style

They key change that marked the advent of the Georgian style was the use of joiner's work in the finish of the building. In the most limited sense, joiner's work is wooden construction that employs a framework of wooden members attached to one another by means of mortise-and-tenon joints, with wooden panels inserted in the spaces enclosed by the framework. A paneled door is joiner's work, as is the paneled breastwork around a fireplace, paneled wainscoting, or a paneled interior window shutter. In eighteenth-century usage, joiner's work was broadened to

Exploded view of the upper corner of an eighteenth-century door. Such doors are usually made with a tenon that extends through the full width of the stile or side member. Tenons may be held in place by thin wedges driven above or below them, as well as by the pins shown here. Drawing by author.

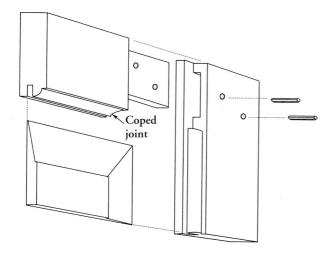

Coped joint

include applied moldings, planed boards used as flooring or casings, window sashes, or any other woodwork, other than carving, visible to the eye in a finished room or on the finished exterior of a building. Thus, the *Builder's Dictionary* of 1734 tells us that a surveyor who is employed to measure and appraise joiner's work "ought to measure where[ever] the Plane touches."

Whereas the seventeenth-century house was finished by planing and chamfering the exposed frame, by hanging board-and-batten doors, and by erecting walls of planed sheathing boards or plaster, the Georgian house was finished by covering the frame with casings, by applying moldings, by hanging paneled doors, and by erecting walls of paneling or plaster. In the Georgian house, the finish completely hides the structure.

Paneling. Georgian paneling is characterized by a recognizable style that seldom varies except in the richest houses. Whether the paneling is employed in doors, paneled walls, or wainscoting, the stiles (vertical members) and the rails (horizontal members) have a fairly large quarter-round molding planed into their inner edges, where the panel is held. The panel itself has a flat surface or field, but its margins are cut with a shouldered bevel, tapering from the full thickness of the panel to a feather edge that slips into a groove cut into the stiles and rails adjacent to the quarter-round molding.

When paneling is used as breastwork on the wall of a room or as wainscoting, the back side is hidden from view. In such cases, the planing on the back is usually rough, often not fully removing the marks of the mill saw. When used as a door, paneled work is, of course, carefully planed on both sides.

Moldings. Second only to paneled work in defining the character of the Georgian building is the molding. Moldings tend to be few in number and weak in profile in those seventeenth-century houses in which they appear at all, but the Georgian house displays a much broader repertoire of moldings. Except for the quarter-round that appears on the stiles and rails of paneled work, the Georgian molding is usually an applied member, shaped from a separate piece of wood and nailed in place. By combining a limited number of moldings of standard profiles, the joiner was able to assemble impressive architectural features such as heavy cornices, staircases, mantelpieces, and frontispieces or doorways.

Carving. Georgian houses in a few areas might benefit from the services of the carver as well as the joiner. Carvers were most likely to be found in seaports, where they could supplement architectural work with ship's carving. Where carvers were to be found, however, they would almost certainly be called on from time to time to embellish a building. Carving differs from joinery in that the carver uses knives, chisels, and gouges to create three-dimensional features from wood. Whereas joiner's work is almost completely fashioned by the plane or the molding tool, the carver works mostly freehand after laying out his design.

The simplest form of architectural carving is the enrichment of moldings. This consists in the cutting of bas-relief decoration into the plain surface of a standard molding,

Paneled chamber, said to date from 1772, Gilman-Clifford House ("Gilman Garrison"), Exeter, New Hampshire. This room, of unusual elaboration, includes the richest features of Georgian joiner's work: six-panel doors, bolection architraves, fluted and cabled pilasters on paneled pedestals, and a full entablature at the ceiling. The Franklin stove dates from the mid-1800s. Photograph by L. C. Durette, 1936. Library of Congress, Prints and Photographs Division, Historic American Buildings Survey, Reproduction Number HABS, NH, 8 – EX, 2.

Panel raising plane by Downing Amsden (working between 1807 and 1828), Lebanon, New Hampshire. The vertical scoring iron ahead of the skewed primary blade nicks the wood to cut the vertical shoulder of the panel's feather edge. Photograph by Bill Finney, courtesy of New Hampshire Historical Society.

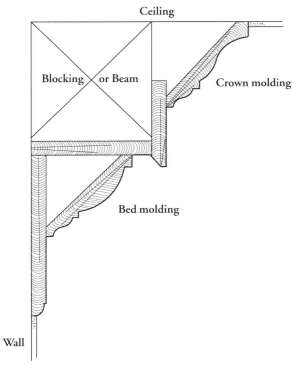

Ceiling

Blocking   or Beam

Crown molding

Bed molding

Wall

(*Left*) Section through a Georgian cornice. A full cornice is composed of a double ogee crown molding (*top*), a fascia or corona (the vertical surface), and an ovolo-and-ogee bed molding (*bottom*). Although made of a few boards nailed together, such a cornice gives the impression of weight and solidity. Drawing by author.

(*Opposite*) Detail of the mantelpiece from the Wentworth-Coolidge Mansion, Portsmouth, New Hampshire, circa 1753. The upper part of the double ogee molding at the top has been enriched with leaf ornamentation; the ovolo bed molding with egg-and-dart; and the lower ogee with a tongue ornamentation that the Dunlap joiners of New Hampshire called the "flowered O G." Photograph by Charles S. Parsons, circa 1975.

thus creating a rich, patterned effect. Eighteenth-century architectural guidebooks, which illustrated several patterns of enrichment according to Renaissance practice, made it clear that certain carved patterns were appropriate for certain molding profiles. For the half-round, a series of round beads or elongated cylinders, or both combined, were the appropriate decoration. For the S-curved cyma, or ogee,

one of several forms of leaf ornament was proper. For the ovolo, or quarter-round, the egg-and-dart was the traditional enrichment.

A greater challenge to the carver was the creation of the carved capitals that topped columns or pilasters in some of the classical orders. The Ionic, the Corinthian, and the Composite orders display increasingly complex capitals, and the full and proper embellishment of each order calls for enriched moldings in the entablatures above the columns as well. In addition, the entablature of the Corinthian order may have carved modillions, or brackets, beneath the projecting cornice.

Interior cornice, Macpheadris-Warner House, Portsmouth, New Hampshire, 1716–1719. Although composed of a series of thin boards and moldings, classical cornices achieve an appearance of massive solidity. This cornice and the paneled wall below it were decorated with painted graining by John Drew, the master builder of the house. Photograph by author.

Carved Ionic capital by William Dearing (1759–1813), St. John's Church, Portsmouth, New Hampshire, 1807. Carved architectural features appear only in those locales where carvers lived or where builders could order carved components from a distance. Photograph by author.

A still broader field of expression for the carver occurred in those few Georgian houses that adopted elements of rococo decoration. The rococo was a fanciful European style of ornament that began to appear in England in the 1740s. As employed by the English and by American craftsmen who copied designs from English architectural books, the rococo was a carver's style that called for the addition of vegetative ornament to an underlying structure of classical forms. In furniture the style is typified by the designs of Thomas Chippendale. In architecture the rococo was conveyed to Americans through several illustrated books written by the English author Abraham Swan. The most often copied of Swan's plates are designs for mantelpieces; in these the fireplace openings may be flanked by carved "trusses" or vegetative volutes, and the shelves are often supported by friezes that are decorated with swags of flowers or with interlaced foliage. Needless to say, such displays of carving are confined to a few port cities.

Americans were generally late in adopting the rococo style. The first American edition of Swan's *British Architect*, originally published in London in 1745, appeared in Philadelphia in 1775. Another American edition was published in Boston as late as 1794.

The Adam, or Federal, Style

By that time, New Englanders were beginning to turn to other British books for a foretaste of a new style that would dominate the first three decades of the nineteenth century. This was neoclassicism, which derived its inspiration from recent archaeological discoveries in southern Italy rather than from the buildings of the Renaissance of the sixteenth century. Seeing the newly uncovered buildings of Rome or the recently excavated houses of the long-buried Roman city of Pompeii, European architects began to develop new architectural forms based on direct observation of ancient buildings rather than on the work of Renaissance architects.

British Sources. The foremost British architect who worked in the neoclassical mode was Robert Adam. Following a visit to Italy in the 1750s, Adam developed a strong personal style as an architect and by the 1770s had become Great Britain's most fashionable designer. Adam introduced a wide range of decorative techniques, most of them based on his observations of ancient buildings. These included delicate moldings, applied swags and festoons of flowers and drapery, thin colonnettes, medallions

displaying idealized classical figures, classical vases and urns, and a vivid use of contrasting colors and patterns. Adam was fascinated with the internal geometry of buildings, creating vistas to be seen along an axis extending from room to room. He often employed oval or octagonal rooms, semicircular niches in rectangular rooms, and varied ceiling heights that impressed the viewer with changes in shape and volume as he progressed from space to space.

Little if any of this innovation was known to Americans before the Revolution. By the 1780s, however, the

---

Plate illustrating decorated cornices from William Pain, *The Practical Builder* (London, 1774; Boston edition, 1792). The repetitive carved or molded ornamentation illustrated in Pain's books, derived from the work of the British architect Robert Adam, included fanciful forms not seen in earlier Georgian books. Pain's books were influential in the formation of the American Adam, or Federal, style.

first hints of the new style began to be felt in New England, sometimes mixing their influence with the laggard arrival of the rococo style of the earlier half of the century. Because few Americans enjoyed access to the great British houses in which Adam's genius was displayed, especially in the years following the Revolution, the source of inspiration and imitation was the English architectural guidebook. As had happened earlier in the century, the architectural book, especially the book intended for the craftsman rather than the wealthy patron, exerted a strong influence on both American householders and on the craftsman who had to master an unfamiliar new style.

The most influential British author in the transmission of the style of Adam to the new United States was William Pain. Pain had been publishing guidebooks for rural architects and builders since the late 1750s, teaching the principles of architecture according to Palladio, the Renaissance architect whose designs had most influenced British (and American) design throughout the earlier eighteenth century. In 1774, Pain published *The Practical Builder, or Workman's General Assistant*, followed in 1788 by *The Practical House Carpenter, or the Youth's Instructor*. Both books included plates and details that reflected the new work of Robert Adam, very different in feeling from older Palladian designs. Evidence of the use of these details begins to appear in New England by the late 1780s. *The Practical Builder* was republished in Boston in 1792, and a Boston edition of *The Practical House Carpenter* followed in 1796.

As transmitted to New England by Pain and as developed by native designers and craftsman, the Adam style had to be simplified and adapted to the scale and materials of American buildings. This process began during the 1790s, although many New England houses built during that decade show little, if any, evidence of the new style. When the style finally flowered during the late 1790s and early 1800s, it was regarded by New Englanders as the Roman style, in distinction from the traditional Georgian style. Today we call the American version of the Adam style the Federal style.

Among the ideas conveyed by the plates in Pain's books was a new form of decoration. Based on the contemporary practice of Robert Adam and other British designers of the period, Pain's ornament is repetitive, often taking the form of leaf ornament carved or cast onto the surface of crown moldings. A favorite device is the use of repeated gouged flutes to enliven flat, vertical surfaces that would have been left plain in Georgian design or of fret dentils or

drilled holes that utilized simple means to provide a dazzling visual effect unknown in earlier work. In combination, these details create a delicate, busy surface that is noticeably distinct from the heavy moldings and plain flat surfaces of Georgian detailing.

Pain also offered new motifs that caught the eye of American craftsmen. Architectural guidebooks that were favored during the Georgian period had illustrated mantelpieces that were massive and often sculptural in design (see figure, page 161). By contrast, Pain offered mantelpiece designs that relied on delicate colonnettes and thin cornices and shelves, often with a few highlights of delicate carving or cast decoration that portrayed floral designs or idealized classical figures. The cost of the heavy mantelpiece designs of the Georgian period had discouraged the use of such features in all but the wealthiest homes, but Pain's lighter designs could be fashioned by a joiner without the need to add expensive carving.

Another motif that Pain illustrated, in many variations, was a new type of frontispiece, or doorway. Where the classic Georgian doorway normally had a solid entablature above the door (sometimes varied with a rectangular transom sash above the door itself), Pain introduced a doorway with a semicircular fanlight, filled with fanciful tracery of various patterns, that projected upward into the pediment. Offering both a modern appearance and improved illumination of the stair hall within, the Pain-type doorway immediately began to appear on New England houses.

Through Pain's books, the ideas of Robert Adam began to be felt and copied in New England during the 1790s. Because Pain's books were adapted to the needs of the joiner, they had a powerful influence in conveying the new style. Although Charles Bulfinch of Boston and a few other New England gentleman architects of the 1790s had begun to design buildings whose overall appearance reflected some familiarity with contemporary British work, much of the essence of the Federal style lies in its detailing. Gentlemen architects were far more concerned with the overall appearance of their buildings than with the details. Their drawings seldom indicate any of the latter, nor, given the class divisions of the period, is it likely that a gentleman would have had much familiarity with the building trades. It was therefore crucial that the craftsman develop an ability to provide all the components, such as a modern door, window sash, or mantelpiece, that were appropriate to an overall design. The books of William Pain

(*Right*) Chimneypiece design from William Pain, *The Practical House Carpenter* (London, 1788; Boston edition, 1796). Pain's books introduced the Adam-style mantelpiece, with delicate proportions and features but without the ponderous overmantel panels of earlier periods, to the rural English and American builder.

(*Below*) Frontispiece, or doorway, design from William Pain, *The Practical Builder* (London, 1774; Boston edition, 1792). The Pain-type doorway, with a semicircular fanlight projecting upward into the tympanum of the pediment, became a hallmark of the early Adam, or Federal, style in New England, eventually being supplanted by doorways with semi-elliptical fanlights and sidelights.

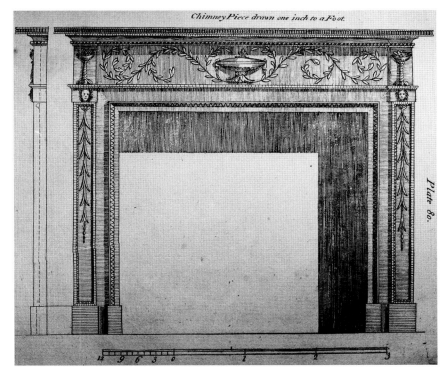

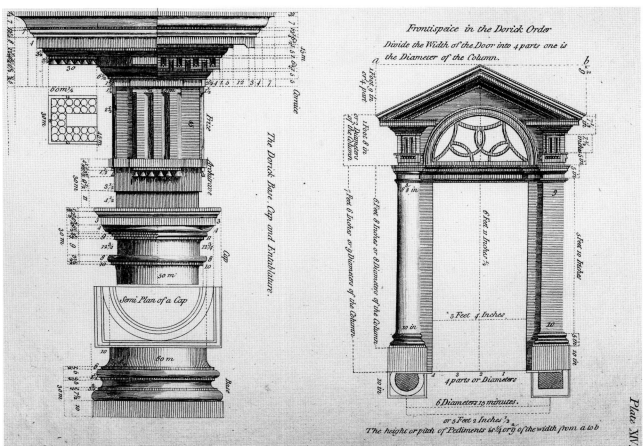

were essential in showing the American craftsman how the British joiner fleshed out the grand ideas of architects like Adam.

This was all the more important because, in New England, it was usually the joiner who designed buildings. Although there were a few gentlemen who acted as amateur designers, most people turned to a building tradesman for help in designing a fashionable house, business block, or public building. In almost every recorded instance, it was the leading joiner on a job who provided the plan. In a few cases, some of these craftsmen provided plans for buildings on which they were not employed themselves, thereby acting as architects in the modern sense.

The American Federal Style. In one extraordinary case, New England witnessed the appearance of a native-born joiner who became an author and whose books adapted Pain's ideas to New England practice. Asher Benjamin (1773–1845), a native of Connecticut, published his first book in 1797, thereby becoming the first American to issue an original work on architecture. Benjamin was a joiner, not a gentleman, and had an intense curiosity about the methods and details of construction. His books were written for his fellow craftsmen, and conveyed in published form the kind of information that must have been passing among the building fraternity by word of mouth or by example since the first of Pain's ideas had arrived in New England.

Benjamin's first volume was entitled *The Country Builder's Assistant: Containing a Collection of New Designs of Carpentry and Architecture, Which will be particularly useful, to Country Workmen in general.* It was published in

Greenfield, Massachusetts, a town in the Connecticut River valley, and its thirty engraved plates document how far some of the ideas of William Pain had spread by 1797.

Transformation of Joiner's Work. Benjamin illustrated many new ideas that are recognizable as hallmarks of Federal-style detailing, in contrast to Georgian detailing. His four- or six-panel doors have flat panels, not feather-edged or raised panels. The stiles and rails around each panel are no longer decorated by a plain quarter-round molding but now display ogee or ovolo-and-fillet moldings that give a markedly different effect. Some of these doors, like some British doors of the same period, have an applied astragal molding that sets off a field inside the margins of the flat panels; in some British work, this inner field might be painted with a decorative scene or motif. Benjamin illustrated a number of six-panel doors, always with the two small panels at the top, in contrast to the usual Georgian practice of placing the small panels at the center of a six-panel door.

Other plates in *The Country Builder's Assistant* illustrate several variations of the Pain-type frontispiece, embellished with Tuscan, Doric, Ionic, and Corinthian columns. Still others show several patterns for delicate mantelpieces in the neoclassical mode, two of them embellished with swags of flowers or classical urns. A master craftsman like Samuel McIntire of Salem, Massachusetts, often duplicated such details in carved wood. Most joiners of the period, however, would have bought molded "composition" figures or festoons, which were available from importers or from specialized manufacturers in Boston, and then glued these features to the wooden mantelpiece.

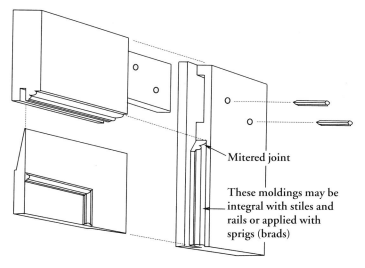

Mitered joint

These moldings may be integral with stiles and rails or applied with sprigs (brads)

Exploded view of the upper corner of a Federal-style door. Such doors retained the construction methods of the eighteenth century but usually had the flat faces of the panels exposed on the principal side of the door, with more elaborate moldings on the stiles and rails. In costly buildings, bead or astragal moldings might be applied to the panel faces. Drawing by author.

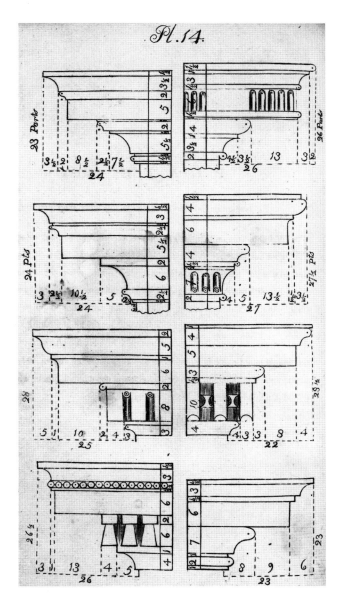

Plate from Asher Benjamin's *Country Builder's Assistant* (Greenfield, Massachusetts, 1797), showing fancy cornices. Benjamin adapted the decorated cornices illustrated by William Pain by using dentils, drilled holes, and gouged fluting in place of the more expensive carving or composition ornament shown by the British author. Photograph courtesy of the New Hampshire Historical Society.

rooms of those buildings. The backband moldings of Benjamin's architraves are of a more complex profile than had been seen in Georgian work. The result is that door, window, and fireplace casings of the Federal style are much more complex and varied in design than those of the Georgian era.

Similarly, Benjamin took the cornice and chair rail prototypes illustrated in William Pain's *Practical Builder* and *Practical House Carpenter* and translated them into designs of greater use to American joiners. Where Pain had shown moldings enriched with carving or with applied composition ornament, Benjamin left his moldings free of enrichment, knowing that few American craftsmen had access to such embellishment. To achieve an effect of complexity and pattern comparable to Pain's, Benjamin suggested decorating the flat surfaces with gouged flutes, with drilled holes, or with bits of molding cut to short lengths and applied to the surface like lattices. Benjamin also illustrated the use of rope moldings and strings of wooden balls, both of which were apparently being manufactured by specialists and are often seen as parts of cornices and chair rails in more elaborate houses along the seacoast.

Another new fashion that Benjamin illustrated was the narrow window sash muntin, shown in conjunction with six-over-six sashes with large glass sizes. Where Georgian muntins were often an inch in width, Benjamin's muntin profiles were less than five-eighths of an inch wide. Where Georgian muntins were almost always of a standard ovolo-and-fillet profile, Benjamin illustrated not only that profile but also a cove-and-astragal and a plain astragal muntin. The thinner muntins and larger glass illustrated in *The Country Builder's Assistant* may reflect the fact that, by the 1790s, New England–made crown glass was newly available from the successful Boston Crown Glass Manufactory, established in 1787. The availability of locally made glass presumably encouraged the use of larger panes than had been common when all window glass was imported.

In part, Benjamin's *Country Builder's Assistant* reflected

In addition to major features like doorways and mantelpieces, *The Country Builder's Assistant* illustrated an array of smaller details. Together, these represented a radical departure from Georgian traditions. Benjamin's architraves, or casings for doors, windows, and fireplace openings, are very different from their heavy Georgian predecessors. Many of them are double, having two flat surfaces separated by a molding, rather than the one undivided band. While double architraves had been seen in the grander Georgian houses, they were rare in more ordinary dwellings of the eighteenth century. Following publication of Benjamin's book, double architraves began to be much more common in ordinary buildings, or at least in the best

The Evolution of Style ❧ 109

practices that were already current among the best joiners in the mid-1790s. In part, as the title suggests, the book instructed country workmen, who were isolated from contact with the coast or with urban centers, in the latest fashions for building. In either case, a radical change in joinery became evident throughout New England in the late 1790s and early 1800s. *The Country Builder's Assistant* had an immense effect, helping to sweep aside the style of the eighteenth century and providing detailed instructions, written by an American for Americans, for executing the style that was to dominate the first thirty years of the nineteenth century.

Benjamin's second book had an equal effect. No longer content to be a country workman, Benjamin moved to Boston in 1803. There he was exposed not only to the ideas of architects like Charles Bulfinch and Peter Banner but also to the traditions and trade practices of a building fraternity of great sophistication.

Benjamin published his second book, *The American Builder's Companion*, in Boston in 1806. Again in this volume, Benjamin illustrated fancy cornices, chair rails, and double architraves. In some cases these are embellished with gouged and drilled ornament or with applied wooden beads and rope molding. In others, the cornices are heavy

Plate 26

(*Right*) Plate from Asher Benjamin's *American Builder's Companion* (Boston, 1806) showing fancy cornices. By the time of publication of his second book, Benjamin had developed his cornice designs to include greater projection, the use of Grecian molding profiles, and ornaments such as rope moldings, wooden beads, and triangular drops called guttae. Photograph courtesy of the New Hampshire Historical Society.

(*Opposite*) Cornice with applied lattice moldings and chip carving, Hart House, Portsmouth, New Hampshire, circa 1800. Also shown are characteristic Federal-style double door casings and a flat-paneled door with applied bead or astragal moldings. Photograph by Arthur Haskell, 1934. Courtesy of the Society for the Preservation of New England Antiquities.

Floor plan, two-story Federal-style house. This characteristic plan, with two rooms and a stair hall on each floor and a kitchen wing, derives from the earlier hall and parlor house. By replacing the older central chimney with chimneys located against exterior walls, the plan provides for a central stair hall within the one-room depth of the house. Drawing by author.

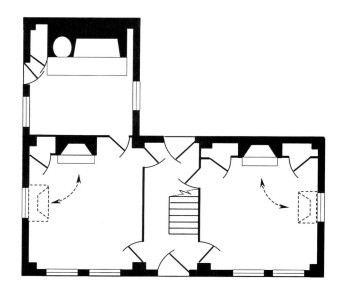

Ham-Woodbury Mansion, 1809, Portsmouth, New Hampshire. The three-story dwelling is a common form of large Federal period house in most of coastal New England and in some inland locales. This house was unusual in having floor-length windows and wrought-iron balconies on its facade. Photograph by L. C. Durette, 1936. Library of Congress, Prints and Photographs Division, Historic American Buildings Survey, Reproduction Number HABS, NH, 8 – PORT, 123.

Nathaniel G. Upham House, Concord, New Hampshire, 1831. The Federal period saw a marked increase in brick houses in northern New England. One of the house types introduced during the 1820s retained the traditional five-bay front but oriented the gable roof to create a pediment over the facade. Because of its suggestion of a temple front, this design remained popular during the Greek Revival period, beginning in the 1830s. Photograph by Bill Finney.

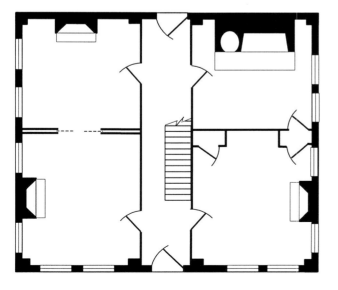

Floor plan, three-story Federal-style house. Large, three-story houses of the Federal period usually have four chimneys and sometimes have sliding doors that allow front and rear rooms to be opened into a single large space. Drawing by author.

with composition ornament, and this may be attributed to the fact that in Boston, unlike most rural locales, several stucco workers and manufacturers of composition ornament were plying their trade. One of these men, Daniel Raynerd, was Benjamin's coauthor of the first edition of *The American Builder's Companion*.

Because Boston was becoming a city of brick at the time that Benjamin authored his second book, the volume contains many details appropriate to brick buildings. Among these are windows with deep embrasures, common in brick houses, and an arched doorway adapted to a masonry building. These features made the volume all the more influential, as brick became fashionable in rural locales as well as in cities and villages.

Together, *The Country Builder's Assistant* and *The American Builder's Companion* established the Federal style as the pervasive method of building both elaborate and simple dwellings across New England. The old style of raised-panel door was replaced with the flat-panel style. Delicate mantelpieces became common, and even bedchambers, which formerly had seldom had a shelf above a fireplace, were now routinely fitted with a mantel. The idea of a full wall of breastwork or paneling quickly faded into history. Instead, the new fashion called for plastered walls above a wooden wainscot, and the latter was often made from wide, flat boards, although in grander houses it might be composed of stiles, rails, and flat panels. Room cornices, when employed at all, tended to be of a shallow but ornate design that projected rather far out onto the ceiling but not far down the wall.

Changes in Floor Plan. Houses changed in form as well as detail under the influence of the Federal style. Whereas Georgian houses were almost always heated by a central chimney or by two chimneys placed on either side of a central stair hall, the Federal-period house shows much more flexibility of floor plan. While conservative dwellings, especially in the country, might retain the form of the story-and-a-half "Cape Cod" house or the two-story, central-chimney plan, many houses began to appear in which the chimneys were placed against the outer walls or even incorporated into those walls in the case of brick buildings. Buildings with such floor plans have more chimneys than did their Georgian predecessors—from two to four or five—but each chimney is a slim stack that does not intrude into the floor space within the building. In coastal towns, where merchants had the money to pay

for imposing effects, this permitted the use of spiral staircases or grand, open stair halls or of pairs of rooms that could be thrown into one by opening sliding pocket doors. In coastal areas the three-story house became commonplace among the mercantile class, whereas houses of this scale had been rare in the eighteenth century.

The Greek Revival Style

Even as the style of Robert Adam was at its peak, some European and British designers were arguing in favor of a fully Grecian style of building: a Greek revival in architecture. While the necessary information for such a style was available to Americans in the form of a number of British treatises on Greek architecture, New England buildings show little evidence of the abandonment of the Federal style or the advent of the Greek, until the late 1820s or early 1830s. Structures built during that period often show a combination of Federal and Greek Revival details, sometimes vacillating from one style to the other in different rooms within the same building.

Several factors combined to draw the attention of Americans toward Greek architecture during the 1820s. First, the Greek style became known to Americans through buildings constructed here by the British immigrant Benjamin Henry Latrobe, beginning with the Bank of Pennsylvania in 1798, and by his students Robert Mills and William Strickland. These structures were unlike anything seen previously in the United States and attracted widespread notice. Second, Americans were caught up in the plight of the modern Greeks, who in the 1820s were engaged in a war to wrest themselves free from Turkish domination. Tales of Turkish cruelty and of the plight of Greek refugees gave birth to Greek relief societies in many American communities and to a deep admiration for Greek culture, ancient and modern.

By the 1820s, Greek architecture had attracted enough popular interest that Asher Benjamin included plates illustrating the Greek orders in the 1826 edition of *The American Builder's Companion*. Four years later, Benjamin published a new book, *The Practical House Carpenter* (1830), entirely in the Greek Revival style, noting in the introduction that "since my last publication, the Roman school of architecture [the Federal style] has been entirely changed for the Grecian."

Benjamin illustrated no house designs in *The Practical*

House Carpenter, nor did he in any of his following three books. Rather, he concentrated on designs for doorways, interior doors and casings, mantelpieces, baseboards, and cornice moldings. Perhaps this was a tacit recognition of the fact that in New England the Greek Revival style is often expressed more in detail than in overall house form. The New England landscape contains few of the classic Doric or Ionic temples seen in other parts of the eastern United States. Rather, the Greek Revival style in this region is applied to a variety of house forms. Some of them have their principal entrances in the gable end, thereby giving a mild suggestion of the facade of a Greek temple. But Grecian detailing is as often seen on vernacular house types, including story-and-a-half Cape Cod cottages and large, two-story farmhouses that echo the form of the double house of the eighteenth century. In cases where Greek Revival detailing was applied to story-and-a-half houses, common practice during the 1830s and later was to lengthen the wall posts and elevate the eaves well above the attic floor. Such a knee wall raised the eaves well above the first-floor windows, allowing the dwelling to be em-

Margaret Porter House, circa 1837–1840, Walpole, New Hampshire. In its most fully developed form, the Greek Revival house assumed the form of a classical temple. More common were houses with Grecian detailing and a gable end as a facade but without the full portico. Photograph by Ned Goode, circa 1959. Library of Congress, Prints and Photographs Division, Historic American Buildings Survey, Reproduction Number HABS, NH, 3 – WALP, 8.

---

bellished with heavy wooden trim suggestive of the massive entablature of a Greek temple.

Similarly, the front door designs given by Benjamin after 1830 suggest the post-and-beam construction of Greek temples. Most Greek Revival doorways have heavy pilasters at each side, surmounted by massive, wooden, three-part entablatures that evoke the feeling of stone construction. Sidelights and rectangular transom sashes above the door openings are particularly common at this period, supplanting the semicircular or elliptical fanlights that had been favored on Federal-style frontispieces.

Whether intended for exterior or interior use, Greek Revival doors are typically much bolder and simpler than

their Federal-style counterparts. Many doors of the period have raised panels but no moldings around the panels. Others have very heavy Grecian ogee moldings—flat S-curved moldings that are a major hallmark of the style—applied around the margins of the panels. Greek Revival doors may have wide horizontal panels, equal to the combined width of two vertical panels, placed at the top or the middle of the door; thus, five-panel doors appear for the first time.

During the latter 1830s, the airtight stove began to replace the open fireplace in many homes. Even so, people of the 1830s and later were often reluctant to relinquish the mantelpiece as a focal point of the room. Whether surrounding a fireplace or used with a stove, the Greek Revival mantelpiece typically displays a massive design quite unlike that of its Federal-style predecessor. The shelf is usually a heavy, square-edged plank, while the pilasters that support it may be plain, undecorated boards or may be ornamented somewhat like the pilasters of an exterior doorway. Heavy, turned Doric columns may support the shelf.

Huckins House, Tamworth, New Hampshire, circa 1845. Many Greek Revival houses maintained the center chimney plan of the traditional Cape Cod dwelling. These dwellings were often built with a knee-wall frame that elevated their eaves well above the first-story windows, allowing them to be embellished with a deep classical entablature. Photograph by author.

The advent of the Greek Revival style coincided with the slow abandonment of wainscoting in rooms. Because they may form the only trim at the bottom of the room, Greek Revival baseboards are often taller, heavier, and capped with a more massive molding than Federal-style baseboards.

The Greek Revival style also saw the introduction of plaster room cornices, which had been uncommon before the 1820s and remained an urban feature. As ornamental plaster detailing became more common, ceiling rosettes or "center pieces" were often installed in the best rooms as a point of support for chandeliers. These typically have molded acanthus leaves or other vegetative ornament and often contrast with the plainness of other features in a room.

As the Federal style had introduced slimmer window muntins and new muntin patterns, the Greek Revival style added still other profiles (see figure, page 147). Buildings of the 1830s through the 1850s may retain the old ovolo-and-fillet pattern, now usually with a Grecian ovolo rather than a plain quarter-round and sometimes only half an inch in width. The rather rare cove-and-astragal muntin may persist. New patterns particularly associated with the Greek Revival style include a "Gothic" profile and a straight beveled pattern. All these muntins tend to be thin and to be used with relatively large panes of glass in more fashionable homes. In country dwellings, small panes may persist, with more panes per sash. Poorer grades of glass, with bubbles and ripples, may be employed.

The Greek Revival style is often a style of great plainness. Sometimes, curved moldings are dispensed with altogether, with flat casings and square-edged boards being used for all trim. In such cases, the Grecian style seems to be the antithesis of the ornate Federal style that preceded it.

But Greek Revival buildings could be exuberantly ornamental. Asher Benjamin illustrated a number of entrance frontispieces, mantelpieces, and interior details that were decorated with honeysuckle ornaments, Greek key ornaments, and other decorative devices that had been discovered on ancient Greek temples. In New York City, another author, Minard Lafever, published his own carpenter's guidebooks to compete with those of Benjamin. Lafever's *The Young Builder's General Instructor* (1829), *The Modern Builder's Guide* (1833), and *The Beauties of Modern Architecture* (1835) illustrated a more florid Grecian style than was favored in Boston. Lafever's designs are rich in anthemion ornaments, based on the stylized honeysuckle, and with Grecian consoles and antefixes of the richest design.

Such ornaments, especially when used repeatedly in bands and friezes, would have challenged the most skillful and industrious carver. Thanks to the manufacturers of molded composition ornamentation, however, the skills

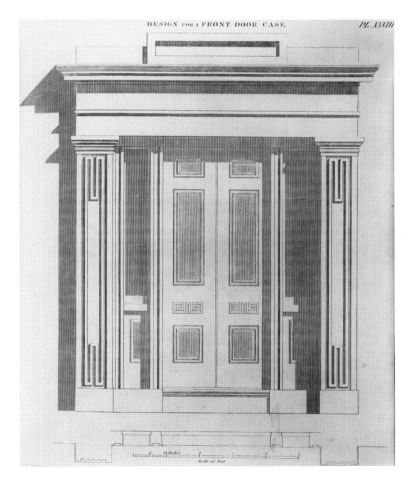

DESIGN FOR A FRONT DOOR CASE.   PL. XXXII.

Plate from Asher Benjamin, *The Practical House Carpenter* (Boston, 1830), illustrating a frontispiece, or doorway, in the Greek Revival style. This pattern of doorway or a simplified version of it was one of the most common entrance designs from the 1830s until the mid-1800s. Photograph courtesy of the New Hampshire Historical Society.

of the carver were not needed to realize the most elaborate of Benjamin's or Lafever's designs. In Boston, New York, and other urban centers, manufacturers of composition and papier-mâché ornaments rapidly changed their molds from Adamesque to Grecian and proceeded to issue great quantities of attractive ornamentation that could be attached to woodwork or ceilings. When covered with paint, these Grecian motifs appeared to be integral with the surface to which they were applied.

While one may encounter Grecian designs of the more highly ornamented type anywhere in northern New England, some of the most sumptuous appear in western Vermont. As in other aspects of the building trades, artisans there were apparently influenced more by New York than by Boston. Some of New England's most ambitious Grecian temples and some of the most richly embellished interiors are to be found in towns like Burlington, Orwell, Cornwall, Arlington, and Sudbury.

Romantic Styles

Asher Benjamin wrote a total of seven books between 1797 and 1843, most of them passing through several editions. Like the books written by a host of British authors before him, Benjamin's volumes were addressed mainly to the workman. Although we know that Benjamin's writings also had an important influence on private householders who were planning their dwellings, Benjamin's descriptions and diagrams were highly technical and were little calculated to help ordinary readers form ideas of architectural taste.

In 1842, just before the last of Benjamin's volumes arrived at the booksellers, an entirely new kind of architectural volume appeared in the United States. This was *Cottage Residences*. It was written by Andrew Jackson Downing, a native of Newburgh, New York, the son of a nurseryman and an extraordinarily appealing writer. Downing's book was the first American publication to discuss domestic architecture in terms that were understandable and appealing to the householder; it was all the more revolutionary for its frequent discussion of household affairs and arrangements that were of special interest to women. *Cottage Residences* was the first American book to discuss the purposes, arrangement, and aesthetics of dwelling houses. It was the first to link the design of a house to the economic circumstances, personal interests, and fam-

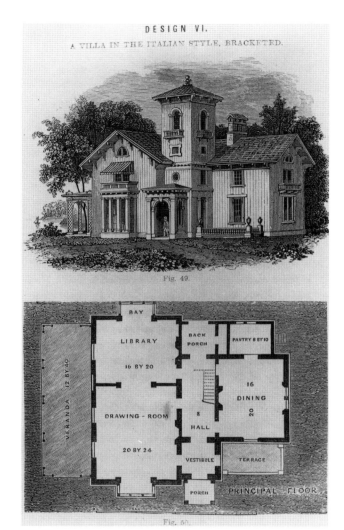

Plate from Andrew Jackson Downing, *Cottage Residences* (New York, 1842), illustrating a villa in the Italian style. Houses of this pattern, though ambitious in scale and design, were not uncommon in New England's manufacturing centers. The balconies, bay windows, porches and verandas offered a connection with nature.

ily life of its owners. It was the first to urge the installation of mechanical contrivances for running water and plumbing and for improved comfort, convenience, and ventilation. It was the first to link the house and its grounds through thoughtful discussions of horticulture and landscaping and of features like bay windows and porches that allowed the building and its setting to interact and to function as a single composition.

From the standpoint of architectural style, *Cottage Residences* was of revolutionary importance because it intro-

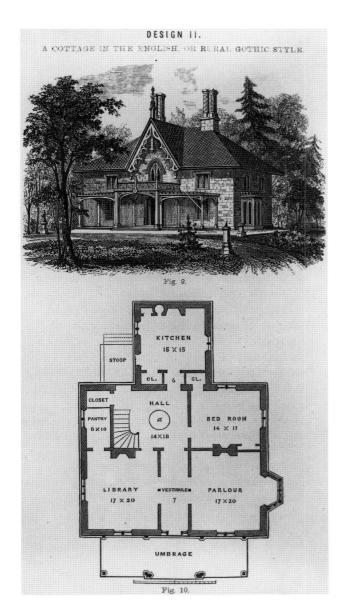

DESIGN II.

A COTTAGE IN THE ENGLISH, OR RURAL GOTHIC STYLE.

Fig. 9.

KITCHEN
15 X 15

STOOP

CL.   6   CL.

CLOSET

HALL

PANTRY
6 X 10

BED ROOM
14 X 17

14 X 18   a

LIBRARY
17 X 20

VESTIBULE
7

PARLOUR
17 X 20

UMBRAGE

Fig. 10.

duced and advocated a wide range of romantic building designs, completely repudiating the classicism of the Greek Revival. Downing's work may be regarded as the seed from which all the romantic and picturesque house types of the latter half of the nineteenth century germinated in the United States. Most of the ideas that Downing discussed

Plate from Andrew Jackson Downing, *Cottage Residences* (New York, 1842), illustrating plans for the grounds of a rural cottage. Downing was a landscape architect whose first book, *A Treatise on the Theory and Practice of Landscape Gardening* (1841), passed through nine American editions. Downing's architectural theories were imbued with sensitivity to horticulture.

Plate from Andrew Jackson Downing, *Cottage Residences* (New York, 1842), illustrating a cottage in the English or rural Gothic style. Downing's praise of the Gothic created a fashion for that style in the United States. Most Gothic cottages were built of wood by local carpenters and lacked the solidity of this masonry house.

and advocated are current today, taken for granted as we plan our houses and yards.

Downing was greatly influenced by European writers who had developed elaborate theories of aesthetics. These theories could be applied equally well to the criticism of landscape paintings, to analysis of the emotional effects of natural settings on the human mind, or to the design and enjoyment of cultivated grounds and of buildings placed within those grounds. To Downing, a building should suit the convenience and practical needs of the owner, but its appearance or style should also evoke feelings of aesthetic

pleasure and should bring to mind associations with other places and other times.

The building and its landscape should be a single work of art. As a nurseryman, Downing was probably the first American writer who was equally knowledgeable and persuasive in discussing both buildings and plants. As a resident of the beautiful Hudson River valley, Downing was familiar with a long-cultivated landscape that was almost English in its picturesqueness. Almost every one of Downing's suggested designs for a house was accompanied by an equally detailed suggestion for its grounds. Downing's preference for house styles that offered porches, pergolas, terraces, balconies, and bay windows allowed his structures to be integrated with their gardens. No longer was there a clear boundary between indoors and outdoors. The house was designed with regard for the view from its rooms, for the pleasures of being half inside, half outside on a porch or loggia, and for the appearance of the building when viewed as an architectural feature from the grounds.

Downing had a special aversion to certain types of houses. The building type that offended him the most was

Joseph Burbeen Walker tenant cottage, Concord, New Hampshire, circa 1855. Built for a farm manager, this cottage was copied from the design "A Symmetrical Bracketed Cottage" in Downing's *Architecture of Country Houses* (New York, 1850), a book that further explored the author's theories of architecture and landscaping. Library of Congress, Prints and Photographs Division, Historic American Buildings Survey, Reproduction Number HABS, NH, 7 – CON, 6–1. Photograph by Gerda Peterich, circa 1964.

---

the wooden Grecian temple, painted stark white, with bright green window blinds — the very epitome of the Greek Revival house in its most fully idealized form. The repeated censure that Downing aimed at this particular style of building undoubtedly had much to do with the eclipse of the Greek Revival style by 1850. Downing's recommendation of soft earth colors for the exteriors of houses gave birth to the paint schemes that dominated the rest of the century.

Downing had several house types to recommend in place of the Greek temple. Among his favorites, for both small cottages and grander country houses, were dwellings based on English precedent. The smaller of these are symmetrical; the larger tend to be asymmetrical but balanced in composition. Most have deeply overhanging roofs, some have bracketed eaves, and some have Gothic detailing. Among his designs for larger houses, Downing favored villas in the Italianate style, since these offered the opportunity for towers that both provided vistas of distant landscapes and permitted a certain expression of self-importance on the part of the owner.

The revolutionary idea that a homeowner might choose among several styles for his dwelling differed radically from American attitudes prior to the 1840s. Up to that time, there had been a single style for all buildings: Georgian or Federal or Greek Revival. Some buildings might display a style in fuller form than others; in humble homes the style might be evident only in the type of door or window sash that was employed. After Downing, however, several styles were possible; and both homeowner and builder had to strive to make all elements of a house consistent and harmonious with the style that had been selected for a particular house—or else to mix features of differing styles with a deliberate effect in mind. This was the birth of the eclectic attitude toward house design that has pervaded American architecture ever since.

One of Downing's maxims was that the house ought to express the personality of the owner. Some of this expression could be external, as in a prominent tower that bespoke the owner's stature in the community. Some could be internal, as in the provision of a library or study for thoughtful or literary inhabitants. Downing was the first American writer to urge the dedication of a room in each house to study and reading. He also recommended a linkage between the purpose of a room and its decoration. "Thus," he wrote, "the hall will be gray and simple in character, a few plain seats its principal furniture; the library sober and dignified, or bookish and learned in its air; the dining-room cheerful, with a hospitable sideboard and table; the drawing-room lively or brilliant, adorned with pictures or other objects of art, and evincing more elegance or gayety of tone in its colors or furniture."

Design for a suburban residence in the French Second Empire style, by Isaac H. Hobbs, architect of Philadelphia. Hobbs's plan was one of many house designs published in the influential *Godey's Lady's Book*, a magazine that had a powerful effect in promoting architectural fashion and in involving women in decisions affecting domestic building. *Godey's Lady's Book*, vol. 76, no. 451 (January 1868).

Other writers would elaborate these ideas to a great degree later in the century.

Downing was also the first to recommend mechanical devices to lighten the burden of running the household. He recommended pumps, aqueducts, cisterns, and plumbing systems to supply water not only to the kitchen but also to bathing rooms and water closets. He recommended dumb waiters to allow kitchens to be placed in basements yet deliver hot food to first-floor dining rooms. In his second book, *The Architecture of Country Houses* (1850), Downing devoted space to other midcentury concerns, including the central heating and ventilation of houses. The idea of exhausting "vitiated" air, laden with carbon dioxide from human respiration, and of replacing it with fresh outside air became a subject of interest to nearly every architectural writer after Downing. Many nineteenth-century houses (and schools and hospitals) made careful provision for this constant flow of outside air, much to the vexation of people in the late twentieth century who tended to seal buildings against air infiltration in the interest of "energy efficiency."

Downing introduced a number of other new subjects in *The Architecture of Country Houses*. He recommended

SUBURBAN RESIDENCE.
Designed expressly for Godey's Lady's Book, by ISAAC H. HOBBS, *Architect, Philadelphia.*

One of the most widely built mail-order house plans ever produced was the "Popular Modern Eight-Room Tower Cottage" by Palliser, Palliser and Company of Bridgeport, Connecticut, and New York. This advertisement states that "over 75,000 copies of this plan have been sold and a large number built . . . some towns having two or three of them." From *Palliser's New Cottage Homes and Details* (New York, 1887).

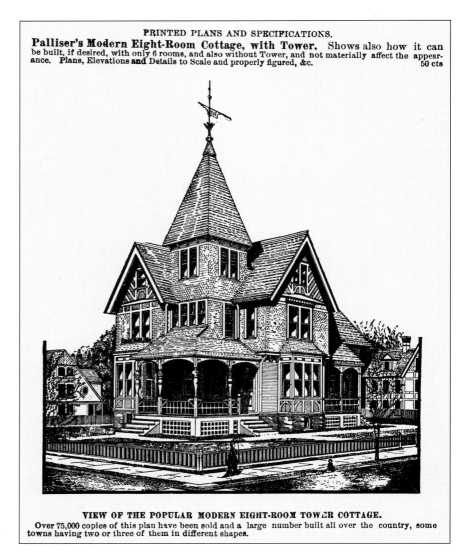

PRINTED PLANS AND SPECIFICATIONS.

Palliser's Modern Eight-Room Cottage, with Tower. Shows also how it can be built, if desired, with only 6 rooms, and also without Tower, and not materially affect the appearance. Plans, Elevations and Details to Scale and properly figured, &c. 50 cts

VIEW OF THE POPULAR MODERN EIGHT-ROOM TOWER COTTAGE.
Over 75,000 copies of this plan have been sold and a large number built all over the country, some towns having two or three of them in different shapes.

staining and varnishing interior trim, both hardwood and softwood, rather than covering it with paint, thereby encouraging the late-nineteenth-century fashion for varnished woodwork. He praised the idea of papering walls with inexpensive wallpapers, a fashion that has persisted down to the present time. Although Downing had disparaged wooden houses in his first book, he acknowledge in his second that Americans favored this kind of construction and discussed the use of patterned wall and roof shingles, exterior stucco, board-and-batten siding, and other features that became hallmarks of dwellings in the next half-century.

Downing's two books on architecture passed through a total of twenty-three editions, most of them published after his premature death in a steamboat accident in 1852. Downing's influence on American architecture was perva-sive. While it is rare to find individual houses in city or country that are exact copies of the plates in his books, it is also rare to find buildings after 1850 that do not reflect his ideas. After Downing's death, a number of other writers, including his English partner, Calvert Vaux, and another English immigrant, Gervase Wheeler, continued in his tradition. Vaux, Wheeler, and others wrote books addressed to men and women who wanted their homes to meet their own needs and at the same time to reflect good taste as defined by theorists of the time.

The idea that house design should be the study of ordinary Americans, not just builders or architects, was reinforced by periodicals like *Godey's Lady's Book*, a highly popular magazine that regularly published house designs by leading urban architects, with thoughtful descriptions of the virtues of each plan. The special interests of women were further addressed by *The American Woman's Home*, by sisters Catharine Beecher and Harriet Beecher Stowe. Published in 1869, this volume dealt little with the aesthetic aspects of house design but devoted a great deal of thought to efficient household planning, mechanical contrivances, and good ventilation.

By 1873, when a new and expanded edition of Downing's *Cottage Residences* appeared, the editors had added a number of new designs that showed the effect the book had had over its thirty years of influence. These included examples of the mansard-roofed French Second Empire style and of the asymmetrical and picturesque English Queen Anne style, which would shortly evolve into the American version so characteristic of the 1880s and 1890s. One author who contributed to the definition of the American Queen Anne style was native-born Henry Hudson Holly, whose *Modern Dwellings* of 1878 promoted the style and discussed its key features, including fireplaces, elaborated staircases, towering pilastered chimneys, and varied exterior wall coverings.

Mail Order House Plans. By the time that Holly's *Modern Dwellings* was published, other enterprising architects had discovered a new way to convey architectural ideas to the American public. This was the mail-order house plan. Such plans were offered by architects, or associations of architects, through books or catalogs that illustrated perspective renderings and floor plans of houses of

Design No. 123 by Boston architect Frank L. Smith. This rendering suggests the sophistication that characterized many mail-order house plans by the late nineteenth century. With its dramatic silhouette, its broad porches and balconies, and its varied roof planes and wall textures, this design embodies most attributes of the Queen Anne style. From *Homes of To-Day* 1, no. 1 (January 1888).

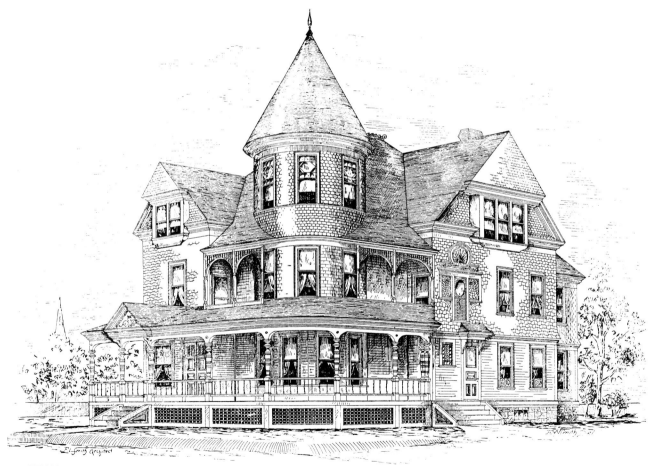

PERSPECTIVE VIEW.

DESIGN NO. 123.

SCIENTIFIC AMERICAN.

Building Edition.

A COLONIAL RESIDENCE AT PRINCETON, N.J.

No 130   AUGUST 1896.

MUNN & CO., PUBLISHERS, NEW YORK

COPYRIGHT 1896, BY MUNN & CO.

$ 2.50 A YEAR.   SINGLE COPIES 25 CTS.

361 BROADWAY.

various sizes, styles, and costs. Detailed working drawings, sometimes with lists of all materials required for construction or with suggested painting schemes, could be ordered through the mail.

Such services were particularly valuable to people who lived in rural areas, far from an architect's office, but who wanted a house of a more sophisticated style than could be supplied by a country builder. In New England, many houses built from mail-order plans are to be found in country settings, although most are seen in small villages,

---

(*Opposite*) Colonial revival house illustrated in the *Scientific American, Building Edition* for August 1896. The colonial style became increasingly popular during the 1890s. Lacking an understanding of the differences between Georgian and Federal-style buildings, architects of the period combined the two styles in their designs.

(*Below*) Design No. 119 by architect David S. Hopkins. This well-developed design in the shingle style illustrates how architects as far away as Michigan had mastered and were purveying designs that might appeal to a New England client. From Hopkins, *Houses and Cottages*, Book No. 9 (Grand Rapids, Michigan, 1893).

where they usually represent the most elaborate and imposing dwelling in a neighborhood.

The leading pioneers in the mail-order house plan business, in the late 1870s and early 1880s, were the partnership of George and Charles Palliser of Bridgeport, Connecticut, and the Cooperative Building Plan Association of New York, founded by Robert W. Shoppell. They were joined in the late 1880s by George F. Barber of Knoxville, Tennessee, whose fanciful Queen Anne designs found favor in some New England towns.

The astonishing amount of thought and writing that followed Downing's first book of 1842 gave rise to a very different architectural landscape in the latter half of the nineteenth century than in the first half. Multitudes of styles were presented to any prospective homeowner. The range of possible styles was increased by the ever increasing supply of architectural materials, ranging from machine-made millwork to hardware, from furnaces and boilers to bathroom fixtures, from larger sizes of glass to new types of tiles and terra cotta. Substitution of the balloon frame for mortise-and-tenon framing encouraged an ever increasing complexity of house forms.

Between the Civil War and the end of the nineteenth century, several major house styles had become well de-

First Floor Plan.

Second Floor Plan.

HOUSES AND COTTAGES.   **DESIGN NO. 119.**   *D. S. HOPKINS, Architect*

fined. Beyond these lay an almost infinite range of exotic styles or of combinations of several styles in one building. The favorite house types of the latter half of the century included the French Second Empire or mansard-roofed dwelling, usually relatively narrow and tall, as befits a house form deriving from urban roots in Paris; the Queen Anne house, recognizable more for its variety of roof planes, wall coverings, and gables and turrets than for any one hallmark; the colonial revival style, which gained favor after the centennial of the Declaration of Independence in 1876 and made undifferentiated use of Georgian and Federal-style features; and the shingle style, especially popular in New England. Shingle-style houses often combined colonial and Queen Anne exterior details but placed them on a structure of infinitely varied shape, usually with broad, low roof planes, a few dormers, a massive brick chimney or two, and most important, walls clad in dark-stained or gray wooden shingles.

Downing had favored balance rather than strict symmetry in house design. Most of the major styles that appeared during the latter half of the nineteenth century moved still further toward strong asymmetry. Only the

French Second Empire style, which derives from a nineteenth-century revival of a seventeenth-century French fashion, adhered to a rather rigid symmetry in its facade, often displaying a front that is three, rather than five, bays in width. A house of this type, with a central doorway, naturally tends to perpetuate the formal central–stair hall plan common in Georgian and Federal-style buildings. The other major post–Civil War styles, however, moved toward an ever more flexible and open floor plan and overall design. Even the colonial revival style, while tending toward outward symmetry, often employs a highly imaginative and flexible room layout.

Central Heating and the Open Plan. Much of this flexibility was due to improvements in central heating. The use of fireplaces for heat absolutely requires that each room be shut while there is a fire in the hearth. Open doors invite drafts throughout the entire building and greater than necessary heat loss up the chimney. For reasons of aesthetics and health, Downing favored the continued use of fireplaces, as did many of the writers who followed him. Despite the fact that parlor stoves and

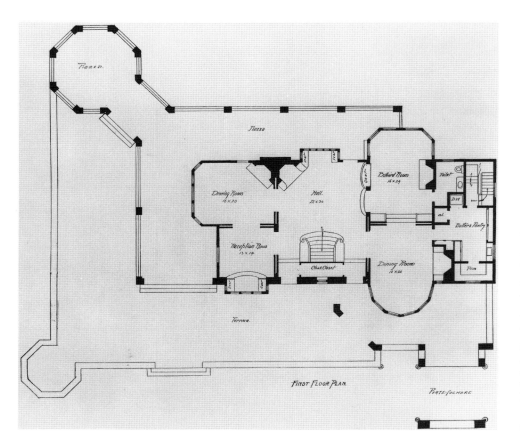

Floor plan of a shingle-style house by architect Charles P. H. Gilbert. With its expansive terraces and porches, its varied rooms connected by sliding doors, its four fireplaces, and its window seats and inglenooks, this house was the ultimate realization of the architectural and horticultural theories of Andrew Jackson Downing of sixty years earlier. *Scientific American, Building Edition,* September 1899.

kitchen ranges were widely available by 1840, American architectural theorists either paid little attention to these devices or openly disapproved of them. Writers often claimed that stoves superheated the air and helped to concentrate and render even more toxic the poisons that were supposed to be released by human respiration. These writers approved of fireplaces precisely because they required enormous quantities of outside air for good operation, thereby carrying off the vitiated air within an occupied room.

As central heating became more feasible during the 1850s, however, the need to compartmentalize a house began to fade. Warmth in late-nineteenth-century houses was produced in the basement, in a steam boiler or a hot-air furnace, and was distributed more or less evenly throughout the building. With a uniform internal atmosphere, a house could be regarded as a series of specialized but interrelated spaces rather than as a series of compartments. Sliding doors or curtained openings could connect parlors, libraries, and dining rooms, inviting easy passage between them. Stair halls, often equipped with built-in benches, alcoves, and fireplaces, could share their architectural elaboration with adjacent rooms through wide connecting portals. Vistas could open from one end of a building to the other, with a bay window in a parlor reflecting another in a dining room at the opposite side of the house. Typically, the kitchen was the only area of a large late-nineteenth-century dwelling that was isolated from the rest of the house, thereby confining cooking odors and noise.

This newfound freedom of internal planning invited connections with the outdoors to a degree that Downing could never have imagined. Towers and bay windows projected outward from the main block of the house. Recessed second-floor openings or balustraded porches atop window bays brought air and sunshine into bedchambers.

Sleeping porches—screened recesses opening off second-floor bedrooms—permitted open-air rest in warm weather, something unheard-of in any prior age in New England. Wide, sheltering piazzas, often extending around two or even three sides of the house, blurred the distinction between outdoors and indoors in temperate weather and excluded the hot summer sun from the interior of the house. And as will often be seen in the now-venerable trees and shrubs that surround late-nineteenth-century homes, Downing's emphasis on landscaping continued and increased, with an ever greater availability of new species and varieties.

Twentieth-Century Styles

The arrival of the twentieth century brought middle-class Americans many of the architectural luxuries formerly available only to the wealthy. The idea of the mail-order house plan, which had provided well-to-do Americans of

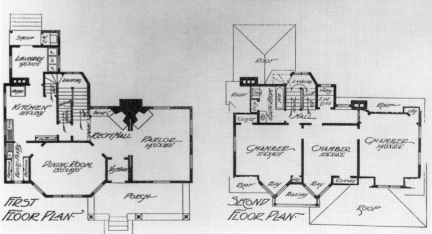

A suburban residence in the shingle style by architect W. L. Price, Philadelphia. By the late 1800s, many magazines and journals had followed *Godey's Lady's Book* in focusing attention on architectural design and building products. Among the most influential was *Scientific American*, which in 1885 began to publish a monthly "Building Edition." *Scientific American, Building Edition,* May 1896.

the 1870s and 1880s with elaborate designs even in the absence of a local architect, was increasingly adapted to less elaborate house types. The elaborate Queen Anne and shingle-style mansions that had predominated in many early mail-order plan books gave way to more modest cottage designs, still thoughtfully designed by experienced architects but now intended to be constructed for $1,500 instead of $10,000.

Methods of purveying plans for small houses multiplied before the turn of the twentieth century. An increasing number of architects and mail-order plan companies issued books of mail-order house plans during the late 1800s and early 1900s. Grand Rapids, Michigan, already a center of the American furniture industry, began to take its place alongside eastern centers as a source of mail-order designs. By the early 1890s, Grand Rapids designers David S. Hopkins, Frank P. Allen, and William K. Johnston had all issued books of well-designed Queen Anne and shingle-style houses. Their entrepreneurial spirit presaged Michigan's dominance in the arena of "pre-cut" houses in the early twentieth century.

Several late-nineteenth-century entrepreneurs developed large businesses writing and publishing books that combined general advice on house building with catalogs of house plans. The Radford Architectural Company of Riverside and Chicago, Illinois, published several collections of one hundred house plans, selling their hardbound books for one dollar—"one cent per house." The same company published an encyclopedia of building, a book of architectural details, and manuals on contracting and estimating. Similarly, Fred T. Hodgson of Chicago issued several books of house plans, but he was also a prolific writer on carpentry, joinery, stair building, the use of the steel square, and masonry.

In 1886, Robert W. Shoppell of New York began to publish an architectural quarterly, *Shoppell's Modern Houses.* Following his example, several other mail-order architects issued their own inexpensive monthly or quarterly periodicals, filled with new designs. Frank L. Smith of Boston began his quarterly *Homes of To-Day* in 1888, and George F. Barber of Tennessee began to publish his monthly *American Homes* in 1895. By the second decade of the twentieth century, magazines like *The National Builder* and *Building Age,* read almost exclusively by contractors, offered house designs in every issue, complete with detailed estimates of labor and materials for each dwelling. Continuing the tradition established more than half a century earlier by

Compliments of

BUCK LUMBER COMPANY

Rutland, Vt.   Telephone 260

Plan service book inscribed with the name of Buck Lumber Company, Rutland, Vermont. Although this book is designed to reassure clients by implying the proprietorship of a local company, it was actually compiled, published, and copyrighted by C. Lane Bowes of Hinsdale, Illinois, in 1927 and distributed to lumber dealers across the nation.

Godey's Lady's Book, magazines like *Ladies Home Journal,* read largely by women, offered similar mail-order plans.

The architects or companies who drew most designs that were offered through mail-order catalogs or magazines were clearly identified by name. By the 1920s, however, several companies developed catalogs of anonymously drawn house plans and distributed these catalogs through local lumber and millwork dealers, usually with the local firm's name printed on the cover. These catalogs were clearly meant to help local suppliers sell the building materials needed to construct the designs. Perhaps for that reason, the cost of plans was kept low, $20 being a typical charge for a set of documents that included floor plans, elevation drawings, sections, large-scale details, full lists of materials, specifications, and a contract. It is difficult to identify the self-effacing designers who worked for these "plan services," but some of the leading purveyors of lumber dealers' plan books were C. Lane Bowes of Hinsdale, Illinois; the Michigan Retail Lumber Dealers' Association; the Wood Homes Bureau of Cleveland, Ohio; and Standard Homes Company of Washington, D.C. Most plan services designed their houses to utilize framing materials of standard lengths and doors, windows, and cabinetry of stock designs, thus keeping construction costs as low as possible.

Pre-Cut Houses. The early twentieth century also saw the birth of prefabrication and modular construction in the American housing industry. Around the turn of the century, Ernest F. Hodgson of Boston began to market small, modular or panelized buildings that included vacation cottages and, eventually, year-round homes. By the second decade of the century, Sears, Roebuck and Company of Chicago was marketing similar "Simplex" panelized structures. The products of both companies consisted of wall and roof sections that were bolted together to create rigid, weather-tight, and self-supporting structures. Although Sears reduced its Simplex line to a few garages by the late 1920s, Hodgson Homes was still manufacturing panelized buildings in the 1960s.

An idea that filled a far more complex need was the pre-cutting of house parts to create house kits that were standardized in their components yet could adapt to a myriad of floors plans and styles. Such buildings typically started with mail-order plan books that resembled the already familiar catalogs of the late 1800s. But while those catalogs had offered plans that were to be built of locally procured materials, the new catalogs offered both plans and "knocked down" houses that were shipped from vast, efficient factories to customers anywhere within reach of rail or freight delivery. The buyer needed only to follow the plans and instructions and nail together an architect-designed house that was built of the best materials, precisely pre-cut.

The concept of pre-cut houses began in Bay City, Michigan, in the heart of the great midwestern lumber-producing region. The pioneers were the brothers William J. and Otto E. Sovereign, who adapted an already proven technique of pre-cutting and shipping boat kits to the production of complete houses. Beginning in 1907 as the North American Construction Company, the brothers began to market their "Aladdin" garages, boathouses, and summer cottages. Within a few years, the company

Aladdin's Famous Board *of* Seven

Master Designers, Builders and Manufacturers

BEFORE this Board of Seven comes every Aladdin house for the acid test of perfection. No detail escapes the keen and searching analysis of these experts. The designer must prove his plans to the complete satisfaction of, First, the Master Designer, for accuracy; Second, the Master Builders, for practicability, strength, and structural harmony; Third, Factory Experts, for elimination of waste, standardization of lengths, and economy of costs. Unless the cost of these high-priced men's time could be spread over a hundred or more houses of each design the cost would be prohibitive. But when they spend two or more hours' valuable time on the design, drawings, and cutting sheets of an Aladdin house the cost is not all charged to that *one house,* but to *several hundred* houses of that *same design* sold during the year.

Description of "Aladdin's Famous Board of Seven" from Aladdin Homes catalog No. 28 (1916). The North American Construction Company of Bay City, Michigan, promised buyers that the high price of designing, estimating, and producing every part of each Aladdin Home was distributed over the cost of hundreds of homes of the same pattern rather than charged to a single customer.

---

was offering dozens of "Readi-Cut" dwellings of one and two stories in several styles, operating from large Bay City mills, with additional mills in Oregon, cutting Douglas fir, and in Florida and Louisiana, cutting southern yellow pine.

The North American Construction Company soon had local competition. In 1914 the Lewis Manufacturing Company of Bay City, formerly associated with the Sovereign brothers in lumber milling, separated to begin its own line of pre-cut "Lewis Homes of Character," impelling the Sovereigns to reorganize their company as Aladdin Homes. Another Bay City manufacturer, International Mill and Timber Company, began to produce pre-cut "Sterling Homes" by 1915. Farther afield, the Gordon-Van Tine Company of Davenport, Iowa, manufacturers of millwork, developed a line of pre-cut houses after 1910, and the Ray H. Bennett Lumber Company of North Tonawanda, New York, was producing "Better Built" pre-cut homes by the 1920s.

By far the most serious competition in the pre-cut housing industry came from the two American mail-order titans: Sears, Roebuck and Company and Montgomery Ward. Sears entered the home construction business in 1908, when it augmented an older line of millwork with a catalog of plans for "Modern Homes," providing plans, specifications, and lists of materials for one dollar, to be refunded if the customer built with Sears materials. It appears that Sears did not produce fully pre-cut buildings until 1916, after the firm had purchased several lumber mills and woodworking plants. Given the huge scale of Sears's catalog market, it is not surprising that the retailing giant eventually dominated the pre-cut home business. By 1939, Sears claimed that over 100,000 families were then living in its "Honor-Bilt Modern Homes." Because of its already extensive inventory of home furnishings and finishes, Sears was able to provide not only the house but everything in it, including the paint and wallpaper. The last Sears houses were marketed in 1940. Many were built in New England.

Montgomery Ward, Sears's chief rival, entered the mail-order building plan business in 1910. By 1918 the company

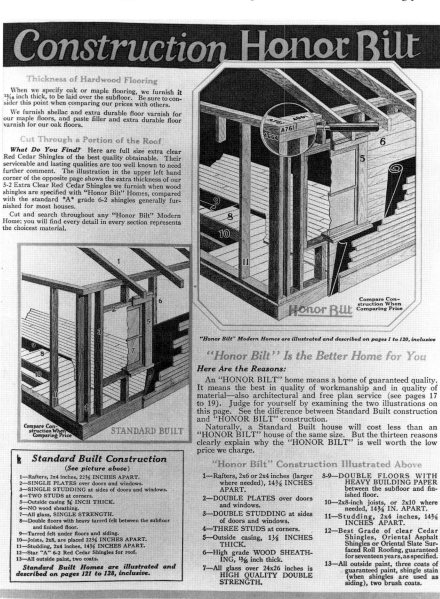

Description of "Standard Built" and "Honor Bilt" construction, from a Sears, Roebuck house catalog of the 1920s. Sears emphasized the superior design and quality of materials supplied with every pre-cut "Honor Bilt" home.

was marketing its "Wardway Homes" in both "Ready Cut" and "Un-Cut" versions. Uncut materials were cheaper and permitted easy alteration of the designs, but pre-cut materials saved greatly on labor, making the finished house less expensive in the end. Montgomery Ward continued to sell houses until 1931.

Manufacturers of pre-cut houses needed to standardize as many building components as possible in order to reduce waste of materials and to increase the efficiency of their mills. Their estimators carefully calculated the cost of everything they would have to buy and fabricate, including the waste in cutting each piece to size. They then prepared packing lists for the customer. These lists included notes explaining the stenciled markings on each component, essential in assembling the house. Wherever possible, manufacturers used lumber of standard mill-run dimensions, planning their buildings to reduce or eliminate extra cutting and waste.

The Western, or Platform, Frame. With few exceptions, if any, manufacturers of pre-cut homes adopted the

The Dutch colonial style became highly popular for small houses during the early twentieth century. It was characterized by a gambrel roof, usually punctuated by broad shed dormers, and often had a fireplace chimney, a glazed sun porch, and an open piazza. "The Georgian" design from Ray H. Bennett Lumber Company, "Bennett Better Built Homes" catalog No. 38, 1928.

___

western, or platform, method of framing their houses. Some textbooks on building construction still ignored the platform frame as late as the 1930s, but the use of this frame by the major midwestern housing manufacturers during the first decades of the century undoubtedly encouraged its adoption for all houses, not just pre-cut dwellings, in conservative New England.

Early Twentieth-Century Houses. The early twentieth century saw the introduction of a number of styles that were especially adapted to the small, middle-class house of three or four bedrooms. Among the most popular was the one-and-a-half- or two-story "Dutch colonial" house, a dwelling with a broad gambrel roof, often pierced by a wide shed dormer that admitted ample light into the bedchambers. Although such houses tended toward symmetrical designs, they were often varied by the addition of an expansive brick chimney, serving both the basement furnace and a fireplace in the living room, rising against the exterior wall at one end of the house. Many had a onestory glazed sun porch or a screened porch attached to one of the gable ends. Most tended to favor interior woodwork of a classical design, either varnished or painted as the owner's taste might dictate. Acknowledging the new availability of home delivery, at least in urban or suburban areas, many of these small houses have semienclosed back

porches with niches for iceboxes and, often, with little doors for milk delivery or for placing blocks of ice into built-in refrigerators. They frequently have special windows for easy delivery from coal wagons directly into enclosed bins or rooms in the cellar.

Another very popular small house was the bungalow. As a house type, the bungalow derives from low, open, tropical dwellings with deeply overhanging roofs. Although bungalows were popular in several countries in the early twentieth century, the term tended to define rather different types of houses in different parts of the world. The American bungalow, popular from coast to coast, evolved into a distinctive range of small house types. Most

The bungalow was one of the most popular American house types of the early twentieth century, described in countless books and articles and celebrated in its own magazine, which began publication in 1912.

of them are one and a half stories high, with broad roof planes that shelter an open front porch and offer constricted but adequate bedroom space above the first story. Roofs project well beyond wood-shingled or stuccoed walls. Rafter tails are exposed and painted rather than enclosed in the traditional classical cornice, or triangular wooden brackets support the projecting eaves.

The bungalow was especially associated with the American manifestation of the international Arts and Crafts style of the late 1800s and early 1900s, and its interior woodwork therefore tended toward the simple forms and varnished finishes that characterized that style. In New England, however, the bungalow also suggested a kinship with the earlier shingle style, a regional favorite that had already established the shingled wall and the broad roof plane as comfortable symbols of domesticity.

The bungalow and the shingle-style home had many characteristics in common, and perhaps these shared attributes permitted a tropical house form to find ready acceptance in a cold climate. On average, bungalows have less floor area and were less costly than the typical two-and-a-half-story shingle-style dwelling, but they retained some of the interior features that had endeared the shingle style to New Englanders. Like their shingle-style predecessors, New England bungalows are usually clad in dark-stained shingles and have a prominent porch. Like earlier New England homes, bungalows usually have a living room fireplace, often accompanied by a built-in seat, or inglenook. They retain wide openings between stair hall, living room, and dining room, offering inviting vistas and glimpses from room to room, even in a small house. Many display long-familiar bay windows or sideboard niches in their dining rooms. Like other small houses of the early years of the century, before electricity was commonly used for anything but lighting, bungalows often have special provisions for delivery of ice, milk, and coal.

Another house type that gained widespread favor throughout the United States after the first decade of the twentieth century was referred to in its time simply as the "square" house. The square house is a two-story dwelling covered by a hipped roof, usually with a front dormer to light the attic and sometimes with dormers on other slopes of its pyramidal roof. The square house usually has a full-width front porch, and its walls are often divided into two zones by an encircling wooden belt, with one story clapboarded and the other shingled. Praised in its own time for its economy of materials and its efficient use

The CARLISLE

A SQUARE house that is "different looking." This is due partly to the artistic arrangement of porch and windows, and partly to the contrast between the shingles of the upper story and the clapboard of the lower.

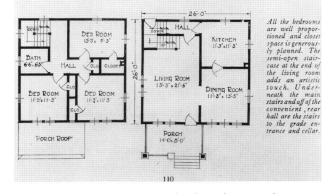

All the bedrooms are well proportioned and closet space is generously planned. The semi-open staircase at the end of the living room adds an artistic touch. Underneath the main stairs and off of the convenient, rear hall are the stairs to the grade entrance and cellar.

110

The "square house" became popular throughout North America during the early twentieth century as a dignified, roomy, but unpretentious family dwelling. Its boxlike form was often varied by different wall coverings on each story. "The Carlisle" from Lewis Manufacturing Company, *Homes of Character* (Bay City, Michigan, 1920).

of space, the square house is often regarded as a typical midwestern or prairie farm home, but it attained popularity in New England as well.

Beginning in the 1920s, a variety of "Tudor" or "English style" cottages became popular. Often characterized by asymmetrical front gables with steeply pitched, low-sweeping roofs that enveloped the bottom of broad fireplace chimneys, these cottages sometimes had clipped end gables that suggested the soft roof lines of thatched cottages.

Many other popular styles are reflected in the plan

books and pre-cut house kits of the decades before World War II. Together, these many designs reveal national tastes and fashions, not regional ones. The early twentieth century saw the rise of architectural and manufacturing forces that obliterated regionalism in American design. The new housing industry marshaled scores of anonymous architects to design houses and employed thousands of workers to manufacture standardized woodwork and pre-cut buildings of every type. While local builders and lumberyards might prosper under these conditions, there would be little local character in the suburbs that emerged under the influence of so gigantic an industry.

Despite the loss of regional character in American houses of the early twentieth century, these dwellings as a group are among the best planned and most comfortable houses ever built. Immense experience in design and manufacturing was brought to bear on the housing industry at this period. Such an investment could hardly fail to fulfill at least some of the promises that were made in virtually every plan book or catalog of pre-cut houses. Small houses of the first half of the twentieth century typically contain excellent materials, judicious planning, and finish of high quality. Thanks to a full century's analysis and writing, beginning with Andrew Jackson Downing, designers of the early twentieth century knew what made a home attractive, convenient, and enduring. In its sheer volume, its quality of design, materials, and workmanship, and its adaptation to the needs of the middle class, our housing stock of the period from the 1880s through World War II must always be regarded as one of our proudest legacies as a nation.

The Tudor house, with its characteristic sweeping front gable and massive fireplace chimney, became a popular small-house style in the 1920s. Its gables were sometimes clipped to suggest the soft outlines of a thatched roof. "The Morrison" from Standard Homes Company, *Better Homes at Lower Cost*, Book No. 12 (Washington, D.C., 1928).

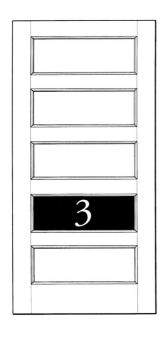

How to Date a Building: The Evolution of Key Features

Moldings

Georgian Moldings. Georgian molding profiles derive from profiles used by the ancient Romans and employed in the Italian Renaissance during the fifteenth and sixteenth centuries. Introduced to England in the first half of the seventeenth century for royal commissions by architects like Inigo Jones, such moldings were not seen in vernacular buildings in England for many years. It was not until 1700 or later that they appeared in New England. Yet when they arrived in New England, these moldings duplicated those employed in classically derived buildings all over Europe. In architecture, the Renaissance arrived in New England with the advent of the eighteenth century.

The standard Roman moldings have Greek, Latin, or Italian names. They are the *ovolo*, or quarter-round; the *torus*, or large, projecting half-round; the *astragal*, or small, projecting half-round; the *bead*, or small half-round, set below the surface; the *cyma*, or large S-curve (also called the *ogee* when of small size); the *cavetto*, or cove; and the *scotia*, or scooped molding. These few contours, separated from one another by flat bands, or *fillets*, make up Georgian molded features. The standard room cornice, for example, has a crown molding in the form of a *cyma recta*, or upright S-curve, separated by a fillet from a *cyma reversa*,

or reversed S, all planed out of one board. This board is nailed between the ceiling and the front face (or *fascia*) of a box. Below the box, between its bottom surface (or *soffit*) and the wall of the room, is a bed molding fashioned from another board shaped into an ovolo, separated by a fillet from another cyma reversa. The entire construction, though made of a few simple parts, appears substantial and complex and adds both visual interest and dignity to the room in which it is installed. The same form of cornice may be installed under the eaves of a house or at the top of a frontispiece, or doorway.

Similarly, most joiners of the Georgian period employed a small cyma, or ogee, molding as the trim on the outer edge of door and window casing, both inside the house and outside. This is called the backband molding. Most employed a bead to mark the edge of a board when that board forms the flat portion of a door or window casing or is set vertically against a wall as the bottom margin of a cornice or as a simple baseboard. These uses of simple moldings are illustrated in the "Casings, or Architraves" section.

Some applications call for a few special moldings. The cap of the handrail of a Georgian staircase, for example, usually has a serpentine top to fit the hand. Below the upper surface, on each side of the cap, is a torus, or half-round.

Below this is a fillet and a cavetto, and below the cavetto is an astragal and fillet. Below this molded cap is the vertical side of the rail itself. The same set of moldings is usually employed as a chair rail, which may be placed above wainscoting or may be applied across the flat middle rail of a paneled wall (see figure, page 170).

Although the handrail cap is complex in appearance, it is fashioned from only a few moldings. Another favorite molded feature of early Georgian joiner's work is likewise complex and imposing in effect but composed of only a few individual moldings. This is the *bolection*, a projecting feature that is most often employed as an enframement of panels, especially before 1750 or so. The bolection always features a bold torus, or projecting half-round, which is sometimes merged with an ogee, or S-curve. The outer margin of the bolection is usually terminated with another, smaller torus and a fillet or bead. Such moldings are sometimes nailed to the stiles and rails of regular paneling to throw a deep shadow around the panels; sometimes the bolection itself supports the panel above the surface of the stiles and rails, giving a bold, baroque appearance to the breastwork. Very large bolections are sometimes seen as enframements for fireplace openings; small ones were often used as picture frame moldings in the eighteenth century.

Working with this rather small repertoire of moldings, the joiner of the eighteenth century was able to produce rooms, mantelpieces, and doorways of powerful effect. This effect increased with enlarged scale and with the repetition of elements, such as ranges of panels in a wall or wainscoting or the consistent use of heavy room cornices. Since repetition of elements entailed increased labor, the

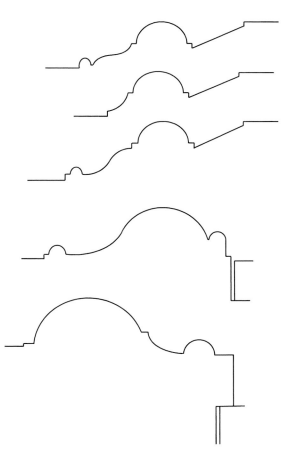

Various bolection molding profiles used as panel enframements and door casings. *Top*: panel moldings; *bottom*: door casings. Drawing by author.

most impressive Georgian houses are, of course, those of wealthy patrons who could pay for massive building frames and for the months of joiner's labor necessary to clothe those frames with impressive woodwork. But even the home of an eighteenth-century family of modest means will normally exhibit its Georgian character and its general date of construction in the pattern of its doors, window sashes, casings, and other molded surfaces.

Federal-Style Moldings. One of the most subtle yet revolutionary characteristics of the Federal style was the transformation of the molding profiles used in New England houses. Throughout the Georgian period in New England, all molding profiles had been based on profiles given by Renaissance authorities or by English authors who had written guidebooks either for gentlemen or for workmen. These molding profiles were based on Roman

The basic molding profiles. *Top row, left to right:* ovolo; ogee: cyma reversa; ogee: cyma recta. *Bottom, left to right:* torus; bead or astragal; cavetto; scotia. Drawing by author.

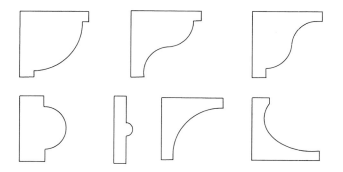

precedent. Most of them were composed of segments of circles. Thus, for example, a Roman ogee molding is composed of two connected arcs that, together, create an S curve. A Roman ovolo is a quarter of a circle.

Writing for the craftsmen whose hand tools produced moldings, the New England author Asher Benjamin devoted a great deal of attention to molding profiles. Benjamin altered the classic molding profile in a way that gave his moldings a very different visual effect from those of the eighteenth century. In both of his first two books,

---

Plate from Asher Benjamin, *The American Builder's Companion*, second edition (Charlestown, Massachusetts, 1811), illustrating Grecian molding profiles. Benjamin added this plate to the second edition to instruct joiners and plane makers in graphic methods of laying out the beautiful conic sections that characterize Grecian moldings. Photograph courtesy of the New Hampshire Historical Society.

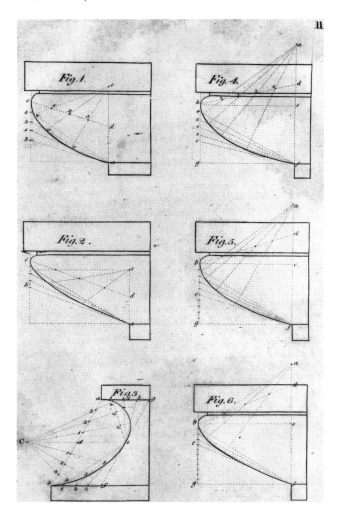

Benjamin drew attention to the idea of curving moldings inward at the top, where they meet the fillet above them. Moldings with this inward curve or reversal of their profiles are called quirked moldings. Quirked moldings had earlier been illustrated in the British books of William Pain. Benjamin explained the beauty of the quirked molding by noting that "their quirks ought to be large, and as many as the cornice will admit of, as the principal beauty of plain cornices depends upon the shadows of their quirks."

In the second edition of *The American Builder's Companion* (1811), Benjamin moved beyond the quirked molding and recommended a completely different set of profiles, those of the Grecian moldings. In making this change, Benjamin was echoing recommendations that the British architect Robert Adam had made almost forty years earlier. Although much of Adam's work took its inspiration from Roman structures, Adam was particularly enamored of the Greek moldings being studied and published by his friend James Stuart. In 1774, Adam wrote: "The mouldings in the remaining structures of ancient Rome are considerably less curvilineal than those of the ancient monuments of Greece. We have always given a preference to the latter, and have even thought it advisable to bend them still more in many cases, particularly in interior finishings, where objects are near, and ought to be softened to the eye."

Unlike the Roman molding, the Grecian molding is based on conic sections, not portions of circles. As Asher Benjamin explained it, "if mouldings are only composed of parts of a circle, and straight lines, they are called Roman; because the Romans, in their buildings, seldom, or never, employed any other curve for their mouldings than that of a circle; but if a moulding is made of a part of an ellipsis, or a parabola, or an hyperbole, the mouldings are then in the Grecian taste; hence it appears, that mouldings of the Grecian taste, are of a much greater variety than those of the Roman." Benjamin accompanied his description with plates showing joiners how to lay out Grecian moldings, thereby enabling them to make or obtain molding tools with the new profiles.

Benjamin's persuasive advocacy of the Grecian molding transformed almost every molded contour seen in American Federal-style buildings. Like the work of Robert Adam, the American Federal style combined motifs derived from Roman buildings with molding profiles from Greece. Grecian moldings pervade the style, appearing in tiny size around door panels, in medium size under man-

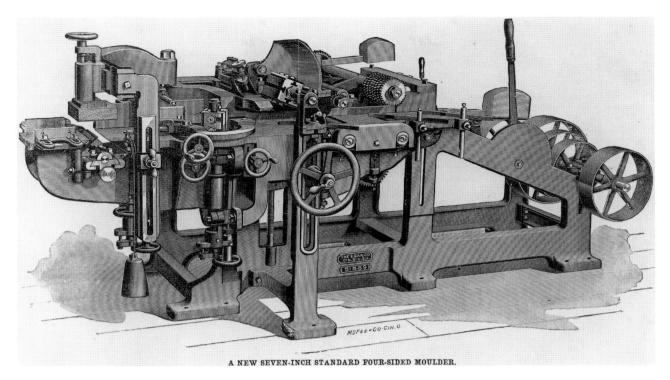

A NEW SEVEN-INCH STANDARD FOUR-SIDED MOULDER.

telshelves or in room cornices, and in huge scale in the cornices of houses and church steeples.

Every joiner who made the transition from the Georgian style to the Federal had to equip himself with an entirely new set of molding tools. This effort and expense ensured that joiners became particularly sensitive to the Grecian moldings and used them with intelligence and good effect. The Federal style owes much of its beauty to the pervasive use of these subtle contours.

Greek Revival Moldings. The advent of the Greek Revival style in New England around 1830 naturally called for the continued use of Grecian molding profiles. The Greek Revival was a style of deliberate plainness, a style that shunned the delicacy and elaboration of the Federal style in favor of coarser and more robust forms that suggest an architecture of stone rather than of wood. Greek Revival moldings tend to copy the contours that were actually employed on Greek temples. Such moldings tend to be flatter and larger in scale than the Grecian moldings of the Federal style. They tend to be used more sparingly than before and to be separated more widely by flat surfaces.

As the Greek Revival style evolved in New England, many joiners adopted moldings of even more severe flatness or angularity than true Grecian moldings. Writing in

Four-sided molding machine made by the Egan Company, Cincinnati, Ohio. Egan and J. A. Fay and Company merged to become "the world's oldest and largest manufacturers of woodworking machinery." This versatile molding machine is typical of the equipment that shaped the complex moldings of the late nineteenth century. *Scientific American, Building Edition,* August 1896.

the 1830s, the Boston author Edward Shaw noted in his book *Civil Architecture* that such moldings were derived from Grecian molding profiles but pointed out that their contours had been altered to achieve a somewhat different visual effect. Shaw described these new profiles simply as "modern mouldings."

Late-Nineteenth-Century Moldings. Once the Roman and Greek moldings had been understood and employed by builders, little more could be done except to combine their contours in various ways. The mid-nineteenth century saw the elaboration of moldings for various uses. A new fascination with the picturesque found the broad, flat moldings of the Greek Revival to be too austere. Architects and woodworkers adopted new and more elaborate profiles for cornices, chair rails, baseboards, casings, and most other features. Whereas older moldings had been executed in pine and painted, interior moldings of the latter part of the nineteenth century were increasingly fashioned from hardwoods and varnished. Outside, the picturesque styles demanded eaves brackets, elaborate door and window enframements, and even roof pinnacles and decorated barge boards. Andrew Jackson Downing's books began a flood of publications that recommended ever

more complex types of ornament. Many post–Civil War authors filled their books with plates illustrating molded ornamentation of unprecedented complexity.

In response to the need for such details, the late nineteenth century saw a major change in the production of molded woodwork. With the advent of ever more versatile molding machines, or shapers, the potential for variation

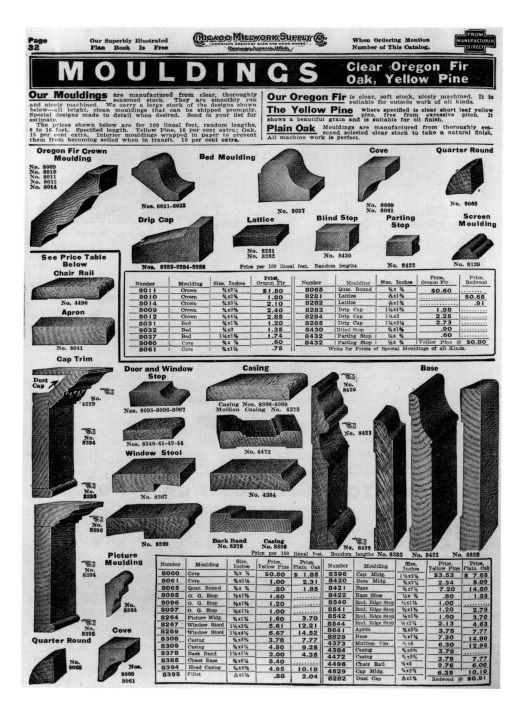

Some of the moldings of the 8000 series of standardized profiles, which remained dominant throughout the first half of the twentieth century. Chicago Millwork Supply Company, catalog No. 367, March 1, 1927.

in molding profiles multiplied far beyond the already wide range possible with hand molding tools. Woodworking machinery quickly evolved beyond the planers and shapers needed for the production of simple moldings or of matched (tongue-and-groove) sheathing. New machines became capable of shaping four sides of a molding in one pass, accommodating hardwood stock and producing shapes with such precision that several moldings could be fitted together to make complex architectural features. With a simple change of knives on a rotary cutter, endless combinations of curves could be combined in a single molding.

Standardized Moldings. By the late 1800s the American building industry began to recognize this potential for variety as a mixed blessing. Endless variation in molding profiles had the potential of engendering chaos. When machine-made moldings were ordered from different suppliers, it was important that moldings of a given profile match one another. As early as the late 1870s, the Universal Catalogue Bureau of Dubuque, Iowa, issued such catalogs, imprinting their covers with the names of subscribing lumber dealers to develop local allegiance to the nationwide standard. By 1880, standard molding series were developed under such designations as the 4000, 5000, 7000, and 8000 series. The 8000 series remained the standard throughout the first half of the twentieth century. Although the 8000 series has been largely supplanted, some of its moldings remain in production with the same profiles and dimensions they have had for a full century.

Doors

The door is one of the most necessary components of a building and one of the most diagnostic of the period and style of the structure. From the introduction of the first joined and paneled doors into New England around 1700, doors have been among the most complex features of any building and, along with the window sash, one of the most heavily used. Doors have to be light yet strong, capable of enduring tens of thousands of careless openings and closings over many centuries. The fact that we currently have thousands of doors doing good service after 250 or even 300 years attests to the successful design of the joined door.

A joined door, like any piece of joined construction, is composed of a framework of members that are connected by mortise-and-tenon joints. In a door, as in paneling, the horizontal members of the framework are called rails, and the vertical members are stiles. These pieces are grooved or plowed on their inside margins to receive the edges of panels that fill the voids enclosed by the joined framework.

In order for the panels to possess strength and rigidity and yet have edges thin enough to fit within the grooves on the stiles and rails, the edges of most handmade panels of the 1700s and early 1800s are planed to a thin feather edge. In doors of the 1700s the feathered edge is normally exposed on the primary face of the door. The flat area that is bordered by the feather edge, a rectangle of uniform thickness, is called the field of the panel. Doors or wainscoting with the feathered edge exposed on the face are often referred to as raised-panel joinery. In doors of the early 1800s, fashion dictated that the primary face of the door have flat panels. In most doors of this period, the feathered edge is placed to face the back, or secondary side, of the door.

Panels in doors or wainscoting are not attached to the stiles and rails, but "float" within the restraining grooves. This method of construction allows the wide board of the panel to shrink and expand somewhat with changes in humidity and yet not split or buckle. Evidence of this movement over the years will usually be seen as a ridge of paint on the feathered edge of the panel, adjacent to the stile or rail, especially noticeable in dry weather. When the panel has shrunk to the greatest degree in very dry weather, a thin line of unpainted wood may be exposed to view.

The inside edges of the stiles and rails are usually molded. The molding that decorates the stiles and rails of a door is an important indicator of the period and style of the door. On more elaborate doors, like those connecting well-finished rooms and hallways, the stiles and rails may be molded on both sides and the panels may be feather-edged on both sides so that the door looks the same from the room or the corridor. In rare instances, occurring just before 1800, when the Georgian style was giving way to the Federal, doors may actually be two-faced, with one side looking backward to the older style and the other side reflecting the incoming style. In less elaborate situations, only one side of the door has moldings. The door is hung so that, when closed, the molded side faces the space that is considered the more important. Closet doors, for example, seldom if ever have moldings on the side facing the closet.

The arrangement of panels in a door may differ according to the pretentiousness of the house. The standard Georgian door, for example, has four panels, separated by a wide latch rail. Many houses, especially at or near the seacoast, display doors with six or eight panels, arranged in various configurations, presumably according to the preference and pocketbook of the householder. These panel arrangements seem to have little to do with the period of a house but rather reflect the owner's taste and the amount of money available to pay the joiner. One of the earliest Georgian houses in northern New England, the MacPheadris-Warner House in Portsmouth, New Hampshire, was finished in 1716 by an immigrant joiner from the London area. It has eight-panel doors. Doors of a very similar pattern appear in the Governor John Langdon House in Portsmouth, finished seventy years later by the London joiner's grandson.

The detailing of stiles, rails, and panels in doors will usually be reflected in other joinery in a given room or in an entire building. Interior window shutters, for example, may be regarded as small doors made to cover windows. Their detailing will almost invariably reflect that of the doors in a room, especially on the side that is visible when the shutters are closed. Wainscoting, or breastwork (the panels above and around a fireplace), also will reflect the detailing seen in the doors.

Georgian Doors.

The earliest joined doors, of which a few examples have been found near the seacoast, date from about 1705. Earlier doors were mostly made of boards, held together with battens. The first joined doors have mortise-and-tenon stiles and rails that are plowed with grooves for the feather edges of panels, which are made exceptionally wide. Instead of having moldings that are integral with the stiles and rails, these doors have an applied molding that is nailed to the stiles and rails and rests against the wide bevel of the panel, permitting the latter to shrink and swell. A molding with a complex profile, dominated by a projecting half-round, is called a bolection. Bolection moldings occur most frequently during the first half of the eighteenth century.

Later doors occasionally have panels supported by applied and grooved bolection moldings rather than by the stiles and rails. The use of bolection moldings to lift the fields of panels above the plane of the stiles and rails is

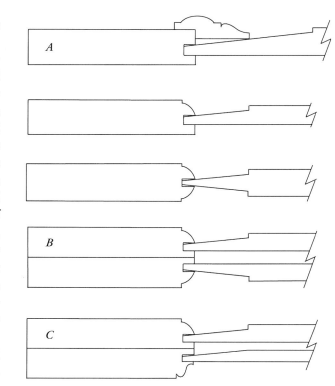

Cross sections of characteristic Georgian doors: (*A*) before 1715; (*B*) double exterior door; (*C*) double door, Georgian-Federal transition. Drawing by author.

more commonly seen on fixed wainscoting than on movable doors (see figure, page 137).

More generally, however, doors of the 1700s have a simple quarter-round, or ovolo, molding planed into the stiles and rails. In simple doors, this molding appears on one side only. On more elaborate doors, especially doors leading from a stair hall to an important room, the molding will appear on both faces of the door, and the panels will be feather-edged on both faces. Such doors look the same from the stair hall or the room.

Exterior doors of the 1700s, especially the heavy front doors of Georgian houses, also may have ovolo moldings and feather-edged panels exposed on both faces. This is sometimes accomplished by nailing two doors back-to-back, thus creating a heavy door of extra thickness and creating an air space that protects the inner panels from the effects of weather.

Federal-Style Doors.

The remarkable and pervasive transformation that marked the advent of the Adam, or Federal, style in the United States around 1800 was ac-

Cross sections of characteristic Federal-style doors. The top five images show door stiles with integral moldings whereas the bottom image has an applied molding. Drawing by author.

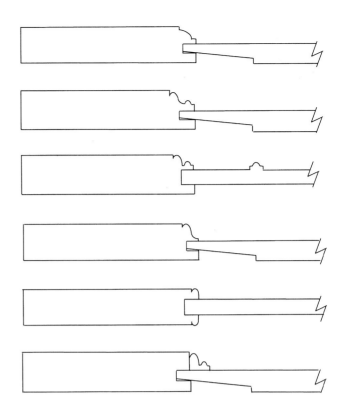

companied by an immediate change in door design. Flat panels replaced feather-edged panels; the feather edge (if any) was placed toward the back, or secondary, face of the door. The quarter-round, or ovolo, stile and rail molding gave way to a number of complex moldings, many of them having "Grecian" profiles—sections of ellipses or parabolas. The panel arrangement changed on many doors. While the standard four-panel door remained common, six-panel doors became characteristic of the Federal style. Six-panel Federal-style doors almost always have a pair of small panels at the top, with two pairs of longer panels below. Because this arrangement creates a cross in the stiles and rails of the upper part of the door, Federal-style doors have often been described as "Christian" doors by twentieth-century house restorers. The characteristic Adam, or Federal, style of panel arrangement is strictly an embodiment of style, with no religious significance.

As noted above, the transition from Georgian-style doors to Federal-style doors just before 1800 was sometimes reflected in houses where one room or stair hall would retain the feather-edged panels of the older style, and other rooms would reflect the incoming style. Because the characteristic panel arrangements of Georgian- and Federal-style doors are different, the stiles and rails on one face cannot serve on the other side. Such double-faced

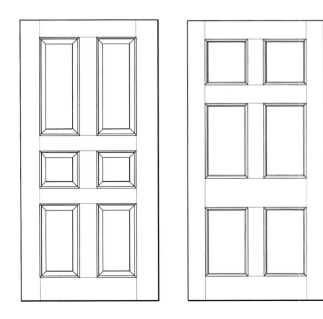

doors were often made by sandwiching two thin doors together. Characteristically, all joiner's work in the rooms on opposite sides of such double doors reflects the style of the face of the door seen in that room. Wainscoting and window shutters on one side would have raised panels, while comparable features on the other side would have flat panels.

Federal-style doors display a greater variety of details than do Georgian doors. The moldings that decorate their stiles and rails may be ovolos, ovolos and beads, or ogees. Despite their complexity, these moldings are usually planed into the stiles and rails as integral features. Occasionally, one will find separate moldings that have been applied to plain stiles and rails with sprigs (brads). It had been common to fashion the intersection of the quarter-round Georgian moldings by coping the rail moldings against the stile moldings with a hollow gouge, but the greater complexity of the Federal-style moldings often makes coping difficult or impossible. Such moldings are simply mitered at the corners (see figure, page 108).

Panel arrangements of six-panel Georgian (*left*) and Federal-style (*right*) doors. Drawing by author.

Greek Revival Doors. Just as doors were changed radically by the advent of the Adam, or Federal, style, they again underwent a transformation with the arrival of the Greek Revival style around 1830. Unlike the change of thirty years earlier, this was an evolution toward simplicity. Greek Revival doors are usually four- or five-panel units. When they have four panels, these doors have smaller panels at the bottom and long ones above. Because the rail that separates these two sets of panels is often below the level of the traditional latch rail, latches or locks on Greek Revival doors are often mounted on the door stile, above the rail.

Many Greek Revival doors have no moldings around their panels; stiles and rails have slightly beveled edges. When moldings are used, they are wide Grecian ovolos or ogees, applied with brads. Panels may be flat or may have a raised field. Most Greek Revival panels do not have feathered edges; the field, if any, is formed by rebating the margins of the panels.

Four-panel doors, with the smaller panels at the bottom and with applied Grecian ogee moldings around the panels, were fashionable for a long time. Introduced around 1830, such doors continued to be made for a full century.

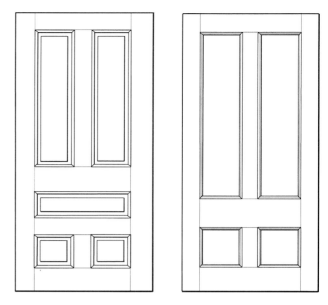

Panel arrangements of characteristic Greek Revival–style doors. Drawing by author.

Late-Nineteenth-Century Doors. Common doors of the latter part of the nineteenth century tended to retain the four- or five-panel arrangements that had been introduced with the advent of the Greek Revival style. The continuing development of woodworking machinery, especially four-surface molding machines, made such doors a standard factory product. Molding machines easily produced the various profiles of "sticking," or moldings, that were applied to the stiles and rails, and they coped and tenoned the ends of the rails for a perfect fit with the machine-mortised stiles.

The end of the nineteenth century saw the introduction of a new style of door that endured, in ever decreasing use, for a full century. This was the five-cross-panel door. As its name implies, such doors have five panels of equal size arranged one above the other. Usually made from softwoods like southern yellow pine, Douglas fir, or Ponderosa pine, such doors were usually given a clear finish that emphasized the grain of the wood. Five-cross-panel doors were considered appropriate for almost any middle-class house, being used equally in Arts and Crafts bungalows, colonial revival, Tudor, square, or any other type of

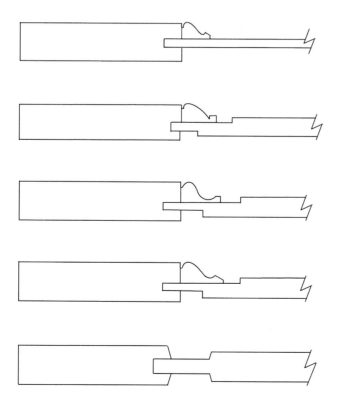

Cross sections of characteristic Greek Revival–style doors. Drawing by author.

dwelling. Manufacturers of pre-cut houses normally supplied such doors as stock items.

Early-Twentieth-Century Doors. Among the machines that were brought to a high degree of perfection in the early years of the twentieth century were those needed in the commercial production of plywood. Large veneer-cutting lathes, in particular, permitted the peeling off of wide veneers of immense lengths, even from huge logs of Douglas fir from Washington and Oregon. These veneers could be glued under pressure to form plywood sheets that greatly exceeded comparable pieces of solid wood in

strength and stability under varying environmental conditions.

The introduction of plywood as a commercial product greatly changed the production of doors. Three-ply panels became far more common than panels of solid wood. Being cut from logs that had been turned against a cutter on lathes, the face veneers of such panels exhibited grain patterns that were never seen in ordinary sawing. Cut as a veneer, even a fairly bland wood like Douglas fir exhibited an attractive and endlessly varied figure.

Manufacturers of doors took advantage of the strength and attractiveness of three-ply panels. Interior doors of

(*Right, top*) Panel arrangements of characteristic late-nineteenth and early-twentieth-century doors: (*left*) five cross panel door; (*right*) "colonial" door. Drawing by author.

(*Right, bottom*) Panel arrangements of characteristic late-nineteenth and early-twentieth-century doors: (*left*) two-panel door; (*right*) "miracle" door. Drawing by author.

(*Below*) Cross sections of characteristic late-nineteenth and early-twentieth-century doors. (*A*) through (*D*) have integral moldings; (*E*) has an applied flush molding; (*F*) is a "miracle" door. Drawing by author.

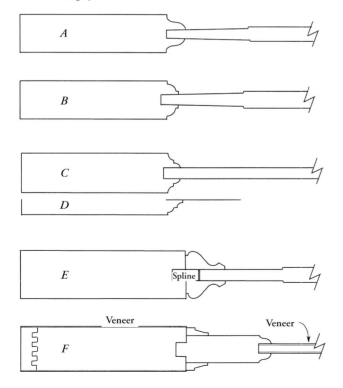

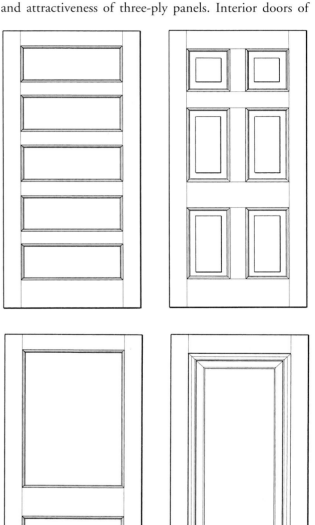

the early twentieth century, intended to have a varnished finish, often had stiles and rails of solid, quarter-sawn Douglas fir or Ponderosa pine, with panels of rotary-cut fir. The most common of such doors were five-cross-panel units. Taking advantage of the strength and rigidity of plywood, the millwork industry also developed two-panel and one-panel doors during the first decade of the century. One- and two-panel doors often had face veneers of birch, gum, or other hardwoods and usually had stiles and rails of glued softwood cores, veneered in the appropriate hardwood. All three types usually had cove-and-bead or bead-and-cove sticking on their stiles and rails.

One of the more popular forms of one-panel door during the early decades of the twentieth century was the "miracle" door. Inexpensive but attractive, miracle doors usually had stiles and rails of pine. Within this framework was an inner frame that held a single plywood panel faced in rotary-cut Douglas fir, birch, gumwood, or some other species with an attractive figure.

Windows

The Window Sash as a Character-Defining Element. Few elements of a building contribute more to its architectural character than do the window sashes. The character of the sash is obvious from the exterior even when (as was often the case) its exterior face was painted black or another dark color. There is a great difference between a window opening filled with twelve-over-eight sashes and one filled with two-over-two sashes.

The character of the sash is even stronger from within the building, where the grid of muntins interposes itself between the eye and the view from the window. The inner faces of the muntins are molded, and the profiles of these moldings evolved over time, contributing much to the expression of style or period in a structure. As indicated on the chart on page 147, the muntin profile provides a useful means of dating a building as well as helping to define the aesthetics of the window and the room.

Yet sashes are meant to be looked through. It is easy to look past the grid of muntins and to ignore their beauty and the size and character of the glass. Perhaps because sashes are largely transparent, they are often undervalued as a contributing element to the style and character of a building. People often assume that all old windows are much alike or that the character of the sash is unimpor-

tant. Coupled with the common idea that old sashes are loose, fragile, and drafty, the assumption that they are insignificant makes the sash the most vulnerable and most often replaced element of a historic building.

In fact, the character of the sash has always been integral to the style of the building. While that fact may have been missed by the owner of a building, it was not lost on the architect or joiner (finish carpenter). In compiling the first American builder's guidebook, *The Country Builder's Assistant* (1797), joiner Asher Benjamin signaled his break with the eighteenth century by illustrating three new muntin profiles that were appropriate for the incoming Federal style of architecture. As shown in the chart on page 147, new sash designs appeared every ten or fifteen years during the nineteenth century, lending their character to succeeding architectural styles.

Any historic building with its original sashes and glazing therefore retains a higher degree of architectural integrity than a comparable structure in which the sashes have been replaced. Where original sashes survive, their preservation should be a paramount concern of the building's owner.

A Brief History of the Sash. The sliding window sash was introduced into the British colonies of North America just after 1700. Prior to that time, window openings had been filled with casements. Casements are sashes that are hinged on their sides to open outward. The lights, or panes of glass, in casement sashes (called quarrels) were usually small and diamond-shaped. The quarrels were held within a latticework of lead members, called cames, which have an H-shaped cross section. To stiffen the somewhat flexible assemblage of cames and quarrels, a few wooden sticks were placed across the sashes between the outer stiles of the casements, and the lead was wired to these stiffeners at intervals.

The sliding sash first appears in written records in Boston and Philadelphia just after 1700. The sliding sash that appeared with the advent of the Georgian style is composed of a framework of outer horizontal members, or rails, and of vertical members, or stiles. Within this outer frame are a series of subdivisions created by the addition of vertical and horizontal members called muntins. The joints that attach stiles and rails at the outer corners of the sash are mortised and tenoned and secured by small pins. Some early sliding sashes were apparently filled with leaded glass, but most were glazed with square lights of glass.

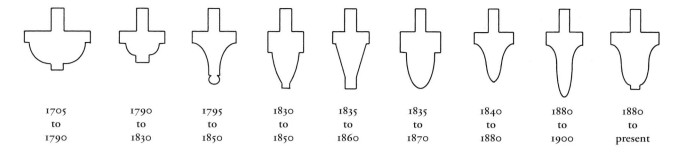

1705 to 1790	1790 to 1830	1795 to 1850	1830 to 1850	1835 to 1860	1835 to 1870	1840 to 1880	1880 to 1900	1880 to present

The accompanying chart shows the profile or cross-sectional shape of the earliest muntins. This profile remained relatively unchanged until near the end of the eighteenth century, although every joiner had his own set of tools, and different sets of sash-molding planes were seldom exactly alike. Thus, there is some variation in this early cross-sectional profile and all later muntin profiles. This variation diminished when machine-made sashes were introduced in the latter half of nineteenth century.

The eighteenth-century muntin was heavy and thick, interposing a strong grid between the occupant of a room and the outdoors. Because of the high cost of large sheets of early glass, panes were usually small (often seven by nine inches or eight by ten inches). The proportion of wood to glass in early sashes was quite high and tended to diminish

The evolution of window muntin profiles, 1705 to the present. Drawing by author.

---

through the nineteenth century as larger glass sizes and thinner muntin profiles were progressively introduced.

For the most part, eighteenth-century window sashes were not counterbalanced by weights. The upper sashes in a pair were usually fixed in place, supported by strips of wood placed below their sides in the window openings. Only the lower sashes could open. They slid up and down between the strips of wood that supported the upper sashes and similar strips of wood, called sash stops, that were nailed against the sides of the window frames. The lower sashes slid upward against the inner faces of the fixed upper sashes and the sash stops; the latter created a groove or channel that restrained and guided the moving sash.

Because sashes were usually not counterbalanced, they were held open, or partly open, by sticks or other props placed beneath them or by spring catches of various designs attached to their side members, or stiles.

Occasionally, one will encounter an extraordinary eighteenth-century dwelling in which the movable lower window sashes were counterbalanced by weights that are attached to the sashes by cords. These cords run over a wooden sheave set into the tops of the side frames of the windows, allowing the weights to rise and fall in pockets on each side of the window opening. Such early weights are almost always found to be of cast lead. In contrast to later, cast-iron window weights, which are usually round in cross section, older lead window weights were usually square or rectangular in cross section. These rare counter-

Window weights of the eighteenth through the twentieth centuries. The two lead weights with the wooden sheaves at the left date from about 1740. The two lead weights at the right date from about 1800. The cylinder at the bottom is a cast-iron weight of the twentieth century. Photograph by author.

balanced windows of the eighteenth century gave rise to the common double-hung windows of the latter part of the nineteenth century, described below.

The idea of double-glazing window openings with storm sashes is largely a late-nineteenth-century development that coincided with greater use of central heating. A few storm sashes, having the same muntin profiles and glass sizes as the main sashes, have been noted on very costly eighteenth-century houses, but it is not certain whether these were original or later additions. In general, folding or sliding interior window shutters were the main defense against cold night air during most of the nineteenth century.

Evolution of Muntin Profiles. The earliest sliding sashes, introduced to North America shortly after 1700, had heavy muntins that were often over an inch in width. The interior face of each muntin has an ovolo, or quarter-round, molding on each side of a central fillet. The wide moldings of eighteenth-century sashes are usually integral with the sash bars or muntins, but instances have been noted on the New Hampshire seacoast where these moldings were bradded or glued to flat bars. Eighteenth-century muntins were often relatively shallow in relation to their width, so the sashes were not excessively thick. The considerable width of the muntins, however, combined with the tendency to use small lights of glass in these early windows, gives eighteenth-century sashes a heavy appearance that is quite noticeable from inside or outside a building. The typical Georgian muntin profile varied little during the eighteenth century, although the width of the muntin might range between an inch and an inch and a half.

Although there is no hiding the heavy grid of muntins in early sashes when seen from within a building, painters often took steps to diminish the effect of heavy sash bars and small lights of glass as seen from the outside. Records make it clear that the outside faces of such windows were often painted black, clearly an attempt to disguise the heavy grid of bars against the dark void of the room within. This practice continued throughout the nineteenth century, although in Victorian times sashes might be painted dark red or green or some other color that contrasted yet harmonized with the color of the exterior window casings and of the body of the building.

Photographic evidence from the 1840s onward shows, however, that exterior window casings were often painted white, frequently in contrast to unpainted clapboards or to

clapboards painted with inexpensive red or yellow ochre. In such cases, the outside faces of sashes were usually painted white as well. Thus, two contrasting approaches to the exterior treatment of multi-paned sashes—one intended to hide the sash bars and one to emphasize them—flourished simultaneously during the 1700s and early 1800s.

The evolution of the muntin profile after the end of the eighteenth century was generally one of increasing delicacy. At the same time, production of window glass in the United States reduced the cost of glazing and permitted sashes to have fewer but larger lights. Thus, window openings tended to become larger, sashes became lighter and held larger panes, and the interiors of buildings generally became brighter. This increasing illumination was characteristic not only of rooms but also of entries or stair halls. The late 1700s saw the introduction of fanlights in doorways, or frontispieces. After 1800, these windows became larger, often taking the form of a wide semi-ellipse. Sidelights flanking doors also became popular at this time, and fanlights often spanned not only the door opening but also the sidelights on each side of the door. In contrast to the dark entries of the 1700s, in which a small transom sash above the door was the only illumination provided, this new fashion filled hallways with light.

The advent of the Federal style in the late 1700s and early 1800s was accompanied by several patterns of window muntin. The most common type, popular until about 1830, was nearly identical in profile to the heavy muntin of the 1700s but was smaller in dimension. Its profile consists of quarter-round moldings and flat fillets. Another muntin type, first seen just before 1800, had a cove-and-bead profile. Generally restricted to more expensive buildings or urban areas, this profile is much less common than the traditional quarter-round-and-fillet pattern.

The quarter-round-and-fillet pattern did not disappear with the advent of the Greek Revival style in the 1830s. Instead, it evolved, adopting an elliptical molding in place of the quarter-round.

The Greek Revival style was, however, accompanied by alternate muntin profiles that were noticeably different from those seen earlier. Perhaps the most distinctive was the flat, angular profile. Like some moldings seen in Greek Revival joinery, this muntin relies on its faceted surfaces rather than on curves for its character. This type of muntin is often seen in conjunction with woodwork that is similarly decorated with flat surfaces rather than with curved moldings.

Also popular during the Greek Revival period, as well as in buildings of a Gothic character, is the Gothic muntin. Often assuming the profile of a rounded or pointed arch, this simple muntin appeared in the late 1830s and persisted from the 1840s through the 1860s.

A profile that enjoyed nearly the longevity of some of the older quarter-round-and-fillet shapes was the sharp ogee muntin. Composed of S-curved moldings that meet in a knife edge, this was the sharpest and thinnest profile ever used in American windows. First seen in Greek Revival buildings by about 1840, the sharp ogee muntin persisted up to the turn of the century, appearing in six-light sashes in the earlier years and in two-light sashes at the end of the century. When used in large sashes, as in churches or public buildings, this muntin profile is usually given added depth to compensate for its inherent weakness in the face of the wind pressures that larger windows must resist.

Another muntin profile that has enjoyed a popularity rivaling that of the earliest quarter-round-and-fillet muntins is still in use today. This is the ogee-and-fillet profile, first seen in early colonial revival buildings. Having a strong cross section, this profile came into its own as two-over-two sashes became popular in the late 1800s. The shallow ogee, or S-curved, molding of this muntin bears a superficial resemblance to the early quarter-round-and-fillet designs, making the new profile ideal for buildings in the colonial style or for use with any other architectural style. The profile is often seen in modern windows with true divided lights and is most commonly encountered in the ever popular Brosco sashes, available in configurations ranging from two lights to multiple lights.

Because window sashes are fragile and easily damaged by neglect, they frequently deteriorate more quickly than other elements of a building. Because they strongly reflect the architectural style of a given period, sashes were often replaced during remodeling even if they had not deteriorated beyond usefulness. Thus, it is not unusual to find old buildings with sashes that are much later in date and style than the majority of other architectural features.

In such cases, it is often of great interest to learn the original style of sash in a building. It will often be found that a few original sashes were left in place in some out-of-the-way location. Odd-sized windows in the back of the building or attic windows too high up to catch the eye are often found to be the only survivors from an otherwise complete renewal of sashes. Also likely to survive are original sashes that are fixed in place and part of a larger architectural feature, or sashes of a size that could not be replaced by stock units of a later period. Thus, transom sashes above a doorway are among the most likely to escape replacement, as are elaborate arched sashes from a Palladian window or a stair landing. One such relic from the original period of construction is enough to indicate the earliest muntin profile of a building.

Older sash styles are seldom available in the retail trade. Almost every style of sash that has ever been made, however, can be acquired on custom order from specialized sash factories or from joiners who have revived the art of making sashes by hand.

How Window Sashes Are Made by Hand. A window sash is one of the most delicate and complex building components made by the joiner. Each muntin is a thin piece of wood stock, molded on one side and rebated on the other to receive glass and putty. Each muntin must intersect and be fitted to other muntins and to the outer stiles and rails of the sash. The stiles and rails, in turn, must be firmly mortised and tenoned together at the corners to create a rigid frame. If the sash is counterbalanced, recesses for the sash cords must be plowed into the sides of the unit.

Because the inside face of the muntin is molded, the end of every horizontal muntin must be coped and tenoned to fit against the molded surface of every vertical muntin or against the two stiles on the sides of the sash. The two horizontal rails must be coped and tenoned to the sides of the stiles at each corner of the sash. And each vertical muntin must be coped and tenoned to the upper or lower rail of the sash. A six-light sash has twelve of these complex intersections; a twelve-light sash has twenty.

Because the ends of intersecting sash members must be coped and tenoned, sash-molding planes were sold in pairs. The principal plane cut the molded inside face of the muntin, stile, or rail. The sash-coping plane shaped the coped joint at the ends of the members, cutting across the end grain of a board before the board was ripped into thin muntin stock. After the coped joint was cut, the board was sawn into thin strips that were transformed into muntins through the use of the principal sash plane.

Because the making of a sash by hand is painstaking and delicate work, joiners of the 1700s or early 1800s devised a fair method of charging for their labor. They billed a customer by the number of "squares of sashes," or openings for lights of glass, that they fabricated. The more openings for glass that were required, the more expensive the joiner's labor on the sash. Thus, a pair of twelve-light sashes would be more expensive than a pair of six-light sashes for a given window opening. Conversely, smaller panes of glass might be cheaper than larger panes, so the ultimate cost of a pair of sashes depended both on the joiner's work and on the cost of glass. As larger panes of glass became cheaper, the cost of windows became cheaper, since the use of larger panes meant fewer squares of sashes in each window unit and thus reduced the joiner's charges.

A building owner had two countervailing concerns in filling his windows. First, because the joiner charged for his work by squares of sashes, a six-light sash cost less than a nine-light sash. On the other hand, English glass was priced at so much per square foot, so the greater proportion of wood in a window, the less the cost of the glass. A nine-light sash has about 20 percent more wood in its muntins than does a six-light sash of the same dimensions, thus offering a small savings in glass. Beyond that, however, larger sizes of glass were not available in all areas of New England, especially in inland locales. Thus, the tendency throughout most of the eighteenth century, or until New England glass was available at the end of the century, was toward smaller panes except in the richest houses. Seven-by-nine-inch glass was probably the most common, with eight-by-ten-inch glass seen in the more ornate houses.

Throughout the eighteenth century and much of the nineteenth, the outer frames (the stiles and rails) of window sashes were mortised and tenoned together at the corners and held by wooden pegs or pins placed through each joint. In most cases, the muntins were simply tenoned into the stiles and rails; due to their small dimensions, these tenons were not pinned. Likewise, horizontal muntins were simply tenoned into the vertical muntins without pins or nails, with the entire window assembly depending for its tightness on the pinned joints at the four corners.

Because an "open," or unglazed, sash is made of thin members pinned together at only four points, the entire unit is often slightly flexible until it is glazed. The insertion of glass and putty stiffens the sash into a unit that will retain its rigidity despite being raised and lowered thousands of times over the years.

The type of glazier's putty used throughout most of our history has been whiting or chalk (calcium carbonate)

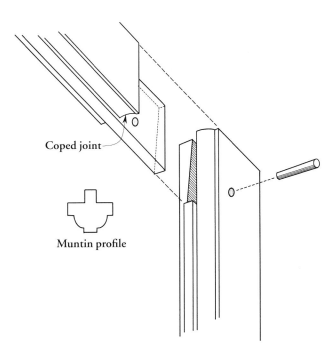

Coped joint

Muntin profile

Exploded view of the upper corner of an early-nineteenth-century window sash, showing the coping of the window rail against the molded side of the stile. Drawing by author.

mixed into a paste in linseed oil. Powdered white lead, which has a drying effect on linseed oil, was often added to the mixture in small quantities to make the putty harden more quickly in the sash and thus allow the unit to be primed with paint soon after glazing.

Window Hardware. Most eighteenth- and early-nineteenth-century windows have little or no hardware. Wooden sashes of this period merely slide up and down in their grooves, being held open or perhaps wedged shut by sticks placed under or above the movable lower sash.

Occasionally, one will find sashes that have small wrought-iron hooks attached to the lower rails. Staples fixed into the window stools permit the closed window to be hooked shut and locked.

As noted above, a few exceptional houses of the eighteenth century have counterbalanced lower sashes, with cords that run from the movable sash over wooden sheaves in the upper side casings of the windows. Lead weights descending in pockets outside the casings allow heavy sashes to be lifted more easily (see figure, page 147).

This type of counterbalancing was becoming more commonplace by the early 1800s. In 1806, Asher Benjamin illustrated counterbalances for both upper and lower sashes in his second architectural guidebook, *The American Builder's Companion*, thus prefiguring the double-hung sash as it has remained in production and use until recent times. Yet such arrangements were restricted to urban dwellings or the homes of the wealthy. Most dwellings did not have counterbalanced sashes until after the mid-1800s.

As noted above, most windows of an earlier period were held open or partially open by props or notched sticks of various designs. An alternative to such props was the window spring, a device that attached to one of the stiles (side members) of the movable lower sash and snapped into holes or notches cut into the window frame at various heights. Many types of window springs were patented throughout the nineteenth century, and many types are still encountered on old sashes. Probably the earliest pattern of window spring employed in northern New England was called Kennedy's patent. A number of New Hampshire joiners were licensed to use and sell this device in 1803. According to its description, Kennedy's spring "allowed one to raise and lower both the upper and lower Sash, and by the assistance of Springs to support it at any height that is wished."

By 1865 the Russell and Erwin Manufacturing Company of New Britain, Connecticut, published the first extensive American hardware catalog, and this book illustrated no fewer than five styles of window spring. Although window springs serve as locks when the window is closed, the Russell and Erwin catalog also listed sash locks in many designs, most of them intended to be screwed to the upper and lower meeting rails in the same manner as modern helical sash locks.

By 1865, too, the counterbalanced, or double-hung, sash had become commonplace. The Russell and Erwin catalog illustrated iron or bronze sash pulleys and cast-iron sash weights that are virtually indistinguishable from those used throughout the next century.

Most sash hardware of the nineteenth century was simple in design and rugged in construction. Homeowners who are fortunate enough to retain such window fittings should make every effort to preserve and use these easily overlooked legacies from the past.

Casings, Shutters, and Blinds. Although sashes are the principal element of a window, sashes are almost always accompanied by inside and outside casings and often by interior shutters and exterior blinds. Together, these elements make up the full window unit.

Interior window casings, or architraves, almost always reflect the design of door casings in the same rooms. Often as distinctive as are the muntins in the sashes, window casings are important stylistic elements in any room and are a valuable means of dating a window. Because window sashes were more often renewed than window casings, it is often easy to detect replacement of sashes when the casings are of one style and the sashes are of a later style.

Sometimes the remodeling of a room was done with such thoroughness that both widow casings and sashes were replaced. This is particularly commonplace during the Greek Revival period from 1830 to 1850. The Greek Revival style required both window muntins and casings that were distinctively different from those of the Georgian or Federal styles. In order to maintain the harmony of a remodeled room, the molded casings of an earlier period were often supplanted by flat casings when a room was modernized in the new Grecian style.

The same is true on the exterior. It is not unusual to find that an older house was updated with a Greek Revival doorway, or frontispiece. In such cases, the exterior window casings are often found to have been replaced, at least on the front of the house, to harmonize with the character of the new entrance.

Among the features that are often missing or damaged from eighteenth- or early-nineteenth-century windows are interior shutters. Often mistakenly called Indian shutters, these features were not intended to defend a building against attack (for which they would have been useless) but to exclude the cold or to provide privacy in an age before window curtains were common.

Interior shutters were made in three major types. The earliest, simplest, and least likely to survive are hinged shutters that were attached to interior window casings and opened, like a small pair of doors, against the walls on each side of the window. Because these shutters fold into the room, disrupting any piece of furniture that is placed in front of the window, and because they occupy wall space when open, they were often regarded as a nuisance in later times and simply removed. More common in the 1700s than later, such shutters were usually attached with H-hinges, and close examination will often reveal evidence of the hinges on the side casings of a window. Because folding shutters need to lie flat against the wall when open, their window casings seldom had projecting moldings. Thus, absence of moldings, combined with a casing design that provides for a rebate, or recess, around the window opening, are clues that a window may originally have been fitted with folding shutters.

The second type of shutter, which often survives unknown to the modern homeowner, is the sliding type. Fitted into thin pockets behind the wall plaster, sliding shutters can be slid out of sight or pulled partly or entirely across the sashes. Sliding shutters are usually made in two units. One covers the lower sash. A second, sliding on a grooved rail at the height of the meeting rails of the sashes, covers the upper sash. Because the shutter rail was often regarded as a nuisance, it was frequently sawn off and the shutters pushed into their pockets, covered with strips of wood, and forgotten.

The third type of shutter, and the most likely to survive

in use, is the folding shutter set into a deep window embrasure. Found only in more elaborate buildings, such shutters are hinged and fold into two or more leaves. They require a thick wall that offers the depth necessary to house the folded leaves of the shutter at each side of the window. In a framed building, this extra thickness is achieved by double-studding the wall; in a brick building, the thickness of the masonry usually provides most of the depth needed to house such shutters.

Very rarely, one will find window shutters of a different style, perhaps sliding on exposed rails beside a window rather than in pockets within a wall cavity or perhaps lifting upward from a pocket below the window opening. The Shakers sometimes employed both types in their buildings. A few grand houses of the early 1800s had double sets of interior sliding shutters, one set solidly paneled and the second set louvered like exterior window blinds, admitting fresh air while excluding sunlight.

Window shutters of every period were fashioned in harmony with the style of joinery of that period. Their design and details almost always match those of the original doors or other paneling in a given room. Their architectural style will be in harmony with the style of the window muntins unless the original sashes have been replaced.

Exterior window blinds, seldom seen until the end of the eighteenth century, became commonplace during the early nineteenth. In New England, almost all exterior blinds except those on stores or warehouses were of the louvered or "Venetian" pattern. Commercial buildings often had solid, heavy exterior shutters clad with sheets of iron to seal the building against theft or fire.

Louvered blinds served an important purpose. When closed, as they often were much of the time, blinds pro-

NH 26

vided both shade and ventilation, serving a crucial function in keeping house interiors cool. In an age when window screens were uncommon and house flies very plentiful, blinds served a secondary purpose in deterring the entry of flies. Householders in the nineteenth century were highly conscious of the fading effects of sunlight, and window blinds effectively excluded the sun when a room was not in use. Nineteenth-century photographs therefore often show closed blinds even in cold weather, when ventilation was neither needed nor wanted.

Folding window shutters of Georgian profile, Moffatt-Ladd House, 1760–1763, Portsmouth, New Hampshire. Hinged or folding window shutters continued in use throughout much of the nineteenth century. Window embrasures from the Federal period onward usually extend to the floor without window seats. Photograph by Bill Finney.

During the early nineteenth century, blinds were often hung with small strap hinges. These turned on hand-forged pintles that were driven into the window casings. To bear the weight of the blinds and resist the effects of wind on an occasional loose blind, these pintles usually have a curved iron brace that extends below the L-shaped pintle. These braces have a small cusp at their lower end, and a nail driven through a hole in this cusp supplements the support given by the main shaft of the pintle. Later versions of the braced pintle were made of cast iron.

By the mid-1800s a number of patented butts were available to hold blinds. On the blind itself, these replaced the earlier forged strap hinges, which had to be attached at the rails of the blind. By contrast, the butts could be attached at any convenient point. On the window casing, butts allowed convenient installation with gimlet and screwdriver. Some patented butts had self-locking features that secured the blinds in an open or closed position without the need for other hardware.

Because of their fragile nature and exposure to the weather, original window blinds survive in lesser quantities than original window sashes, especially those from the first half of the nineteenth century. In general, the earliest window blinds have heavy stiles and rails. These frames hold thick, fixed louvers whose ends are fitted into slots in the stiles of the blind and are held in place by wooden beads applied over the slots.

Later blinds have thinner louvers, often with rounded rather than sharply beveled edges. By the 1850s, blinds were often made with louvers that are pivoted on dowels attached to their ends. Called rolling slats, these pivoting louvers are stapled to wooden rods that link them together

Sections through characteristic architraves, or casings, of the Georgian period. Drawing by author.

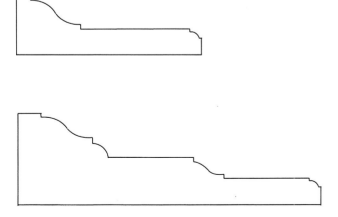

and allow the angle of the louvers to be adjusted to improve ventilation when the blinds are closed.

Throughout much of the nineteenth century, the window blind was the only common adjunct to the window sashes. Window screens made from woven wire cloth were occasionally found, and sometimes the cloth was painted with landscapes that could be seen from outdoors in certain light conditions yet did not obstruct the view from within the house. Wire window screening did not become commonplace until the end of the nineteenth century. Houseflies were a constant annoyance in warm weather and were controlled mostly by sticky flypaper and by "safes"—small screened covers that were placed over exposed food in the kitchen or on the table.

Casings, or Architraves

Georgian Casings. In contrast to the three-dimensional richness of Georgian raised paneling and heavy cornices, door and window casings of the 1700s tended to be rather simple and limited in their variety. Doors, windows, and fireplaces were usually surrounded by casings fashioned from single flat boards with beaded inner edges that define the opening and with backband moldings applied to their outer margins. In the case of window openings intended for hinged interior shutters, casings are usually simple square-edged boards. Such casings have no backband moldings because the projection of such moldings would prevent the shutters from lying flat against the walls of the room.

The standard backband profile until the very end of the eighteenth century is a rather shallow Roman ogee and fillet. In larger and more richly finished houses, this molding may have an additional bead or small quarter-round applied to its inner edge, but any elaboration beyond this is rare in northern New England. In most cases, the outer edge of the casing serves as a stop or ground for the wall plaster, so the backband molding does not project much above the wall plane. The overall appearance of the casing, with its shallow backband, is one of low relief and general inconspicuousness in comparison to nineteenth-century casings.

Two methods were employed to render such casings more ornate. The first was to make the casing "double" by planing it into two distinct planes or fasciae, with the inner plane lower in level than the outer plane and separated from the latter by a narrow ogee molding. The addition of the standard ogee backband to such an architrave provides an enframement with attractive shadow lines.

The second method of enhancing Georgian casings was through carved enrichment. Rarely seen in northern New England except in the grand mansions of the seacoast and in an occasional richly finished inland house, enrichment takes the form of the carving of shallow, repetitive ornamentation on the curved surfaces of moldings. Eighteenth-century British guidebooks, like Abraham Swan's *The British Architect*, illustrated types of carved enrichment appropriate to each molding. The bead, or

Sections through characteristic architraves, or casings, of the Federal period. Drawing by author.

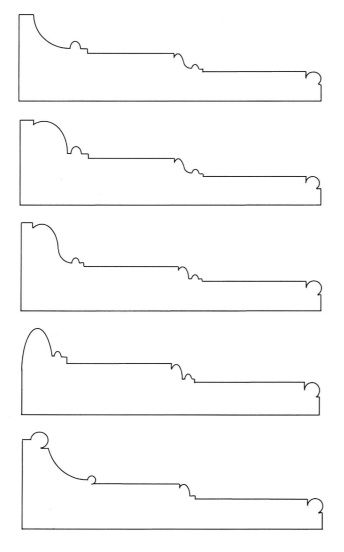

astragal, molding, for example, was appropriately enriched with small carved balls or beads. The ovolo, or quarter round, lent itself to the so-called egg-and-dart ornament. The S-curved ogee was usually enriched with carved leafage or with repetitive incised detailing. One form of the latter, seen both in coastal architecture and in inland furniture made in the late 1700s by the Dunlap family of New Hampshire, was referred to as flowered ogee carving by the joiners themselves. Calling for a heavy investment of a carver's time, enriched architraves are rarely seen in northern New England (see figure, page 103).

Federal-Style Casings. Like doors, Federal-style door casings assumed a far greater variety of profiles than during the eighteenth century. While Georgian architraves were usually simple casings with a beaded inner edge and a plain ogee backband, Federal-style casings exhibited a multiplicity of backband profiles, most based on conic sections (portions of ellipses or parabolas). The more elaborate Federal-style buildings often employ double architraves —casings with two distinct planes separated by moldings—which had been rare during the 1700s. The transition between the two planes of such casings is embellished by delicate Grecian moldings that often match those on the stiles and rails of the doors.

Greek Revival Casings. Characteristic Greek Revival door and window casings are also radically different from anything seen earlier. Instead of being a single or double architrave with an outer backband molding, the new casings are typically a square-edged board with square corner blocks at the upper corners. Into the face of this board is planed a symmetrical set of moldings or fillets or a series of flutes. Depending on the style of the room, fluting may range in profile from shallow to bold. This type of casing is often applied over plaster grounds, and therefore it stands well above the surface of the surrounding wall plaster. Corner blocks tend to be plain in early Greek Revival buildings but impressed with circular bosses or other machine-made or molded relief in later work.

Later Casings. Although the more elaborate Greek Revival casings often have imaginative profiles, casings and other woodwork of very complex molded outlines did not appear until after 1850. The taste for more complex profiles, often executed in hardwoods rather than pine,

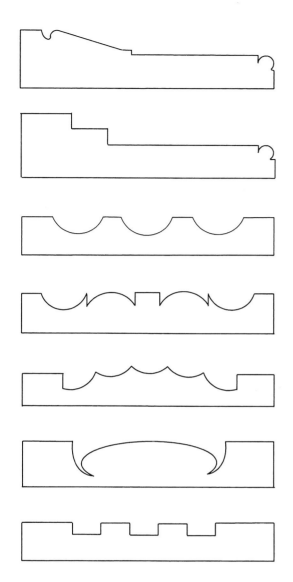

Sections through characteristic architraves, or casings, of the Greek Revival period. Drawing by author.

centers into round bosses or textured panels. Machinery also could produce moldings of such precise dimensions that several could be combined into massive and complex casings that would have been difficult or costly to fabricate with hand tools alone.

Using such moldings, architects and joiners supplemented the standard symmetrical casings of the period with casings having massive, bolection-molded backbands that project boldly above the wall planes. Because most casings of the period after 1850 are nailed to plaster grounds, their full depth, including that of any backband moldings applied to them, stands proud of the wall surface and adds to the impression of massiveness and complexity.

Despite the use of complex architraves in the grander Victorian residences of the later 1800s, the standard casing of the period remained the symmetrically molded board with corner blocks, first seen around 1830. This attractive and utilitarian casing, lending itself to the capabilities of the machine, persisted as the favored form of door and window enframement well into the twentieth century. Varied only by the profile that is planed into its surface, the flat, symmetrical casing is seen in every architectural style of the late 1800s and in most homes, whether colonial, Tudor, or bungalow in style, through the 1920s.

By the 1920s, however, preference was beginning to shift toward another style of casing. Like the symmetrically molded casing with corner blocks, this style of trim had first made its appearance during the Greek Revival period as an alternative style of finish. This style employs matching side casings that support a top casing that may project slightly beyond the edges of the side casings and is

was abetted by the increasing availability and sophistication of molding machinery. Shapers could replicate the wide, molded casings that were favored throughout the latter part of the nineteenth century and could do so more quickly and cheaply than a joiner could fashion such casings with the wide, two-man planes needed for such work. Other machines were developed to ornament the corner blocks used with door and window casings, shaping their

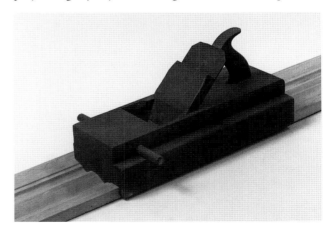

Architraves in the Greek Revival style, with sliding doors in the same style. Door and window openings and chimneypieces in the Grecian style sometimes have a slanted top that suggests the pediment of a Greek temple. William Jones House, Claremont Plains, Claremont, New Hampshire, 1847–1850. Photograph by David S. Putnam.

usually edged with an applied bead at its bottom and a small cap molding at its top. Together, the two side casings, the cap, and the inside stool and apron used on windows are referred to as a side of trim. Such inside detailing remained dominant until after World War II, which brought the advent of the flush door and the simple casing of "clamshell" profile.

An early-twentieth-century side of trim could vary somewhat to reflect the style of the home. Houses that tended toward classical or colonial detailing usually have an ogee-molded cap on the top casing and ogee borders to the sunken panel at the center of the side casings. Bungalows or other houses that express the craftsman style usually have a square-edged cap on the top casing and flat or nearly flat side casings.

Mantelpieces

Fireplaces were essential to heating and cooking from the first settlement of New England until the widespread introduction of airtight cast-iron ranges and parlor stoves in the 1830s. Fireplaces returned to favor in the late nineteenth century for their aesthetic appeal and have remained a desirable luxury ever since. Despite the fact that the open fire has been a fixture in our homes during much of our history, the mantelpiece has not always been present as a distinct architectural feature.

Ordinary houses of the seventeenth and eighteenth centuries seldom had mantelpieces. Except for kitchen fireplaces, most hearths had no shelves above them. Rather, most fireplace openings were defined by a wooden architrave, or casing, that usually duplicated those used around doors and windows in the same room. In a few grand houses of the early 1700s, fireplaces might be bordered by a bolection molding of impressive dimensions, usually much larger than any comparable moldings that might be seen elsewhere in the dwelling. Yet it was rare even in such pretentious houses to find a shelf above such a molding. Rather, the breastwork or paneling of the fireplace wall is

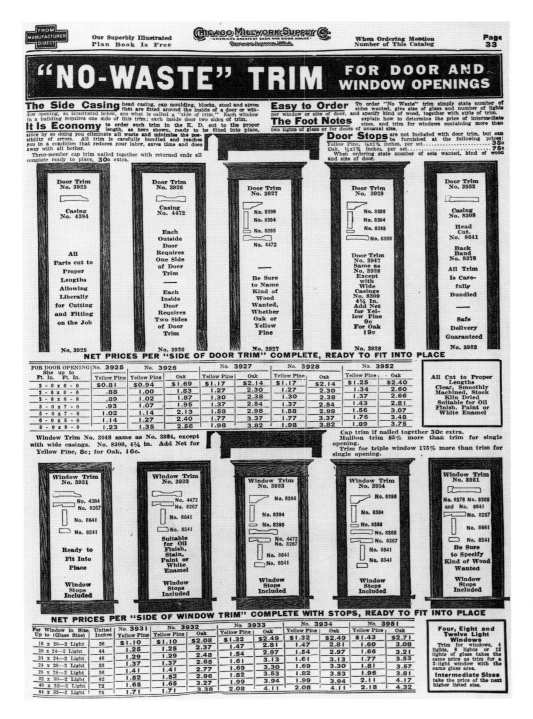

Characteristic architraves, or casings, of the early twentieth century. Shown in the center of the door or window openings are cross sections of each component of that "side of trim." Chicago Millwork Supply Company Catalogue No. 367, March 1, 1927.

Chimneypiece, circa 1753, Wentworth-Coolidge Mansion, Portsmouth, New Hampshire. Executed in pine for the royal governor of New Hampshire, this mantelpiece is a copy of the marble original designed by William Kent in 1725 for Houghton Hall in Norfolk, England. Photograph by Douglas Armsden.

usually continued across the top of the fireplace opening, often with two or three panels ranged horizontally above the hearth. Sometimes, a pair of fluted wooden pilasters separates this zone of horizontal panels from areas of vertical paneling on adjacent areas of the wall, defining the hearth as a distinct area (see figure, page 101).

Kitchen fireplaces, by contrast, often have a mantelshelf, though not a true mantelpiece, set high above the fireplace opening. Household inventories from the eighteenth century suggest that such shelves served several useful purposes, chief among them that of storing the candlesticks of the household. The common nighttime ritual

involved lighting candles at the kitchen fire, carrying them to light the way to the bedchambers, and returning them to the kitchen in the morning (see figure, page 57).

Most British architectural guidebooks of the eighteenth century illustrate highly elaborate mantelpieces. The wide variety of such books that found their way to the colonies must have provoked much interest in New England readers, but the elaborate engraved plates seldom inspired imitation. One exception is an imposing mantelpiece to be found in the rural home of Benning Wentworth, royal governor of New Hampshire between 1741 and 1767. Probably dating from about 1753, this grand feature is a copy in

Plate 64 from William Kent, *The Designs of Inigo Jones* (London, 1727). This plate, or a copy of it in Edward Hoppus' book, *The Gentleman's and Builder's Repository* (London, circa 1737), provided the design for the Wentworth chimneypiece.

pine of the marble mantelpiece of 1725 in Houghton Hall, the home of British first minister Sir Robert Walpole in Norfolk. The reappearance of this grand feature at Portsmouth, New Hampshire, is explained by two things: the availability of an English architectural book that transmitted the design of architect William Kent and the presence of local carvers with the skill to reproduce the design. Legend describes one or two comparable mantelpieces in coastal New Hampshire in the mid-1700s, but none has survived. It is perhaps significant that even Wentworth's house has no other mantelpiece of any kind.

The few eighteenth-century houses that have true mantelpieces usually display much more basic designs, involving little or no carving and relying on moldings to define the fireplace openings and to support a shelf above a wide, flat wooden frieze. Mantelshelves that are encountered in houses built before the 1790s will often be found to have been added later, especially when paneled breastwork remains visible above the shelf.

A radical change began to manifest itself in the 1790s. William Pain's influential Adamesque books, *The Practical Builder* (London, 1774) and *The Practical House Carpenter* (London, 1788), were reprinted in Boston in 1792 and 1796. Asher Benjamin published his *Country Builder's As-*

NH26

sistant in Massachusetts in 1797. All three books contain a variety of designs for mantelpieces. Most of these are delicate designs with flat pilasters at the sides, a frieze ornamented with foliage or a classical urn, and a thin, strongly projecting mantelshelf. Gone were the heavy carved features and overmantel panels that had characterized designs in earlier British books. These new designs could easily be executed by joiners without the need to employ carvers. If carved ornamentation was wanted, it could easily be simulated by the molded composition ornaments that were increasingly becoming available (see figure, page 107).

The mantelpiece became a fashionable feature of the best rooms almost immediately. Even in lesser rooms, like bedchambers, a frieze board, crown molding, and shelf might be added above the traditional architrave around the fireplace opening, creating a basic mantelpiece. In the better rooms of more pretentious houses, designs could be highly elaborate and inventive, sometimes making use of reeding, lattice moldings, and occasional panels of varnished hardwoods. By the turn of the nineteenth century, joiners in several coastal locales had begun to support mantelshelves on pipestem-thin colonnettes, which themselves sometimes whimsically stood on wooden balls. Such attenuated columns became a familiar feature of mantelpieces, even in inland locales, over the next quarter century.

One fashion in mantelpiece decoration during the early 1800s has been largely forgotten. This was the practice of painting wooden mantelpieces black, perhaps to suggest marble. The taste of later generations usually dictated that these black features of the Federal period be overpainted the same color as adjoining woodwork, but evidence of the early black paint will sometimes be encountered. Later generations, unable to account for this early fashion, have invented various legends to explain it. One story is that earlier wooden mantelpieces were painted black in the mid-1800s to resemble the then-fashionable marble or marbleized slate mantels. Another persistent legend states

Mantelpiece, circa 1800, painted black, Pendergast Garrison, Durham, New Hampshire. Although not uncommon in the early 1800s, black mantelpieces have usually been overpainted in lighter colors to match adjoining woodwork. Photograph by L. C. Durette, 1936. Library of Congress, Prints and Photographs Division, Historic American Buildings Survey, Reproduction Number HABS, NH, 9 – DUR.V, 1.

that wooden mantelpieces were painted black in mourning for Lincoln's assassination. In fact, the fashion for black mantelpieces began shortly after 1800, independent of later developments.

The latter years of the Federal period saw the increasing popularity of the cast-iron fire frame in New England. Derived from the Franklin stove, fire frames are decorative iron inserts that were intended to move the fire farther forward on the hearth, heating the room with a small fire and adding the radiation of warmed cast iron to that of the flames themselves.

The dual trends toward smaller, more efficient fires and the use of cast-iron fireplaces had been evolving during the eighteenth century. Benjamin Thompson (Count Rumford), a native of Massachusetts who left New England as a Loyalist and achieved fame as a scientist in England and Bavaria, published plans for a shallow fireplace with flaring cheeks that radiated much of the fire's heat

(*Opposite*) Chimneypiece, Captain Samuel Chauncy House, circa 1808, Portsmouth, New Hampshire. This mantelpiece had lower colonnettes and oval panels of varnished mahogany. The plinths for its upper colonnettes were supported on wooden balls, a fanciful design suggested in Asher Benjamin's *American Builder's Companion* (Boston, 1806). Photograph by L. C. Durette, 1936. Library of Congress, Prints and Photographs Division, Historic American Buildings Survey, Reproduction Number HABS, NH, 8 – PORT, 124.

into the room. To combat the tendency of such shallow hearths to puff smoke into the room with each downdraft in the chimney, Thompson developed the "smoke shelf," a projection just above the throat of the fireplace. This shelf intercepts downdrafts, turning them upward into the current of rising heat and smoke. By the late 1700s most brick fireplaces in new houses were of the Rumford type, with shallow hearths, flaring cheeks, and at least a rudimentary smoke shelf at the backs of their throats.

Meanwhile, Benjamin Franklin had been promoting the idea of a cast-iron stove since the 1740s. Franklin's original "Pennsylvania Fireplace" was a stove with an open front, duplicating the form of a small fireplace. In its original form, Franklin's invention involved bringing fresh air through a tube from outside the house to feed the fire and forcing its smoke to pass downward over a series of baffles behind the fire in order to extract as much heat as possible. While these innovations seldom proved practicable, the idea of a cast-iron fireplace, projecting into the room to radiate its heat and venting its smoke directly into the chimney flue, was widespread by the late 1700s. Foundries

Mantelpiece, 1804, and fire frame, circa 1830, Benjamin Pierce House, Hillsborough, New Hampshire. Installation of fire frames usually reduced the size of a fireplace in height, width, and depth, permitting the room to be warmed with a smaller fire. Photograph by author.

throughout the new United States cast a wide variety of simple "Franklin stoves" of this type (see figure, page 101).

The principles of the Rumford fireplace and the Franklin stove were combined in the fire frame. As usually seen, the fire frame was probably meant to be installed in an existing fireplace to improve its efficiency. Unlike the Franklin stove, the fire frame has no hearth or back. It consists of two curved side pieces that fit into the fireplace, a frieze or hood across the front, and a top plate that locks the sides and frieze together. When installed in an existing fireplace, the unit allows the fire to be brought forward, warming the room by its own radiation and by convection from the exposed iron surfaces. Because the frame is usually smaller than the older fireplace, it encourages a smaller fire. New brickwork, often added to fill up the back of the deeper fireplace, creates a smoke shelf where none may have existed. Depending on their period of manufacture, most fire frames bear attractive cast decoration in the Adamesque or Grecian styles.

The advent of the Greek Revival style saw an evolution in mantelpieces that paralleled that in all other woodwork. The delicate and fanciful designs of the Federal style quickly gave way to much simpler mantelpieces that reflected the aesthetics of the new style. These designs sometimes displayed heavy, turned columns that resembled the Greek Doric order. Sometimes, fireplace openings were bordered by symmetrical casings with corner blocks, much like the door and window casings of the period.

The same period saw the introduction of marble man-telpieces as a fashionable focal point in many homes. Most of these units were not intended to enclose fires fueled by wood. Rather, they held cast-iron inserts and grates for coal fires, taking advantage of the increasing importation of coal from southern states as the century advanced. Although many "marble" mantelpieces are indeed what they seem, others were made from cheaper materials. Vermont and Pennsylvania slate was often marbleized by a secret process that produced a convincing and enduring imitation of marble of various colors and grains. The fashion for stone mantelpieces was strong enough to persuade many householders to remove older wooden mantelpieces and to insert coal grates in fireplaces that had originally burned wood. It is not uncommon to find such mantelpieces in the best rooms of houses that were originally built in the 1700s or early 1800s.

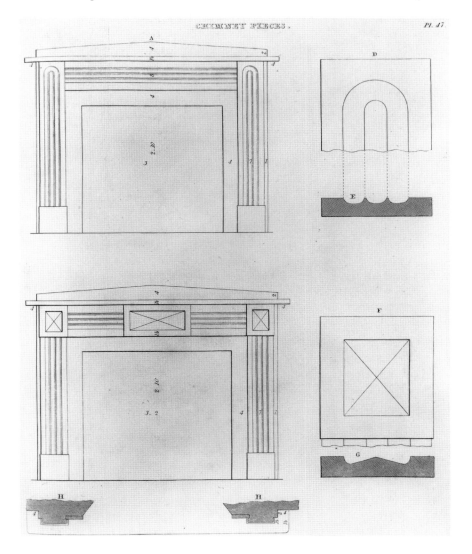

Plate illustrating two designs for chimneypieces in the Greek Revival style, from Asher Benjamin, *The Practice of Architecture* (Boston, 1833). Courtesy of the New Hampshire Historical Society.

Mantelpiece in the Greek Revival style with painted marbling. Exhibiting a peaked board above its shelf, this chimneypiece suggests the low-pitched pediment of a Greek temple. Painted decoration of this type was common during the early nineteenth century but often was overpainted later. Evidence suggests that this mantelpiece never had a fireplace but rather served as an enframement for a stove that stood in the location of the modern radiator. William Jones House, Claremont Plains, Claremont, New Hampshire, 1847–1850. Photograph by David S. Putnam.

Since the advent of the Greek Revival style in the 1830s coincided with the increasing popularity of airtight parlor stoves, some houses of this era were built with stove chimneys, not with fireplaces. So ingrained had the idea of the fireplace become, however, that mantelpieces were usually installed against the walls, in front of the chimneys, framing a stovepipe thimble instead of a hearth. Even as late as 1900, houses with central heating were often equipped with parlor mantelpieces attached to their walls simply as a focal point of the room, with no fireplace or chimney nearby. Bedchambers often had bracketed shelves, reminiscent of the mantelshelf, attached to a convenient wall.

Between the 1830s and the mid-1800s, airtight kitchen ranges and parlor stoves became increasingly varied in their designs and increasingly commonplace as a means of cooking and heating. Many New Englanders were conservative, however, and gave up the idea of the fireplace only reluctantly. Some housewives distrusted the kitchen range, especially for baking. Many houses that were built to be heated with stoves were nevertheless also equipped with a brick oven until well after 1850. Similarly, many New Englanders were reluctant to relinquish the open fire. Both Emerson and Melville wrote in praise of the fire in the hearth. Many people objected to the smell of the hot stove and lamented the entrapment of the dancing flames in an iron box.

Perhaps because of this nostalgia, the fireplace was destined to return to the New England house before the end of the century. No longer a necessity in an age of stoves or central heating, the fireplace was prized for its symbolic suggestion of hearth and home, and for the reveries its flames and embers evoked in the contemplative mind.

Mantelpiece designs after the Civil War partook of the general complexity of all late-nineteenth-century woodwork. The most elaborate examples combined a variety of features, frequently including a tiled hearth, tiled fireplace jambs and lintel, and an overmantel with a plate glass mirror. In addition to the principal mantelshelf, such designs often included supplementary galleries for the display of ceramics or objects of art. The stylistic vocabularies displayed by these features borrow from the myriad of styles that were used and combined during this eclectic era.

The basic elements of tiled hearths and jambs and an overmantel mirror were frequently repeated during the late 1800s and early 1900s in houses of the colonial revival style. Mantelpieces in the colonial style usually tended

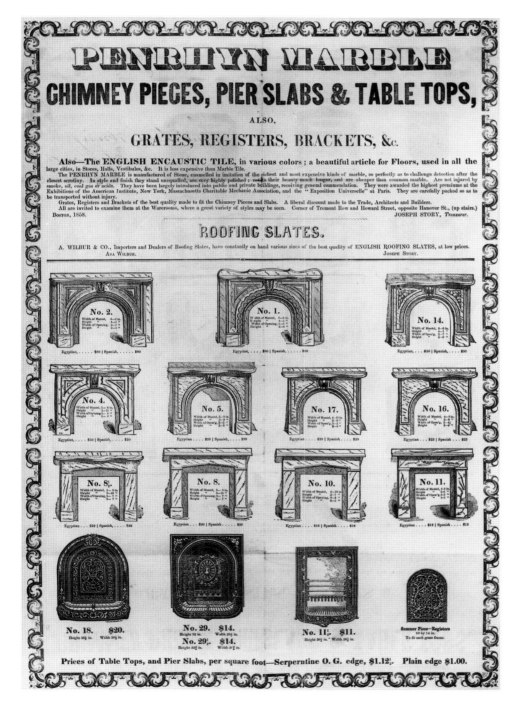

Broadside advertising stone chimneypieces, Boston, 1858. While many mantelpieces were made of true marble, these Penrhyn Marble units were made of enameled slate. Stone chimneypieces were widespread by the 1850s, both in new construction and as additions in remodeled houses.

toward Adamesque or Federal design, having slender colonnettes and an abundance of ribbons or floral swags executed in London putty or one of the other forms of composition ornament that were available at the period.

The craftsman movement, which brought about a general simplification of woodwork during the early 1900s, attained strong expression in the mantelpiece. The image of the open hearth was especially consonant with the craftsman style, and most houses of moderate cost, or higher, were designed with a fireplace in the living room. In keeping with the tenet of honest expression of materials, craftsman fireplaces are often built of exposed brick, topped with a mantelshelf of heavy timber, perhaps supported on brick or timber corbels. Such fireplaces are sometimes flanked by built-in bookcases or accompanied by a cozy seat in a tiny inglenook.

Turnings and Balustrades

It is difficult to make general statements about the evolution of balustrades because these features often reflected the work of individual turners within a local region until the advent of manufactured components in the late 1800s. Turned members tend to be highly individualistic. This fact is recognized by furniture specialists, who can often identify separate cabinet shops, even within the same community, by the distinctive turned legs on early-nineteenth-century tables. Many areas of rural New England apparently sustained no turners, and in such regions no balusters or turned newel posts will be found unless they were brought from elsewhere. It is, nevertheless, possible to trace a general evolution in those areas where turnings are found.

Staircases of the late 1600s and very early 1700s are almost always of the closed-stringer type, with a diagonal stringer enclosing the side of a staircase. In such stairs, the risers and treads are hidden from view by the stringer. Balusters, if they exist, rise from the top of the slanted stringer to the bottom of the handrail. Such balusters often assume the form of an elongated vase, a basic profile that was to persist throughout most of the 1700s. In the turnings of the mid- to late century, the vasiform section no longer stands alone but becomes the dominant portion of a baluster or newel post of much more elaborate profile.

The coastal regions of New Hampshire and southern Maine supported professional turners by the early 1700s.

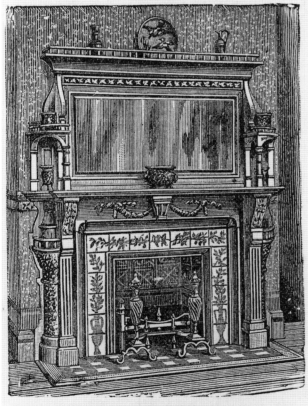

Advertisement for a chimneypiece with an overmantel looking glass. Late-nineteenth-century mantelpieces were often highly elaborate and eclectic in design, serving as the focal point of a room and also providing a setting in which to display china and other collections. *Carpentry and Building* magazine, September 1883.

Advertisement for a chimneypiece in the colonial revival style. From the late 1800s through the early 1900s, mantelpieces displaying classical motifs were popular, appearing not only in colonial revival houses but also in dwellings of other styles. *American Homes* magazine, last quarter (October, November, December), 1895.

At least one of these craftsmen, John Mills of Portsmouth, New Hampshire, had served his apprenticeship in Bristol, England, and brought a sophisticated mastery of his trade when he arrived at Piscataqua about 1725. To Mills and his son Richard may be ascribed most of the distinctive balustrades that distinguish the grander houses of the region during the 1700s. These balustrades have three distinct patterns of balusters on each tread of the stairs. Many have newel posts that duplicate, in enlarged form, either the vasiform or the fluted pattern of baluster. A few have open newel posts that embrace a complex spiral-turned central shaft (see figure, page 41).

Less pretentious houses usually have either vasiform turned newels or square, unturned posts. The vasiform shaft is often supported on a squat, vase-shaped lower turning. The balusters of such staircases closely reflect the double-vase-shaped profile of the newel post in miniature.

The handrails that accompany such newel posts are usually heavy and deep, with a complex cap that is formed by small bolection moldings that are attached to each side and provide a secure grip. Joiners usually finished the wall side of a staircase with a slanted cap that reflects the con-tours of the handrail and echoes its profile. This half-profile therefore functions as a chair rail and is often carried around all the walls of the stair hall as well as up the staircase.

The dominance of the vase-shaped newel post and baluster began to weaken by the 1790s. The arrival of the Federal style saw a growing preference for unfluted columnar newel posts. Asher Benjamin suggested such patterns in *The Country Builder's Assistant* (1797) and *The American Builder's Companion* (1806). Balusters of the early 1800s often take a similar form, becoming elongated columns supported by short vase turnings, although thin and attenuated vasiform balusters also persist during the period.

The advent of the Federal style also saw a deliberate abandonment of turned balusters in some cases. It is not unusual to encounter houses of considerable pretension that have plain balusters of square or rectangular cross-section, often in combination with a delicately turned newel post. Simple round dowels also serve as balusters in some houses in the Federal style, perhaps more frequently during the 1820s and 1830s as that style gave way to the Greek Revival. The option of choosing square or round balusters was welcomed in country areas where no turners were available.

Handrails of the Federal era tend to be more delicate than those of any other period. The Federal style saw a vogue for spiral staircases and for balustrades that ascend in continuous curves without the intermediate support of angle posts. Asher Benjamin and other authors who followed him devoted a great deal of attention to the methods of laying out and constructing such staircases.

Where a turned newel post was wanted, the elongated columnar form persisted until about 1830. At about that time a distinctive change is seen. While the basic elements of the newel post remain the same, the column shaft frequently assumes a swelling outline. This convex profile is strongly associated with the Greek Revival style. Greek Revival buildings often have open porches or colonnades, sometimes one above another on two stories. It is not unusual to find such porches supported by columns of the same distinctive swelling profile.

The period around 1850 saw the next distinctive change

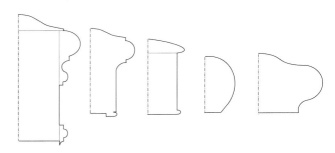

Evolution of handrail profiles, 1750 to 1850: (*left to right*) circa 1750, circa 1795, circa 1810 (sometimes veneered), circa 1810, circa 1850. Drawing by author.

in newel posts. Posts of the mid-1800s are usually much heavier than any seen in earlier times. Such newels are sometimes turned from black walnut or mahogany. Their handrails are broad, fashioned from walnut or mahogany with a simple, serpentine cross-section. Staircases of the period from 1850 to the end of the century tend to have the most massive components and the heaviest appearance of those of any era.

The late 1800s saw a tendency to abandon the turned newel post. Its place was taken by a wide variety of square, paneled, or faceted posts, usually with massive caps and often with enriched moldings and veneers of various hardwoods. As with other elements of late-nineteenth-century architecture, these posts and the elaborately turned balusters that often accompanied them were usually the product of large woodworking factories rather than of local shops.

The end of the nineteenth century was marked by a strong interest in "colonial" design. Architects and woodworkers of the period had not yet perceived the differences between Georgian and Federal detailing. The colonial motifs of this era were therefore classical in feeling, but they often mixed Georgian and Adamesque elements indiscriminately. Being manufactured in large quantities, such detailing was applied to buildings of the colonial revival style and also to houses in the shingle style and the various eclectic mixtures that were common in the late 1800s. Buildings of this period may therefore exhibit staircase designs that suggest the feeling of earlier eras. Despite the pervasive classicism of this period, however, staircases and other elements of the late 1800s and early 1900s are easily distinguished from work of the 1700s and early 1800s.

The early twentieth century saw the introduction of

Evolution of newel post design. *From left to right*: 1750, 1800, 1830, 1850. Drawing by author.

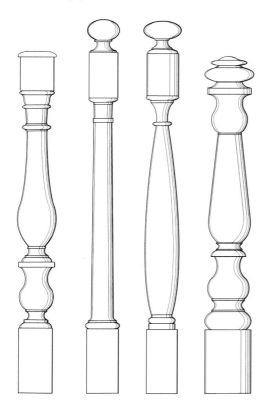

the craftsman style, which was especially suited to the bungalow. As an outgrowth of the international Arts and Crafts movement of the late 1800s and early 1900s, the craftsman style sought to embody simplicity, solid workmanship, and an honest expression of materials and function in all architectural elements. The style used few moldings and little extraneous decoration. Staircases expressed the style through heavy, square newel posts with square caps, square balusters, and angular moldings in place of the coves that are usually applied under the nosing of each tread. Typically, staircases in the craftsman style are varnished, not painted.

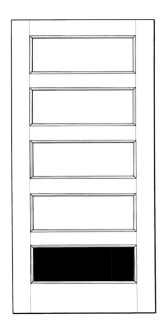

Appendix: The Secretary of the Interior's Standards for the Treatment of Historic Properties

Standards for Preservation

"Preservation" is defined as the act or process of applying measures necessary to sustain the existing form, integrity, and materials of an historic property. Work, including preliminary measures to protect and stabilize the property, generally focuses upon the ongoing maintenance and repair of historic materials and features rather than extensive replacement and new construction. New exterior additions are not within the scope of this treatment; however, the limited and sensitive upgrading of mechanical, electrical, and plumbing systems and other code-required work to make properties functional is appropriate within a preservation project.

1. A property will be used as it was historically, or given a new use that maximizes the retention of distinctive materials, features, spaces, and spatial relationships. Where a treatment and use have not been identified, a property will be protected and, if necessary, stabilized until additional work may be undertaken.

2. The historic character of a property will be retained and preserved. The replacement of intact or repairable historic materials, or alteration of features, spaces, and spatial relationships that characterize a property will be avoided.

3. Each property will be recognized as a physical record of its time, place, and use. Work needed to stabilize, consolidate, and conserve existing historic materials and features will be physically and visually compatible, identifiable upon close inspection, and properly documented for future research.

4. Changes to a property that have acquired historic significance in their own right will be retained and preserved.

5. Distinctive materials, features, finishes, and construction techniques or examples of craftsmanship that characterize a property will be preserved.

6. The existing condition of historic features will be evaluated to determine the appropriate level of intervention needed. Where the severity of deterioration requires repair or limited replacement of a distinctive feature, the new material will match the old in composition, design, color, and texture.

7. Chemical or physical treatments, if appropriate, will be undertaken using the gentlest means possi-

ble. Treatments that cause damage to historic materials will not be used.

8. Archaeological resources will be protected and preserved in place. If such resources must be disturbed, mitigation measures will be undertaken.

Standards for Rehabilitation

"Rehabilitation" is defined as the act or process of making possible a compatible use for a property through repair, alterations, and additions while preserving those portions or features which convey its historical, cultural, or architectural values.

1. A property will be used as it was historically or be given a new use that requires minimal change to its distinctive materials, features, spaces, and spatial relationships.

2. The historic character of a property will be retained and preserved. The removal of distinctive materials or alteration of features, spaces, and spatial relationships that characterize a property will be avoided.

3. Each property will be recognized as a physical record of its time, place, and use. Changes that create a false sense of historical development, such as adding conjectural features or elements from other historic properties, will not be undertaken.

4. Changes to a property that have acquired historic significance in their own right will be retained and preserved.

5. Distinctive materials, features, finishes, and construction techniques or examples of craftsmanship that characterize a property will be preserved.

6. Deteriorated historic features will be repaired rather than replaced. Where the severity of deterioration requires replacement of a distinctive feature, the new feature will match the old in design, color, texture, and, where possible, materials. Replacement of missing features will be substantiated by documentary and physical evidence.

7. Chemical or physical treatments, if appropriate, will be undertaken using the gentlest means possi-

ble. Treatments that cause damage to historic materials will not be used.

8. Archaeological resources will be protected and preserved in place. If such resources must be disturbed, mitigation measures will be undertaken.

9. New additions, exterior alterations, or related new construction will not destroy historic materials, features, and spatial relationships that characterize the property. The new work shall be differentiated from the old and will be compatible with the historic materials, features, size, scale and proportion, and massing to protect the integrity of the property and its environment.

10. New additions and adjacent or related new construction will be undertaken in such a manner that, if removed in the future, the essential form and integrity of the historic property and its environment would be unimpaired.

Standards for Restoration

"Restoration" is defined as the act or process of accurately depicting the form, features, and character of a property as it appeared at a particular period of time by means of the removal of features from other periods in its history and reconstruction of missing features from the restoration period. The limited and sensitive upgrading of mechanical, electrical, and plumbing systems and other code-required work to make properties functional is appropriate within a restoration project.

1. A property will be used as it was historically or be given a new use which reflects the property's restoration period.

2. Materials and features from the restoration period will be retained and preserved. The removal of materials or alteration of features, spaces, and spatial relationships that characterize the period will not be undertaken.

3. Each property will be recognized as a physical record of its time, place, and use. Work needed to stabilize, consolidate and conserve materials and features from the restoration period will be physi-

cally and visually compatible, identifiable upon close inspection, and properly documented for future research.

4. Materials, features, spaces, and finishes that characterize other historical periods will be documented prior to their alteration or removal.

5. Distinctive materials, features, finishes, and construction techniques or examples of craftsmanship that characterize the restoration period will be preserved.

6. Deteriorated features from the restoration period will be repaired rather than replaced. Where the severity of deterioration requires replacement of a distinctive feature, the new feature will match the old in design, color, texture, and, where possible, materials.

7. Replacement of missing features from the restoration period will be substantiated by documentary and physical evidence. A false sense of history will not be created by adding conjectural features, features from other properties, or by combining features that never existed together historically.

8. Chemical or physical treatments, if appropriate, will be undertaken using the gentlest means possible. Treatments that cause damage to historic materials will not be used.

9. Archaeological resources affected by a project will be protected and preserved in place. If such resources must be disturbed, mitigation measures will be undertaken.

10. Designs that were never executed historically will not be constructed.

Standards for Reconstruction

"Reconstruction" is defined as the act or process of depicting, by means of new construction, the form, features, and detailing of a non-surviving site, landscape, building, structure, or object for the purpose of replicating its appearance at a specific period of time in its historic location.

1. Reconstruction will be used to depict vanished or non-surviving portions of a property when docu-

mentary and physical evidence is available to permit accurate reconstruction with minimal conjecture, and such reconstruction is essential to the public understanding of the property.

2. Reconstruction of a landscape, building, structure, or object in its historic location will be preceded by a thorough archaeological investigation to identify and evaluate those features and artifacts which are essential to an accurate reconstruction. If such resources must be disturbed, mitigation measures will be undertaken.

3. Reconstruction will include measures to preserve any remaining historic materials, features, and spatial relationships.

4. Reconstruction will be based on the accurate duplication of historic features and elements substantiated by documentary or physical evidence rather than on conjectural designs or the availability of different features from other historic properties. A reconstructed property will re-create the appearance of the non-surviving historic property in materials, design, color, and texture.

5. A reconstruction will be clearly identified as a contemporary re-creation.

6. Designs that were never executed historically will not be constructed.

SELECTED BIBLIOGRAPHY

American Building Design and Technology, 1600–1925

This bibliography includes books, journal articles, and occasional publications that will be helpful to the reader who wishes to learn more about subjects covered in this book. The bibliography is limited to publications that may be presumed to remain in print or to be found in the collections of larger libraries. Much information in this book derives from publications of the nineteenth and early twentieth centuries. Being rare or ephemeral sources, not normally obtainable by the general reader, these have not been included in the bibliography unless they are available in reprint editions.

The bibliography is arranged according to subject. The following outline may help in locating the resources available for further study of a specific subject.

Architectural History

ARCHITECTURAL AND SOCIAL HISTORY

Andrews, Wayne. *Architecture, Ambition, and Americans.* New York: Harper Brothers, 1955.

Burke, Doreen Bolger, Jonathan Freedman, Alice Cooney Frelinghuysen, David A. Hanks, Marilynn Johnson, James T. Kornwolf, Catherine Lynn, Roger B. Stein, Jennifer Toher, Catherine Hoover Voorsanger, and Carrie Rebora. *In Pursuit of Beauty: Americans and the Aesthetic Movement.* New York: Metropolitan Museum of Art, 1986.

Clark, Clifford Edward, Jr. *The American Family Home, 1800–1960.* Chapel Hill: University of North Carolina Press, 1986.

Clark, Robert Judson, ed. *The Arts and Crafts Movement in America, 1876–1916.* Princeton, N.J.: Princeton University Press, 1972.

Congdon, Herbert Wheaton. *Old Vermont Houses, 1763–1850.* 1946. Reprint, revised, Dublin, N.H.: William L. Bauhan, 1973.

Connally, Ernest Allen. "The Cape Cod House." *Journal of the Society of Architectural Historians* 19 (May 1960): 47–56.

Cowan, Ruth Schwartz. "'The Industrial Revolution' in the Home: Technology and Social Change in the Twentieth Century." *Technology and Culture* 17 (January 1976): 1–23.

Craven, Wayne. *American Art: History and Culture.* New York: Harry N. Abrams, 1994.

Cummings, Abbott Lowell. *Architecture in Colonial Massachusetts.* Boston: Colonial Society of Massachusetts, 1979.

————. *The Framed Houses of Massachusetts Bay*. Cambridge, Mass.: Harvard University Press, 1979.

Davidson, Marshall B., ed. *The American Heritage History of Notable American Houses*. New York: American Heritage Publishing Company, 1971.

Doucet, Michael J., and John C. Weaver. "Material Culture and the North American House: The Era of the Common Man, 1870–1920." *Journal of American History* 72 (December 1985): 560–87.

Downing, Antoinette, and Vincent Scully, Jr. *The Architectural Heritage of Newport, Rhode Island*. 2nd ed. New York: Clarkson N. Potter, 1967.

Early, James. *Romanticism and American Architecture*. New York: A. S. Barnes, 1965.

Fitch, James Marston. *American Building: The Environmental Forces That Shape It*. Boston: Houghton Mifflin Company, 1972.

————. *American Building: The Historical Forces That Shaped It*. 2nd ed. New York: Schocken Books, 1973.

Garrett, Wendell D., Paul F. Norton, Alan Gowans, and Joseph T. Butler. *The Arts in America: The Nineteenth Century*. New York: Charles Scribner's Sons, 1969.

Gebhard, David. "The American Colonial Revival in the 1930s." *Winterthur Portfolio* 22 (summer-autumn 1987): 109–48.

Gottfried, Herbert. "The Machine and the Cottage: Building, Technology, and the Single-Family House, 1870–1910." *IA* 21 (1995): 47–68.

Gowans, Alan. *The Comfortable House: North American Suburban Architecture, 1890–1930*. Cambridge, Mass.: MIT Press, 1986.

————. *Styles and Types of North American Architecture: Social Function and Cultural Expression*. New York: HarperCollins, 1992.

Hamlin, Talbot. *Greek Revival Architecture in America*. 1944. Reprint, New York: Dover Publications, 1964.

Handlin, David P. *The American Home, Architecture, and Society, 1815–1915*. Boston: Little, Brown and Company, 1979.

Hubka, Thomas. *Big House, Little House, Back House, Barn: The Connected Farm Buildings of New England*. Hanover, N.H.: University Press of New England, 1984.

Jordy, William H. *American Buildings and Their Architects: Progressive and Academic Ideals at the Turn of the Twentieth Century*. Garden City, N.Y.: Doubleday and Co., 1972.

Kelly, J. Frederick. *Early Domestic Architecture of Connecticut*. 1924. Reprint, New York: Dover Publications, 1963.

Kimball, S. Fiske. *Domestic Architecture of the American Colonies and of the Early Republic*. 1922. Reprint, New York: Dover Publications, 1966.

Kirker, Harold. *The Architecture of Charles Bulfinch*. Cambridge, Mass.: Harvard University Press, 1969.

Klein, Marilyn W., and David P. Fogle. *Clues to American Architecture*. Washington, D.C.: Starrhill Press, 1985.

Leopold, Allison Kyle. *Victorian Splendor*. New York: Stewart Tabori and Chang, 1986.

Lewis, Arnold, ed. *American Victorian Architecture: A Survey of the 70s and 80s in Contemporary Photographs*. New York: Dover Publications, 1975.

Loth, Calder, and Julius T. Sadler. *The Only Proper Style: Gothic Architecture in America*. Boston: New York Graphic Society, 1975.

Maas, John. *The Victorian House in America*. New York: Hawthorne Books, 1972.

Morrison, Hugh. *Early American Architecture from the First Colonial Settlements to the National Period*. New York: Oxford University Press, 1952.

Mumford, Lewis. *The Brown Decades: A Study of the Arts in America, 1865–1895*. 1931. Reprint, New York: Dover Publications, 1971.

————. *Sticks and Stones*. 1924. Reprint, New York, Dover Publications, 1955.

Pierson, William H. *American Buildings and Their Architects: The Colonial and Neoclassical Styles*. Garden City, N.Y.: Doubleday and Co., 1970.

————. *American Buildings and Their Architects: Technology and the Picturesque: The Corporate and Early Gothic Styles*. Garden City, N.Y.: Doubleday and Co., 1978.

Sanders, Barry. *A Complex Fate: Gustav Stickley and the Craftsman Movement*. New York: Preservation Press/John Wiley and Sons, 1996.

Scully, Vincent. *The Stick Style and the Shingle Style*. New Haven, Conn.: Yale University Press, 1971.

Smith, G. E. Kidder. *A Pictorial History of Architecture in America*. New York: Bonanza Books and American Heritage Publishing Company, 1976.

Stilgoe, John R. *Borderland: Origins of the American Suburb, 1820–1939*. New Haven, Conn.: Yale University Press, 1988.

Thompson, Deborah, ed. *Maine Forms of American Architecture*. Camden, Maine: Downeast Magazine, 1976.

Thornton, Peter. *Authentic Decor: The Domestic Interior, 1620–1920*. New York: Viking Penguin, 1984.

Upton, Dell, and John Michael Vlach, eds. *Common Places: Readings in American Vernacular Architecture*. Athens: University of Georgia Press, 1986.

Whittaker, Craig. *Architecture and the American Dream*. New York: Clarkson N. Potter, 1996.

Wright, Gwendolyn. *Building the Dream: A Social History of Housing in America*. New York: Pantheon, 1981.

Wright, Louis B., George B. Tatum, John W. McCoubrey, and Robert C. Smith. *The Arts in America: The Colonial Period*. New York: Charles Scribner's Sons, 1966.

Anderson, Patricia McGraw, and Josephine H. Detmer. *Portland*. 2nd ed. Portland, Maine: Portland Landmarks, 1986.

Baker, John Milnes. *American House Styles: A Concise Guide*. New York: W. W. Norton & Company, 1994.

Blumenson, John J.-G. *Identifying American Architecture: A Pictorial Guide to Styles and Terms, 1600–1945*. Nashville, Tenn.: American Association for State and Local History, 1977.

Bruhn, Paul A., ed. *Historic Preservation in Vermont*. Shelburne: Preservation Trust of Vermont, 1982.

———, comp. *Vermont's Historic Architecture: A Second Celebration*. Shelburne: Preservation Trust of Vermont, 1985.

Candee, Richard M., ed. *Building Portsmouth: The Neighborhoods and Architecture of New Hampshire's Oldest City*. Portsmouth, N.H.: Portsmouth Advocates, 1992.

Chambers, S. Allen. *Discovering Historic America*. New England ed. New York: E. P. Dutton Company, 1982.

Gilbertson, Elsa. *A Guide to Vermont Architecture*. 1992. Reprint, ed. by Curtis B. Johnson, Montpelier: Vermont Division of Historic Preservation, 1996.

Johnson, Curtis B., ed. *The Historic Architecture of Addison County [Vermont], Including a Listing of the Vermont State Register of Historic Places*. Montpelier: Vermont Division for Historic Preservation, 1992.

———, ed. *The Historic Architecture of Rutland County [Vermont], Including a Listing of the Vermont State Register of Historic Places*. Montpelier: Vermont Division for Historic Preservation, 1988.

Lake Champlain Basin Program. *Around the Lake: Historic Sites on Lake Champlain*. Grand Isle: Preservation Trust of Vermont, 1996.

McAlester, Virginia, and Lee McAlester. *A Field Guide to American Houses*. Nashville, Tenn.: American Association for State and Local History, 1986.

Poppeliers, John, S. Allen Chambers, and Nancy B. Schwartz. *What Style Is It?* Washington, D.C.: Preservation Press, 1977.

Rifkind, Carole. *A Field Guide to American Architecture*. New York: New American Library, 1980.

Tolles, Bryant F., Jr., and Carolyn K. Tolles. *New Hampshire Architecture: An Illustrated Guide*. Hanover, N.H.: University Press of New England, 1979.

Visser, Thomas Durant. *Field Guide to New England Barns and Farm Buildings*. Hanover, N.H.: University Press of New England, 1997.

Walker, Lester. *American Shelter: An Illustrated Encyclopedia of the American Home*. Woodstock, N.Y.: Overlook Press, 1981, 1997.

Whiffen, Marcus. *American Architecture since 1780: A Guide to the Styles*. Cambridge, Mass.: MIT Press, 1969.

Bucher, Ward. *Dictionary of Building Preservation*. New York: John Wiley and Sons, 1996.

Burden, Ernest. *Illustrated Dictionary of Architecture*. New York: McGraw-Hill, 1998.

Carley, Rachel. *The Visual Dictionary of American Domestic Architecture*. New York: Henry Holt and Company, 1994.

Harris, Cyril M. *American Architecture: An Illustrated Encyclopedia*. New York: W. W. Norton, 1998.

———. *Historic Architecture Sourcebook*. New York: McGraw-Hill, 1977.

———. *Illustrated Dictionary of Historic Architecture*. New York: Dover Publications, 1977, 1983.

———, ed. *Dictionary of Architecture and Construction*. New York: McGraw-Hill, 1975.

Isham, Norman Morrison. *A Glossary of Colonial Architectural Terms*. 1939. Reprint, Watkins Glen, N.Y.: American Life Foundation and Study Institute, 1976.

Pevsner, Nikolaus, John Fleming, and Hugh Honour. *A Dictionary of Architecture*. Woodstock, N.Y.: Overlook Press, 1976.

Phillips, Steven J. *Old-House Dictionary: An Illustrated Guide to American Domestic Architecture (1600–1940)*. Lakewood, Colo: American Source Books, 1989.

Putnam, R. E., and G. E. Carlson. *Architectural and Building Trades Dictionary*. 3d ed. New York: Van Nostrand Reinhold Company, 1974.

Building Technology

GENERAL

Condit, Carl W. *American Building: Materials and Techniques from the First Colonial Settlements to the Present*. 2nd ed. Chicago: University of Chicago Press, 1982.

Dietz, Albert G. H. *Dwelling House Construction*. 4th ed., rev. Cambridge, Mass.: MIT Press, 1974.

Elliott, Cecil D. *Technics and Architecture: The Development of Materials and Systems for Buildings*. Cambridge, Mass.: MIT Press, 1992. Includes chapters on wood, masonry, metals, glass, cements, plumbing, lighting, heating, ventilating, air conditioning, fire and lightning protection, elevators, and acoustics.

Friedman, Donald. *Historical Building Construction: Design, Materials, and Technology*. New York: W. W. Norton and Company, 1995. Contains chapters on cast iron facades, steel skeleton framing, floor and wall systems, fireproofing, and other aspects of large building construction.

Hart, David M. *How to Date a House: Part One and Part Two*. Reprint from *Yankee Magazine*, July and November 1976.

Boston: Society for the Preservation of New England Antiquities, n.d.

Jandl, H. Ward, ed., *The Technology of Historic American Buildings*. Washington, D.C.: Foundation for Preservation Technology, 1983. Includes articles on hand-forged hardware, metal roofing, the balloon frame, and nineteenth-century painting.

Jester, Thomas C., ed. *Twentieth-Century Building Materials: History and Conservation*. New York: McGraw-Hill for the National Park Service, 1995. Contains sections on metals, concrete, wood and plastics, masonry, glass, flooring, roofing, siding, and interior and exterior wall coverings.

Kay, Gersil Newmark. *Mechanical and Electrical Systems for Historic Buildings*. New York: McGraw-Hill, 1992.

McDonald, Travis C., Jr. *Understanding Old Buildings: The Process of Architectural Investigation*. Preservation Brief 35. Washington, D.C.: National Park Service, 1994.

Mercer, Henry C. *The Dating of Old Houses*. 1923. Reprint, Watkins Glen, N.Y.: American Life Foundation and Study Institute, 1976.

Simonson, Kaye Ellen. *Maintaining Historic Buildings: An Annotated Bibliography*. Washington, D.C.: National Park Service, 1990.

Peterson, Charles E., ed. *Building Early America: Contributions toward the History of a Great Industry*. 1976. Reprint, Mendham, N.J.: Astragal Press, n.d. Includes articles on wood, brick, stone, iron, concrete, glass, lighting, heating, roofing, building conservation and preservation.

BRICK, TILE, MORTAR, AND CONCRETE

Cowden, Adrienne Beaudet. *Historic Concrete: An Annotated Bibliography*. Washington, D.C.: National Park Service, 1993.

Garvin, James L. "Small-Scale Brickmaking in New Hampshire." *IA* 20:1–2 (1994): 19–31.

Gillespie, Ann. "Early Development of the *Artistic* Concrete Block: The Case of the Boyd Brothers." *APT Bulletin* 11:2 (1979): 30–52.

Grimmer, Anne. *Keeping It Clean: Removing Exterior Dirt, Paint, Stains and Graffiti from Historic Masonry Buildings*. Washington, D.C.: National Park Service, 1988.

Grimmer, Anne, and Paul K. Williams. *The Preservation and Repair of Historic Clay Tile Roofs*. Preservation Brief 30. Washington, D.C.: National Park Service, 1992.

Grimmer, Anne, and Kimberly A. Konrad. *Preserving Historic Ceramic Tile Floors*. Preservation Brief 40. Washington, D.C.: National Park Service, 1996.

Gurcke, Karl. *Bricks and Brickmaking: A Handbook for Historical Archaeology*. Moscow: University of Idaho Press, 1987.

London, Mark. *Masonry: How to Care for Old and Historic Brick and Stone*. Washington, D.C.: Preservation Press, 1988.

Mack, Robert C., de Teel Patterson Tiller, and James S. Askins. *Repointing Mortar Joints in Historic Brick Buildings*. Rev. ed. Preservation Brief 2. Washington, D.C.: National Park Service, 1980.

McGrath, Thomas L. "Notes on the Manufacture of Hand-Made Bricks." *APT Bulletin* 12:3 (1979): 88–95.

McKee, Harley J. "Brick and Stone: Handicraft to Machine." In *Building Early America: Contributions toward the History of a Great Industry*, ed. Charles E. Peterson. Mendham, N.J.: Astragal Press, n.d.

———. *Introduction to Early American Masonry: Stone, Brick, Mortar and Plaster*. Washington, D.C.: Preservation Press, 1973.

Phillips, Morgan W. "Brief Notes on the Subjects of Analyzing Paints and Mortars and the Recording of Moulding Profiles." *APT Bulletin* 10:2 (1978): 77–89.

———. "SPNEA-APT Conference on Mortar, Boston, March 15–16, 1973: Written Summary." *APT Bulletin* 6:1 (1974): 9–39.

Plumridge, Andrew, and Wim Meulenkamp. *Brickwork: Architecture and Design*. New York: Harry N. Abrams, 1993.

Prudon, Theodore H. M. "The Case against Removing Paint from Brick Masonry." *The Old-House Journal* 3 (February 1975): 6–7.

———. "Removing Stains from Masonry." *The Old-House Journal* 5 (May 1977): 58–59.

Ritchie, Thomas. "A History of the Tunnel Kiln and Other Kilns for Burning Bricks." *APT Bulletin* 12:3 (1980): 46–61.

Speweik, John P. *The History of Masonry Mortar in America, 1720–1995*. Arlington, Va.: National Lime Association, 1995.

Thomas, James Cheston. *Restoring Brick and Stone: Some Dos and Don'ts*. Technical Leaflet 81, *History News* 30 (January 1975).

Weaver, Martin E. *Removing Graffiti from Historic Masonry*. Preservation Brief 38. Washington, D.C.: National Park Service, 1995.

Weiss, Norman R. "Cleaning of Building Exteriors: Problems and Procedures of Dirt Removal." *Technology and Conservation* 2/76 (fall 1976): 8–13.

GLASS AND WINDOWS

Bock, Gordon. "New Century Sash: The Fashions and Features behind Post-Victorian Windows." *The Old-House Journal* 25 (January-February 1997): 36–39.

Byrne, Richard O. "Conservation of Historic Window Glass." *APT Bulletin* 13:3 (1981): 3–10.

Fisher, Charles E., III, ed. "Rehabilitating Windows in Historic Buildings: An Overview." In *The Window Handbook: Successful Strategies for Rehabilitating Windows in Historic Buildings*. Rev. ed. Washington, D.C.: National Park Service and The Center for Architectural Conservation, College of Architecture, Georgia Institute of Technology, 1990.

Gilmore, Andrea. "Guidelines for Repairing Historic Windows." *Traditional Building* 9 (January-February 1996): 77, 79.

Kendrick, Gregory D., ed. *The Preservation of Historic Pigmented Structural Glass (Vitrolite and Carrara Glass).* Preservation Brief 12. Washington, D.C.: National Park Service, 1984.

LePre, Vincent. "Window Sash Manufacture." *Building Renovation* (September-October 1993): 55–58.

Meany, Terence. *Working Windows: Repair and Restoration of Wood Windows.* Bothell, Wash.: MeanyPress, 1997.

Myers, John H. *The Repair of Historic Wooden Windows.* Preservation Brief 9. Washington, D.C.: National Park Service, 1981.

National Park Service. *Window Directory for Historic Buildings.* Washington, D.C.: National Park Service, 1992.

New York Landmarks Conservancy. *Repairing Old and Historic Windows.* Washington, D.C.: Preservation Press, 1992.

O'Connor, Richard. "Perfecting the 'Iron Lung': Making the New Window Glass Technology Work." *IA* 23:1 (1997): 6–24. Cylinder glass.

Smith, Baird M. *Conserving Energy in Historic Buildings.* Preservation Brief 3. Washington, D.C.: National Park Service, 1978.

Stumes, Paul. *Reinforcing Deteriorated Wooden Windows.* Preservation Tech Note: Windows No. 14. Washington, D.C.: National Park Service, 1986.

Swiatosz, Susan. "A Technical History of Late Nineteenth Century Windows in the United States." *APT Bulletin* 17:1 (1985): 31–37.

Vogel, Neal A., and Rolf Achilles. *The Preservation and Repair of Historic Stained and Leaded Glass.* Preservation Brief 33. Washington, D.C.: National Park Service, 1993.

Wilson, H. Weber. *Great Glass in American Architecture: Decorative Windows and Doors before 1920.* New York: E. P. Dutton, 1986.

———. *Your Residential Stained Glass: A Practical Guide to Repair and Maintenance.* Chambersburg, Pa.: Architectural Ecology, 1979.

Wilson, Kenneth M. "Window Glass in America." In *Building Early America: Contributions toward the History of a Great Industry,* ed. Charles E. Peterson. Mendham, N.J.: Astragal Press, n.d.

HARDWARE

Buggey, Susan. "A Most Significant Reference Document: A List of Nails and Spikes Required for the Service of the Office of Ordnance, 17 March 1813." Excerpted from "Supplying Building Materials to the British Army in the Colonies: An Illustrated Document." *APT Bulletin* 8:3 (1976): 88–118.

Butter, F. J. *An Encyclopedia of Locks and Builders Hardware.* Willenhall, England: Josiah Parkes and Sons, 1968.

Cotton, J. Randall. "Knobs and Latches." *The Old-House Journal* 15 (November/December 1987): 37–44.

Hennessy, Thomas. *Early Locks and Lockmakers of America.* Des Plaines, Ill.: Nickerson and Collins Co., 1976.

Loveday, Amos J., Jr. *The Rise and Decline of the American Cut Nail Industry.* Westport, Conn.: Greenwood Press, 1983.

Mercer, Henry C. *The Dating of Old Houses.* 1923. Reprint, Watkins Glen, N.Y.: American Life Foundation and Study Institute, 1976.

Nelson, Lee H. "How Hand-Wrought Nails Were Made from Bar Iron in the Eighteenth Century." *CRM* 14:4 (1991): 18–19.

———. "Nail Chronology as an Aid to Dating Old Buildings." Technical Leaflet 15, *History News* 19:2 (1963); revised version printed as Technical Leaflet 48, *History News* 24:11 (1968).

———. "Rediscovering American Hardware." *Historic Preservation* 32:6 (1980): 22–25.

Phillips, Maureen K. "'Mechanic Geniuses and Duckies,' A Revision of New England's Cut Nail Chronology before 1820." *APT Bulletin* 25:3–4 (1994): 4–16.

———. "Mechanic Geniuses and Duckies Redux: Nail Makers and Their Machines." *APT Bulletin* 27:1–2 (1996): 47–56.

Priess, Peter J. *An Annotated Bibliography for the Study of Building Hardware.* Ottawa: Parks Canada, 1978.

———. "Wire Nails in North America." *APT Bulletin* 5:4 (1973): 87–92.

Rolando, Victor. *200 Years of Soot and Sweat: The History and Archeology of Vermont's Iron, Charcoal, and Lime Industries.* Burlington: Vermont Archaeological Society, 1992.

Stevens, John R. "Early Cast Iron Latches." *APT Bulletin* 1:3 (1969): 11–13.

Streeter, Donald. "Early American Stock Locks." *Antiques* 98 (August 1970): 251–55.

———. "Early American Wrought Iron Hardware: Cross Garnet, Side, and Dovetail Hinges." *APT Bulletin* 6:2 (1974): 6–23.

———. "Early American Wrought Iron Hardware—English Iron Rim Locks: Late Eighteenth and Early Nineteenth Century Forms." *APT Bulletin* 6:1 (1974): 40–67.

———. "Early American Wrought Iron Hardware: H and HL Hinges, together with Mention of Dovetail and Cast Iron Butt Hinges." *APT Bulletin* 5:1 (1973): 22–49.

———. "Early American Wrought Iron Hardware: Norfolk Latches." *APT Bulletin* 3:4 (1971): 12–30.

———. "Early American Wrought Iron Hardware: Slide Bolts." *APT Bulletin* 7:4 (1975): 104–22.

———. "Early Wrought-Iron Hardware: Spring Latches." *Antiques* 66 (August 1954): 125–27.

———. "The Historical Development of Hand Forged Builder's Hardware." In *The Technology of Historic American Buildings,* ed. H. Ward Jandl. Washington, D.C.: Foundation for Preservation Technology, 1983.

———. "Some Signed American Rim Locks." *APT Bulletin* 5:2 (1973): 9–37.

———. "Wrought Iron Hardware for Exterior Shutters." *APT Bulletin* 7:1 (1975): 38–56.

Trump, Robert Townshend. "The Carpenter-type Lock." *Antiques* 66 (December 1954): 482.

HEATING, VENTILATION, COOKING, AND PLUMBING

Brewer, Priscilla J. "'We Have Got a Very Good Cooking Stove': Advertising, Design, and Consumer Response to the Cookstove, 1815–1880." *Winterthur Portfolio* 25 (spring 1990): 35–54.

Ferguson, Eugene S. "An Historical Sketch of Central Heating: 1800–1860." In *Building Early America: Contributions toward the History of a Great Industry*, ed. Charles E. Peterson. Mendham, N.J.: Astragal Press, n.d.

Leeds, Lewis W. *Lectures on Ventilation . . . 1866–67.* Watkins Glen, N.Y.: American Life Foundation, 1976.

Ogle, Maureen. "Domestic Reform and American Household Plumbing, 1849–1870." *Winterthur Portfolio* 28 (spring 1993): 33–58.

Stifler, Susan Reed. *The Beginnings of a Century of Steam and Water Heating.* Westfield, Mass.: H. B. Smith Company, 1960.

Stone, May N. "The Plumbing Paradox: American Attitudes toward Late Nineteenth-Century Domestic Sanitary Arrangements." *Winterthur Portfolio* 14 (autumn 1979): 283–310.

Townsend, Gavin. "Airborne Toxins in the American House, 1865–1895." *Winterthur Portfolio* 24 (spring 1989): 29–42.

Walbert, Benjamin L., III. "The Infancy of Central Heating in the United States, 1803 to 1845." *APT Bulletin* 3:4 (1971): 76–88.

LIGHTING

Darbee, Herbert C. *A Glossary of Old Lamps and Lighting Devices.* Technical Leaflet 30, *History News* 20:8 (1965); revised 1976.

Moss, Roger W. *Lighting for Historic Buildings.* Washington, D.C.: Preservation Press, 1988.

Myers, Denys Peter. *Gaslighting in America: A Guide for Historic Preservation.* Washington, D.C.: National Park Service, Technical Preservation Services Division, 1978.

Russell, Loris S. "Early Nineteenth-Century Lighting." In *Building Early America: Contributions toward the History of a Great Industry*, ed. Charles E. Peterson. Mendham, N.J.: Astragal Press, n.d.

———. *A Heritage of Light.* Toronto: University of Toronto Press, 1968.

Union Pacific System. *The Evolution of Artificial Light.* 1893. Reprint, Wethersfield, Conn.: Rushlight Club, 1986.

METALS, ARCHITECTURAL

Dierickx, Mary. "Metal Ceilings in the U.S." *APT Bulletin* 7:2 (1975): 83–93.

Gayle, Margot, David W. Look, and John G. Waite. *Metals in America's Historic Buildings.* Washington, D.C.: U.S. Department of the Interior, Heritage Conservation and Recreation Service, 1980, 1992. Contains articles on the history and use of iron, lead, tin, zinc, copper and copper alloys, nickel and nickel alloys, and aluminum and on their deterioration and preservation.

Peterson, Charles E. "Iron in Early American Roofs." *Smithsonian Journal of History* 3:3 (1968): 42.

Southworth, Susan, and Michael Southworth. *Ornamental Ironwork: An Illustrated Guide to Its Design, History, and Use in American Architecture.* New York: McGraw-Hill, 1992.

Sweetser, Sarah M. *Roofing for Historic Buildings.* Preservation Brief 4. Washington, D.C.: National Park Service, 1978.

Waite, Diana S., ed. *Architectural Elements: The Technological Revolution.* New York: Bonanza Books, 1972. Contains selections from the catalogs of Marshall, Lefferts & Brother (1854); Buffalo Eagle Iron Works (1859); Morris, Tasker & Company (1872); Keystone Mantel and Slate Works (1872); and George O. Stevens (1879).

Waite, John G. *The Maintenance and Repair of Architectural Cast Iron.* Preservation Brief 27. Washington, D.C.: National Park Service, 1991.

PAINT

Albee, Peggy A. "A Study of Historic Paint Colors and the Effects of Environmental Exposures on Their Colors and Their Pigments." *APT Bulletin* 16:3–4 (1984): 3–26.

Bevil, Marianne, Meredith Fiske, and Anne-Leslie Owens. *Painting Historic Buildings: Materials and Techniques.* Washington, D.C.: National Park Service, 1993.

Chase, Sara B. *Painting Historic Interiors.* Preservation Brief 28. Washington, D.C.: National Park Service, 1992.

A Decorator. *Victorian Interior Decoration.* Reprint of *The Paper Hanger, Painter, Grainer and Decorator's Assistant*, 1879. Watkins Glen, N.Y.: American Life Foundation, n.d.

F. W. Devoe Paint Company. *Exterior Decoration. A Treatise on the Artistic Use of Colors in the Ornamentation of Buildings . . .* Philadelphia: Athenaeum of Philadelphia, 1976.

"Exterior Painting." *The Old-House Journal* 4 (Special issue, April 1981).

Gardiner, F. G. *How to Paint Your Victorian House.* Reprint of *How to Paint*, 1897. Watkins Glen, N.Y.: American Life Foundation, 1978.

Hartshorne, Penelope. "Paint Color Research and Restoration." Technical Leaflet 15, *History News* 19 (1963).

Hawkes, Pamela W. "Economical Painting: The Tools and Techniques Used in Exterior Painting in the Nineteenth Century." In *The Technology of Historic American Buildings*, ed. H. Ward Jandl. Washington, D.C.: Foundation for Preservation Technology, 1983.

Marx, Ina Brosseau, Allen Marx, and Robert Marx. *Professional Painted Finishes*. New York: Watson-Guptill Publications, 1991.

Miller, Kevin H. *Paint Color Research and Restoration of Historic Paint*. APT Publication Supplement, 1977.

Mosca, Matthew. "Historic Paint Research: Determining the Original Colors." *The Old-House Journal* 9:4 (1981): 81–83.

Moss, Roger W. *A Century of Color: Exterior Design for American Buildings, 1820–1920*. Watkins Glen, N.Y.: American Life Foundation, 1981.

———, ed. *Paint in America: The Colors of Historic Buildings*. Washington, D.C.: Preservation Press, 1994.

Moss, Roger W., and Gail Caskey Winkler. *Victorian Exterior Decoration: How to Paint Your Nineteenth-Century House Historically*. New York: Henry Holt and Company, 1987.

Park, Sharon C., and Douglas C. Hicks. *Appropriate Methods for Reducing Lead-Paint Hazards in Historic Housing*. Preservation Brief 37. Washington, D.C.: National Park Service, 1995.

Penn, Theodore Zuk. "Decorative and Protective Finishes, 1750–1850: Materials, Process, and Craft." *APT Bulletin* 16:1 (1984): 3–46.

Phillips, Morgan W. "Brief Notes on the Subjects of Analyzing Paints and Mortars and the Recording of Moulding Profiles." *APT Bulletin* 10:2 (1978): 77–89.

Phillips, Morgan W., and Norman R. Weiss. "Some Notes on Paint Research and Reproduction." *APT Bulletin* 7:4 (1975): 14–19.

Reynolds, Hezekiah. *Directions for House and Ship Painting*. 1812. Reprinted, with an introduction by Richard Candee. Worcester, Mass.: American Antiquarian Society, 1978.

Schwin, Lawrence, III. *Old House Colors: An Expert's Guide to Painting Your Old (or Not So Old) House*. New York: Sterling Publishing Company, 1990.

Weaver, Martin E. *Removing Graffiti from Historic Masonry*. Preservation Brief 38. Washington, D.C.: National Park Service, 1995.

Weeks, Kay D., and David W. Look. *Exterior Paint Problems on Historic Woodwork*. Preservation Brief 10. Washington, D.C.: National Park Service, 1982.

———. "Paint on Exterior Historic Woodwork: Identification and Treatment of Surface Condition Problems." *Technology and Conservation* 2/82 (summer 1982): 34–45.

Welsh, Frank S. "Paint Analysis." *APT Bulletin* 14:4 (1982): 29–30.

Winkler, Gail Caskey, and Roger W. Moss. *Victorian Interior Decoration: American Interiors, 1830–1900*. New York: Henry Holt and Company, 1986.

PLASTER, STUCCO, AND COMPOSITION

Cotton, J. Randall. "Composition Ornament." *The Old-House Journal* 21 (January/February 1993): 28–33.

Flaharty, David. *Preserving Historic Ornamental Plaster*. Preservation Brief 23. Washington, D.C.: National Park Service, 1990.

Garrison, John Mark. "Casting Decorative Plaster." *The Old-House Journal* 13 (November 1985): 186–89.

———. "Decorative Plaster: Running Cornices." *The Old-House Journal* 12 (December 1984): 214–19.

Grimmer, Anne. *The Preservation and Repair of Historic Stucco*. Preservation Brief 22. Washington, D.C.: National Park Service, 1990.

Leeke, John. "Saving Irreplaceable Plaster." *The Old-House Journal* 15 (November/December 1987): 51–55.

MacDonald, Marylee. *Repairing Historic Flat Plaster—Walls and Ceilings*. Preservation Brief 21. Washington, D.C.: National Park Service, 1989.

McKee, Harley J. *Introduction to Early American Masonry: Stone, Brick, Mortar and Plaster*. Washington, D.C.: Preservation Press, 1973.

Poore, Patricia. "The Basics of Plaster Repair." *The Old-House Journal* 16 (March/April 1988): 29–35.

Shivers, Natalie. *Walls and Molding: How to Care for Old and Historic Wood and Plaster*. Washington, D.C.: Preservation Press, 1990.

Thornton, Jonathan, and William Adair. *Applied Decoration for Historic Interiors: Preserving Composition Ornament*. Preservation Brief 34. Washington, D.C.: National Park Service, 1994.

Weeks, Kay D. "Forgiving the Lath/Saving the Plaster." *CRM* 12:5 (1989): 9–12.

SLATE ROOFING

Jenkins, Joseph. *The Slate Roof Bible*. Grove City, Pa: Jenkins Publishing, 1997.

Levine, Jeffrey S. *The Repair, Replacement, and Maintenance of Historic Slate Roofs*. Preservation Brief 29. Washington, D.C.: National Park Service, 1992.

Marshall, Philip. "Polychromatic Roofing Slate of Vermont and New York." *APT Bulletin* 11:3 (1979): 77–87.

McKee, Harley J. "Slate Roofing." *APT Bulletin* 2:1–2 (1970): 77–84.

National Slate Association. *Slate Roofs*. 1926. Reprint, Fair Haven: Vermont Structural Slate Company, 1977.

Pierpont, Robert N. "Slate Roofing." *APT Bulletin* 19:2 (1987): 10–23.

Sweetser, Sarah M. *Roofing for Historic Buildings.* Preservation Brief 4. Washington, D.C.: National Park Service, 1978.

Waite, Diana S. "Roofing for Early America." In *Building Early America: Contributions toward the History of a Great Industry,* ed. Charles E. Peterson. Mendham, N.J.: Astragal Press, n.d.

STONE

Armistead, Donald. "Plug and Feather: A Simple Tool, Yet Very Effective." *Chronicle of the Early American Industries Association* 47:2 (1994): 43–45.

Garvin, Donna-Belle. "The Granite Quarries of Rattlesnake Hill: The Concord, New Hampshire, 'Gold Mine.'" *IA* 20:1–2 (1994): 50–68.

London, Mark. *Masonry: How to Care for Old and Historic Brick and Stone.* Washington, D.C.: Preservation Press, 1988.

McKee, Harley J. "Brick and Stone: Handicraft to Machine." In *Building Early America: Contributions toward the History of a Great Industry,* ed. Charles E. Peterson. Mendham, N.J.: Astragal Press, n.d.

———. "Early Ways of Quarrying and Working Stone in the United States." *APT Bulletin* 3:1 (1971): 44–58.

———. *Introduction to Early American Masonry: Stone, Brick, Mortar and Plaster.* Washington, D.C.: Preservation Press, 1973.

Prudon, Theodore H. M. "Simulating Stone, 1860–1940: Artificial Marble, Artificial Stone, and Cast Stone." *APT Bulletin* 21:3–4 (1989): 79–91.

Thomas, James Cheston. *Restoring Brick and Stone: Some Dos and Don'ts.* Technical Leaflet 81, *History News* 30 (January 1975).

Weaver, Martin E. *Removing Graffiti from Historic Masonry.* Preservation Brief 38. Washington, D.C.: National Park Service, 1995.

WALLPAPER

Bradbury, Bruce. "A Laymen's Guide to Historic Wallpaper Reproduction." *APT Bulletin* 16:1 (1984): 57–58.

Frangiamore, Catherine Lynn. *Rescuing Historic Wallpaper: Identification, Preservation, Restoration.* Technical Leaflet 76, *History News* 29 (July 1974).

———. *Wallpapers in Historic Preservation.* Washington, D.C.: National Park Service, Technical Preservation Services Division, 1977.

Hoskins, Lesley, ed. *The Papered Wall: History, Pattern, Technique.* New York: Harry N. Abrams, 1994.

Lynn, Catherine. *Wallpaper in America, from the Seventeenth Century to World War I.* New York: W. W. Norton and Company, for the Barra Foundation/Cooper Hewitt Museum, 1980.

Nylander, Richard C. *Wallpapers for Historic Buildings: A Guide to Selecting Reproduction Wallpapers.* Washington, D.C.: Preservation Press, 1983.

Nylander, Richard C., Elizabeth Redmond, and Penny J. Sander. *Wallpaper in New England: Selections from the Society for the Preservation of New England Antiquities,* with additional essays by Abbott Lowell Cummings and Karen A. Guffey. Boston: Society for the Preservation of New England Antiquities, 1986.

WOOD: STRUCTURE

Forest Products Laboratory. *The Encyclopedia of Wood.* Rev. ed. New York: Sterling Publishing Co., 1989.

Hoadley, R. Bruce. *Identifying Wood: Accurate Results with Simple Tools.* Newtown, Conn.: Taunton Press, 1990.

———. *Understanding Wood: A Craftsman's Guide to Wood Technology.* Newtown, Conn.: Taunton Press, 1980.

Merrill, William. *Wood Deterioration: Causes, Detection and Prevention.* Technical Leaflet 77, *History News* 29 (August 1974).

WOOD: MILLING, CARPENTRY, AND JOINERY

Avrami, Erica C. *Preserving Wood Features in Historic Buildings: An Annotated Bibliography.* Washington, D.C.: National Park Service, 1993.

Ball, Norman S. "Circular Saws and the History of Technology." *APT Bulletin* 7:3 (1975): 79–89.

Curtis, John O. "The Introduction of the Circular Saw in the Early Nineteenth Century." *APT Bulletin* 5:2 (1973): 162–89.

Englund, John H. "An Outline of the Development of Wood Moulding Machinery." *APT Bulletin* 10:4 (1978): 20–46.

Field, Walker. "A Reexamination into the Invention of the Balloon Frame." *Journal of the Society of Architectural Historians* 2 (October 1942): 3–29.

Gilmore, Andrea M. "Dating Architectural Moulding Profiles: A Story of Eighteenth and Nineteenth Century Moulding Plane Profiles in New England." *APT Bulletin* 10:2 (1978): 90–117.

Hindle, Brooke, ed. *America's Wooden Age: Aspects of Its Early Technology.* Tarrytown, N.Y.: Sleepy Hollow Restorations, 1975.

———, ed. *Material Culture of the Wooden Age.* Tarrytown, N.Y.: Sleepy Hollow Press, 1981.

Lewandoski, Jan Leo. "The Plank Framed House in Northeastern Vermont." *Vermont History* 53:2 (1985): 104–21.

———. "Transitional Timber Framing in Vermont, 1780–1850." *APT Bulletin* 26:2–3 (1995): 42–50.

Nelson, Walter R. "Some Examples of Plank House Construction and Their Origin." *Pioneer America* 1:2 (1969): 18–29.

Peterson, Charles E. "Sawdust Trail: Annals of Sawmilling and the Lumber Trade from Virginia to Hawaii via Maine, Barbados, Sault Ste. Marie, Manchac and Seattle to the Year 1860." *APT Bulletin* 5:2 (1973): 84–153.

Phillips, Morgan W. "Brief Notes on the Subjects of Analyzing Paints and Mortars and the Recording of Moulding Profiles." *APT Bulletin* 10:2 (1978): 77–89.

Shivers, Natalie. *Walls and Molding: How to Care for Old and Historic Wood and Plaster.* Washington, D.C.: Preservation Press, 1990.

Sobon, Jack. *The Scribe Rule or the Square Rule? Traditional Timber Frame Layout Systems.* N.p.: Author, 1986, 1987.

Sprague, Paul E. "Chicago Balloon Frame: The Evolution during the Nineteenth Century of George W. Snow's System for Erecting Light Frame Buildings from Dimension Lumber and Machine-Made Nails." In *The Technology of Early American Buildings: Studies of the Materials, Crafts Processes, and the Mechanization of Building Construction,* ed. H. Ward Jandl. Washington, D.C.: Foundation for Preservation Technology, 1983.

———. "Origin of Balloon Framing." *Journal of the Society of Architectural Historians* 40 (December 1981): 311–19.

Zink, Clifford W. "Dutch Framed Houses in New York and New Jersey." *Winterthur Portfolio* 22 (Winter 1987): 265–94. Offers comparisons with New England and *Québecois* framing traditions.

WOOD: ROOFING

Niemiec, S. S., and T. D. Brown. "Care and Maintenance of Wood Shingle and Shake Roofs." Publication #EC 1271. Corvallis: Oregon State University Extension Service, 1988.

Park, Sharon C. *The Repair and Replacement of Historic Wooden Shingle Roofs.* Preservation Brief 19. Washington, D.C.: National Park Service, 1989.

"Roofs." *The Old-House Journal* 11 (Special issue, April 1983).

Waite, Diana S. "Roofing for Early America." In *Building Early America: Contributions toward the History of a Great Industry,* ed. Charles E. Peterson. Mendham, N.J.: Astragal Press, n.d.

Yeomans, D. T. "A Preliminary Study of 'English' Roofs in Colonial America." *APT Bulletin* 13:4 (1981): 9–18.

Mail-Order Plans, Pre-Cut Houses, Prefabrication

Culbertson, Margaret, comp. *American House Designs: An Index to Popular and Trade Periodicals, 1850–1915.* Westport, Conn.: Greenwood Press, 1994.

Garvin, James L. "The Mail-Order House Plan and American Victorian Architecture." *Winterthur Portfolio* 16 (winter 1981): 311–34.

Grow, Lawrence. *Old House Plans: Two Centuries of American Domestic Architecture.* New York: Universe Books, 1978.

Harvey, Thomas. "Mail-Order Architecture in the Twenties." *Landscape* 25:3 (1981): 1–9. (The Architects' Small House Service Bureau, Inc.)

Jones, Robert T., ed. *Authentic Small Houses of the Twenties: Illustrations and Floor Plans of 254 Characteristic Homes.* Reprint of *Small Homes of Architectural Distinction: A Book of Suggested Plans Designed by The Architects' Small House Service Bureau, Inc.,* 1929. New York, Dover Publications, 1987.

Schweitzer, Robert, and Michael W. R. Davis. *America's Favorite Homes: Mail-Order Catalogues as a Guide to Popular Early Twentieth-Century Houses.* Detroit: Wayne State University Press, 1990.

Smeins, Linda E. *Building an American Identity: Pattern Book Homes and Communities, 1870–1900.* Walnut Creek, Calif.: Altamira Press, 1999.

Stevenson, Katherine Cole, and H. Ward Jandl. *Houses by Mail: A Guide to Houses from Sears, Roebuck and Company.* Washington, D.C.: Preservation Press, 1986.

Testa, Carlo. *The Industrialization of Building.* New York: Van Nostrand Reinhold Co., 1972.

Upton, Dell. "Pattern-Books and Professionalism: Aspects of the Transformation of Domestic Architecture in America, 1800–1860." *Winterthur Portfolio* 19 (summer/autumn 1984): 107–50.

Investigation, Restoration, and Maintenance of Buildings

Note: This book focuses on understanding old buildings, not on restoring them. Many books, magazines, and incidental publications deal with the rehabilitation and restoration of structures. Some of those publications reflect the core preservation ethics: research, adherence to evidence, use of traditional methods and materials, and reversibility. Some do not. In consulting the sources listed below, the reader should evaluate their approaches and practices against The Secretary of the Interior's Standards for the Treatment of Historic Properties, *which are given in the* Appendix.

Auer, Michael J. *The Preservation of Historic Barns.* Preservation Brief 20. Washington, D.C.: National Park Service, 1989.

Avrami, Erica C. *Preserving Wood Features in Historic Buildings: An Annotated Bibliography.* Washington, D.C.: National Park Service, 1993.

Bleekman, George M., III, Ann Girard, Karin Link, Donald Peting, Anne Seaton, Jonathan Smith, Lisa Teresi-Burcham, and Richa Wilson. *Twentieth-Century Building Materials, 1900–1950: An Annotated Bibliography.* Washington, D.C.: National Park Service, 1993.

Building Research 1 (September-October 1964). Special issue of the journal of the Building Research Institute on the restoration and preservation of historic buildings; contains articles on historical, architectural, and archaeological research; photography, architectural photogrammetry and measured drawings; and building restoration and maintenance.

Bullock, Orin M., Jr. *The Restoration Manual: An Illustrated Guide to the Preservation and Restoration of Old Buildings.* 1966. Reprint, New York: Van Nostrand Reinhold Co., 1983.

Carosino, Catherine, John Carr, Millan Galland, Janel Houten, Molly Lambert, and Ana Sanchez. *Historic Masonry Deterioration and Repair Techniques: An Annotated Bibliography.* Washington, D.C.: National Park Service, 1993.

Clifton, James R., ed. *Cleaning Stone and Masonry.* ASTM Special Technical Publication 935. Philadelphia: American Society for Testing and Materials, 1986.

Feilden, Bernard M. *Conservation of Historic Buildings.* London: Butterworths, 1982.

Fisher, Charles E., III, and Hugh C. Miller, eds. *Caring for Your Historic House.* New York: Harry N. Abrams, 1998. Contains articles on research and maintenance, interior and exterior woodwork, windows, roofing, plaster, plumbing, heating, cooling, and ventilating systems, paint and wallpaper, and landscaping.

Friedland, Edward P. *Antique Houses: Their Construction and Restoration.* New York: Dutton Studio Books, 1990.

Gayle, Margot, David W. Look, and John G. Waite. *Metals in America's Historic Buildings.* Washington, D.C.: U.S. Department of the Interior, Heritage Conservation and Recreation Service, 1980, 1992. Contains articles on the preservation and repair of iron, lead, tin, zinc, copper and copper alloys, nickel and nickel alloys, and aluminum.

Greater Portland Landmarks. *Living with Old Houses.* Portland, Maine: Greater Portland Landmarks, 1975.

Hanson, Shirley, and Nancy Hubby. *Preserving and Maintaining the Older Home.* New York: McGraw-Hill, 1983.

Howard, Hugh. *How Old Is This House?* New York: Noonday Press, 1989.

Howe, Barbara J., Dolores A. Fleming, Emory L. Kemp, and Ruth Ann Overbeck. *Houses and Homes: Exploring Their History.* Nashville, Tenn.: American Association for State and Local History, 1987.

Hutchins, Nigel. *Restoring Old Houses.* New York: Gramercy Publishing Company, 1985.

Insall, Donald W. *The Care of Old Buildings Today.* London: Architectural Press, 1972.

Jackson, Albert, and David Day. *The Complete Home Restoration Manual.* New York: Simon and Schuster, 1992.

Jandl, H. Ward. *Rehabilitating Interiors in Historic Buildings.* Preservation Brief 18. Washington, D.C.: National Park Service, 1988.

Jester, Thomas C., ed. *Twentieth-Century Building Materials: History and Conservation.* Washington, D.C.: National Park Service, 1995. Contains sections on metals, concrete, wood and plastics, masonry, glass, flooring, roofing, siding, and interior and exterior wall coverings.

Johnson, Curtis B., and Thomas D. Visser. *Taking Care of Your Old Barn: Ten Tips for Preserving and Reusing Vermont's Historic Agricultural Buildings.* Montpelier: Vermont Division for Historic Preservation and Vermont Housing and Conservation Board, 1995.

Johnson, Ed. *Old House Woodwork Restoration: How to Restore Doors, Windows, Walls, Stairs and Decorative Trim to Their Original Beauty.* Englewood Cliffs, N.J.: Prentice-Hall, 1983.

Judd, Henry A. *Before Restoration Begins.* Nashville, Tenn.: American Association for State and Local History, 1973.

Kennedy, Pamela A. *Easy Guide to Rehab Standards.* Providence: Rhode Island Historical Preservation Commission, 1992.

Kirk, John T. *The Impecunious House Restorer: Personal Vision and Historic Accuracy.* New York: Alfred A. Knopf, 1984.

Kitchen, Judith L. *Caring for Your Old House.* Washington, D.C.: Preservation Press, 1991.

Light, Sally. *House Histories: A Guide to Tracing the Genealogy of Your Home.* Spencertown, N.Y.: Golden Hill Press, 1989.

London, Mark. *Masonry: How to Care for Old and Historic Brick and Stone.* Washington, D.C.: Preservation Press, 1988.

MacDonald, Marylee. *Repairing Historic Flat Plaster: Walls and Ceilings.* Preservation Brief 21. Washington, D.C.: National Park Service, 1989.

Maguire, Byron W. *Exterior Renovation and Restoration of Private Dwellings.* Englewood Cliffs, N.J.: PTR Prentice-Hall, 1993.

———. *Interior Renovation and Restoration of Private Dwellings.* Englewood Cliffs, N.J.: PTR Prentice-Hall, 1994.

Matulionis, Raymond C., and Joan C. Freitag, eds. *Preventive Maintenance of Buildings.* New York: Van Nostrand Reinhold, 1991.

McDonald, Travis C., Jr. *Understanding Old Buildings: The Process of Architectural Investigation.* Preservation Brief 35. Washington, D.C.: National Park Service, 1994.

McKee, Harley J. *Introduction to Early American Masonry: Stone, Brick, Mortar and Plaster.* Washington, D.C.: Preservation Press, 1973.

Myers, Denys Peter. *Gaslighting in America: A Guide for Historic Preservation.* Washington, D.C.: Technical Preservation Services Division, National Park Service, 1978.

National Park Service. *Respectful Rehabilitation: Answers to Your Questions about Old Buildings.* Washington, D.C.: Preservation Press, 1982.

Nelson, Lee H. *Architectural Character: Identifying the Visual Aspects of Historic Buildings as an Aid to Preserving Their Character.* Preservation Brief 17. Washington, D.C.: National Park Service, 1988.

Orme, Alan Dan. *Reviving Old Houses.* Pownal, Vt.: Garden Way Publishing, 1989.

Park, Sharon C. *Heating, Ventilating, and Cooling Historic Buildings: Problems and Recommended Approaches.* Preservation Brief 24. Washington, D.C.: National Park Service, 1991.

———. *The Repair and Replacement of Historic Wooden Shingle Roofs.* Preservation Brief 19. Washington, D.C.: National Park Service, 1989.

Poore, Patricia, ed. *The Old-House Journal Guide to Restoration.* New York: Dutton, 1992.

Schwin, Lawrence, III. *Old House Colors: An Expert's Guide to Painting Your Old (or Not So Old) House.* New York: Sterling Publishing Company, 1990.

Seale, William. *Recreating the Historic House Interior.* Nashville, Tenn.: American Association for State and Local History, 1979.

Sherwood, Gerald E. *How to Select and Renovate an Older Home.* New York: Dover Publications, 1976.

Shivers, Natalie. *Walls and Molding: How to Care for Old and Historic Wood and Plaster.* Washington, D.C.: Preservation Press, 1990.

Simonson, Kaye Ellen. *Maintaining Historic Buildings: An Annotated Bibliography.* Washington, D.C.: National Park Service, 1990.

Slaton, Deborah, and Rebecca Shiffer, eds. *Preserving the Recent Past.* Washington, D.C.: National Park Service, 1995. Includes chapters on evaluation of resources, strategies for preservation and re-use, conservation of modern materials, and the history and preservation of curtain wall construction.

Smith, John F. *A Critical Bibliography of Building Conservation.* London: Mansell Information/Publishing, 1978.

Stahl, Frederick A. *A Guide to the Maintenance, Repair, and Alteration of Historic Buildings.* New York: Van Nostrand Reinhold Company, 1984.

Stephen, George. *New Life for Old Houses.* Washington, D.C.: Preservation Press, 1972, 1989.

———. *Remodeling Old Houses without Destroying Their Character.* New York: Alfred A. Knopf, 1978.

Sweetser, Sarah M. *Roofing for Historic Buildings.* Preservation Brief 4. Washington, D.C.: National Park Service, 1978.

Thornton, Jonathan, and William Adair. *Applied Decoration for Historic Interiors: Preserving Composition Ornament.* Preservation Brief 34. Washington, D.C.: National Park Service, 1994.

Timmons, Sharon, ed. *Preservation and Conservation: Principles and Practices.* Washington, D.C.: Preservation Press, 1976. Contains sections on wood, masonry, metals, and paints and varnishes and on standards of education and practice for custodians of old buildings.

Waite, John G. *The Maintenance and Repair of Architectural Cast Iron.* Preservation Brief 27. Washington, D.C.: National Park Service, 1991.

Weaver, Martin E., with Frank Matero. *Conserving Buildings: A Guide to Techniques and Materials.* New York: John E. Wiley & Sons, 1993. Contains sections on inspecting, recording, and evaluating timber, stone, bricks and tiles, cements, metals, paints, glass, slate roofing, wallpapers, and synthetic materials.

Weeks, Kay D., and Anne E. Grimmer. *The Secretary of the Interior's Standards for the Treatment of Historic Properties, with Guidelines for Preserving, Rehabilitating, Restoring and Reconstructing Historic Buildings.* Washington, D.C.: National Park Service, 1995.

Weeks, Kay D., and David W. Look. *Exterior Paint Problems on Historic Woodwork.* Preservation Brief 10. Washington, D.C.: National Park Service, 1982.

Weeks, Kay D., and Diane Maddex, eds. *Respectful Rehabilitation: Answers to Your Questions on Historic Buildings.* Washington, D.C.: Preservation Press, 1982.

Hand Tools: History and Use
(*see also* "Reprints of Early Architectural Sourcebooks")

Bealer, Alex W. *The Art of Blacksmithing.* New York: Funk & Wagnalls, 1969.

———. *The Tools That Built America.* New York: Bonanza Books, 1976.

Dunbar, Michael. *Antique Woodworking Tools: A Guide to the Purchase, Restoration, and Use of Old Tools for Today's Shop.* New York: Hastings House, 1977.

———. *Restoring, Tuning and Using Classic Woodworking Tools.* New York: Sterling Publishing Company, 1989.

———. *Woodturning for Cabinetmakers.* New York: Sterling Publishing Company, 1990.

Garvin, James L., and Donna-Belle Garvin. *Instruments of Change: New Hampshire Hand Tools and Their Makers, 1800–1900.* Concord, N.H.: New Hampshire Historical Society, 1985.

Gaynor, James M., and Nancy L. Hagedorn. *Tools: Working Wood in Eighteenth-Century America.* Williamsburg, Va.: Colonial Williamsburg Foundation, 1993.

Hawley, J. E. *The Blacksmith and His Art.* Phoenix, Ariz.: Author, 1976.

Hummell, Charles F. *With Hammer in Hand: The Dominy Craftsmen of East Hampton, New York.* Charlottesville, Va.: University Press of Virginia for Winterthur Museum, 1968.

Kaufmann, Henry J. *American Axes: A Survey of Their Development and Their Makers.* Brattleboro, Vt.: Stephen Greene Press, 1972.

Kebabian, Paul B. *American Woodworking Tools.* Boston: New York Graphic Society, 1978.

Martin, Richard A. *The Wooden Plane.* N.p.: Early American Industries Association, 1977.

McRaven, Charles. *Country Blacksmithing.* New York: Harper and Row, 1981.

Mercer, Henry C. *Ancient Carpenter's Tools.* Doylestown, Pa.: Bucks County Historical Society, 1960.

Moxon, Joseph. *Mechanick Exercises; or, The Doctrine of Handyworks.* Reprint of 3d ed. (London, 1703). Morristown, N.J.: Astragal Press, 1989.

Pollak, Emil, and Martyl Pollak. *A Guide to American Wooden Planes.* 2nd ed. Morristown, N.J.: Astragal Press, 1987.

Roberts, Kenneth D. *Wooden Planes in Nineteenth-Century America.* 2 vols. Fitzwilliam, N.H.: Ken Roberts Publishing Co., 1975–1983.

Salaman, R. A. *Dictionary of Tools Used in the Woodworking and Allied Trades, c. 1700–1970.* New York: Charles Scribner's Sons, 1975.

———. *Dictionary of Woodworking Tools.* Newtown, Conn.: Taunton Press, 1990.

Sellens, Alvin. *Woodworking Planes: A Descriptive Register of Wooden Planes.* Augusta, Kans: Author, 1978.

Smith, H. R. Bradley. *Blacksmith's and Farrier's Tools at the Shelburne Museum.* Shelburne, Vt.: Shelburne Museum, 1966.

Streeter, Donald. *Professional Smithing.* 1980. Reprint, Mendham, N.J.: Astragal Press, 1995.

Watson, Aldren A. *The Village Blacksmith.* New York: Thomas Y. Crowell Company, 1968.

Welch, Peter C. *Woodworking Tools, 1600–1900.* Contributions from the Museum of History and Technology, Paper 51. Washington, D.C.: Smithsonian Institution, 1966.

Wildung, Frank H. *Woodworking Tools at Shelburne Museum.* Shelburne, Vt.: Shelburne Museum, 1957.

Reprints of Early Architectural Sourcebooks

Aladdin Homes. 1918–19. Reprint, Watkins Glen, N.Y.: American Life Foundation, 1985.

Architectural Record Company. *"Sweet's" Indexed Catalogue of Building Construction for the Year 1906.* Garden City, N.Y.: McGraw-Hill Information Systems Company, c. 1977.

Badger, Daniel D. *Badger's Illustrated Catalogue of Cast Iron Architecture.* 1865. Reprint, with a new introduction by Margot Gayle, New York: Dover Publications, 1974.

Barber, George F. *The Cottage Souvenir.* 1890. Reprint, with introduction by Michael Tomlan, Watkins Glen, N.Y.: American Life Foundation, 1982.

Beecher, Catherine, and Harriet Beecher Stowe. *The American Woman's Home.* 1869. Reprint, Hartford, Conn.: Stowe-Day Foundation, 1975.

Belle, John, John Ray Hoke, Jr., and Stephen A. Kliment, eds. *Traditional Details for Building Restoration, Renovation, and Rehabilitation.* From the 1932–1951 eds. of Ramsey and Sleeper's *Architectural Graphic Standards.* New York: John Wiley and Sons, 1991.

Benjamin, Asher. *The American Builder's Companion.* 1827. Reprint, with an introduction by William Morgan, New York: Dover Publications, 1969.

———. *The Architect, or Practical House Carpenter (1830).* New York: Dover Publications, 1988.

———. *The Works of Asher Benjamin.* New York: DaCapo Press, 1972:

1. *The Country Builder's Assistant* (1797)
2. *The American Builder's Companion* (1806)
3. *The Rudiments of Architecture* (1814)
4. *The Practical House Carpenter* (1830)
5. *The Practice of Architecture* (1833)
6. *The Builder's Guide* (1839)
7. *The Elements of Architecture* (1843)

Berg, Donald J., ed. *Modern American Dwellings, 1897.* Reprint from *Carpentry and Building* magazine. Rockville Centre, N.Y.: Antiquity Reprints, 1981.

Bettesworth, A., and C. Hitch. *The Builder's Dictionary; or, Gentleman's and Architect's Companion.* 2 vols. 1734. Reprint, Ottawa: Association for Preservation Technology, 1981.

Bicknell, A. J. *Bicknell's Village Builder.* Watkins Glen, N.Y.: American Life Foundation, 1976.

———. *Bicknell's Village Builder: Bicknell's Victorian Buildings.* New York: Dover Publications, 1979.

Bicknell and Company. *Victorian Architecture.* Reprint of *Detail, Cottage and Constructive Architecture* (1873) and Comstock, *Modern Architectural Designs and Details* (1881), with an introduction by John Maas. Watkins Glen, N.Y.: American Life Foundation, 1975.

The Carpenter's Company of the City and County of Philadelphia. *Articles of the Carpenter's Company of Philadelphia and Their Rules for Measuring and Valuing Carpenter's Work.* 1786. Reprint, with an introduction by Charles E. Peterson, Philadelphia: Bell Publishing Company [Crown Publishers], 1971.

Cleaveland, Henry W., William Backus, and Samuel D. Backus. *Village and Farm Cottages: The Requirements of American Village Homes Considered and Suggested; With Designs for Such Houses of Moderate Cost.* 1856. Reprint, with an introduction by David Schuyler, Watkins Glen, N.Y.: American Life Foundation, 1982.

Combined Book of Sash, Doors, Blinds, Mouldings. . . . 1898. Reprinted as *Late Victorian Architectural Details,* Watkins Glen, N.Y.: American Life Foundation, 1978.

Comstock, William T. *Country Houses and Seaside Cottages of the Victorian Era.* Reprint of *American Cottages,* 1883. New York: Dover Publications, 1989.

———. *Victorian Domestic Architectural Plans and Details: 734 Scale Drawings of Doorways, Windows, Staircases, Moldings,*

Cornices and Other Elements. Reprint of *Modern Architectural Designs and Details,* 1881. New York: Dover Publications, 1987.

Crom, Theodore R., ed. *Trade Catalogues, 1542 to 1842.* Melrose, Fla.: Theodore R. Crom, 1989. Compilation of British and American trade catalogs, including tools and mathematical instruments.

Cummings and Miller. *Architectural Designs for Street Fronts, Suburban Houses and Cottages* (1868), and Cummings, M. F. *Cummings' Architectural Details* (1873). Reprinted as *Victorian Architectural Details,* Watkins Glen, N.Y.: American Life Foundation, 1978.

A Decorator. *The Paper Hanger, Painter, Grainer and Decorator's Assistant.* 1879. Reprinted as *Victorian Interior Decoration,* Watkins Glen, N.Y.: American Life Foundation, n.d.

F. W. Devoe Paint Company. *Exterior Decoration. A Treatise on the Artistic Use of Colors in the Ornamentation of Buildings. . . .* 1885. Reprint, Philadelphia: Athenaeum of Philadelphia, 1976.

Dow, George Francis. *The Arts and Crafts of New England, 1704–1775: Gleanings from Boston Newspapers Relating to Painting, Engraving, Silversmiths, Pewterers, Clockmakers, Furniture, Pottery, Old Houses, Costume, Trades and Occupations, &c.* 1927. Reprint, New York: DaCapo Press, 1967.

Downing, Andrew Jackson. *The Architecture of Country Houses,* with an introduction by George B. Tatum. New York: Da-Capo Press, 1968.

————. *The Architecture of Country Houses.* 1850. Reprint, New York: Dover Publications, 1969.

————. *Cottage Residences, Rural Architecture and Landscape Gardening.* 1842. Reprinted, with an introduction by Michael Hugo-Brunt, Watkins Glen, N.Y.: American Life Foundation, 1967.

————. *Victorian Cottage Residences.* Reprint of *Cottage Residences* (1873). New York: Dover Publications, 1981.

Eastlake, Charles L. *Hints on Household Taste.* 1878. Reprinted, with an introduction by John Gloag, New York: Dover Publications, 1969.

Ellis, George. *Modern Practical Joinery.* 1908. Reprint, Fresno, Calif.: Linden Publishing Co., 1987.

Eveleth, Samuel F. *School-house Architecture.* 1870. Republished as *Victorian School-House Architecture,* Watkins Glen, N.Y.: American Life Foundation, 1978.

Fisher, Charles E., III, ed. *The Well-Appointed Bath.* Washington, D.C.: Preservation Press, 1989. Reprint of two early-twentieth-century catalogs of bathroom fixtures.

Fowler, Orson S. *The Octagon House: A Home for All,* with an introduction by Madeleine B. Stern. Reprint of the 1853 2nd ed. of *A Home for All; or the Gravel Wall and Octagon Mode of Building New, Cheap, Convenient, Superior, and Adapted to Rich and Poor.* New York: Dover Publications, 1973.

Gordon-Van Tine Architectural Details. 1915. Reprint, Watkins Glen, N.Y.: American Life Foundation, 1985.

Halsted, Byron David. *Barns, Sheds, and Outbuildings.* 1881. Reprint, Brattleboro, Vt.: Stephen Greene Press, 1977.

Holly, Henry Hudson. *Holly's Country Seats* (1863) and *Modern Dwellings in Town and Country* (1878). Reprinted as *Country Seats and Modern Dwellings,* with an introduction by Michael Tomlan, Watkins Glen, N.Y.: American Life Foundation, 1977.

Langley, Batty. *The Builder's Director or Bench-Mate.* 1751. Reprint, New York: Benjamin Blom, 1970.

Langley, Batty, and Thomas Langley. *The Builder's Jewel, or the Youth's Instructor and Workman's Remembrancer.* 1757. Reprint, New York: Benjamin Blom, 1970.

————. *The City and Country Builder's and Workman's Treasury of Designs.* 1750. Reprint, New York: Benjamin Blom, 1967.

Leeds, Lewis W. *Lectures on Ventilation.* 1866–1867. Reprint, Watkins Glen, N.Y.: American Life Foundation, 1976.

Lungwitz, A. *The Complete Guide to Blacksmithing.* 1902. Reprint, New York: Bonanza Books, 1981.

Modern American Dwellings (by numerous architects). 1897. Rockville Centre, N.Y.: Antiquity Reprints, 1981.

Morgan Woodwork Organization. *Homes and Interiors of the 1920s.* Reprint of *Building With Assurance* (1923). New York: Sterling Publishing Company, 1987.

Moxon, Joseph. *Mechanick Exercises; or, The Doctrine of Handyworks.* Reprint of 3d ed. (London, 1703). Morristown, N.J.: Astragal Press, 1987.

Neve, Richard. *The City and Country Purchaser.* Reprint of 2nd ed. (London, 1726). New York: Augustus M. Kelly, 1971.

Nicholson File Company. *A Treatise on Files and Rasps.* 1878. Reprint, Albany, N.Y.: Early American Industries Association, 1983.

Official Chicago Moulding Book (Illustrated) . . . Adopted May 2, 1901 (the 8000 Series of moldings). Included in E. L. Roberts and William L. Sharp, *Number 500 General Catalogue of E. L. Roberts Company* (1903), reprinted as *Roberts' Illustrated Millwork Catalogue: A Sourcebook of Turn-of-the-Century Architectural Woodwork.* New York: Dover Publications, 1988.

Palliser, George. *Model Homes for the People.* 1876. Reprint, Watkins Glen, N.Y.: American Life Foundation, 1978.

Palliser, Palliser & Company. *Model Homes.* 1878. Reprint, Watkins Glen, N.Y.: American Life Foundation, 1978.

Palliser's Late Victorian Architecture. [Contains *Model Homes* (1878) and *American Cottage Homes* (1878), as republished by Palliser, Palliser & Company in 1888 under the title *American Architecture,* and also *New Cottage Homes and Details* (1887)]. Watkins Glen, N.Y.: American Life Foundation, 1978.

Reynolds, Hezekiah. *Directions for House and Ship Painting.* 1812. Reprint, with an introduction by Richard Candee, Worcester, Mass.: American Antiquarian Society, 1978.

Richardson, M. T., ed. *Practical Blacksmithing*. Reprint of the 1889, 1890, and 1891 volumes. New York: Weathervane Books, 1978.

Roberts, E. L., and William L. Sharp. *Number 500 General Catalogue of E. L. Roberts Company*. 1903. Reprinted as *Roberts' Illustrated Millwork Catalogue: A Sourcebook of Turn-of-the-Century Architectural Woodwork*. New York: Dover Publications, 1988.

Roberts, Robert. *The House Servant's Directory*. 1827. Reprint, Waltham, Mass.: Gore Place Society, 1977.

Russell & Erwin Manufacturing Company. *Illustrated Catalogue of American Hardware of the Russell & Erwin Manufacturing Company*. 1865. Reprinted, with an introduction by Lee H. Nelson. N.p.: Association for Preservation Technology, 1980.

Shoppell, R. W., et al. *Turn-of-the-Century Houses, Cottages, and Villas: Floor Plans and Line Drawings from Shoppell's Catalogues*. (Selected designs from *Shoppell's Modern Houses*). New York: Dover Publications, 1983.

———. *Shoppell's Modern Houses*. 1887. Reprint, Rockville Centre, N.Y.: Antiquity Reprints, 1978.

Stevens, John Calvin, and Albert Winslow Cobb. *Examples of American Domestic Architecture*. 1889. Reprinted as *American Domestic Architecture: A Late Victorian Stylebook*, Watkins Glen, N.Y.: American Life Foundation, 1978.

Stickley, Gustav. *The Best of Craftsman Homes*. Santa Barbara, Calif.: Peregrine Smith, 1979.

———. *The Craftsman: An Anthology*. Santa Barbara, Calif.: Peregrine Smith, 1978.

———. *Craftsman Homes: Architecture and Furnishings of the American Arts and Crafts Movement*. Reprint of 1909 *Craftsman Homes*. New York: Dover Publications, 1979.

Swan, Abraham. *The British Architect*. 1758. Reprint, New York: DaCapo Press, 1967.

Union Pacific System. *The Evolution of Artificial Light*. 1893. Reprint, Wethersfield, Conn.: Rushlight Club, 1986.

Vaux, Calvert. *Villas and Cottages*. 1864. Reprint, New York: Dover Publications, 1970.

The Victorian Design Book. Reprint of the *Universal Design Book*, 1904. Ottawa: Lee Valley Tools, 1984.

Vose and Company. *Illustrated Book of Stoves Manufactured by Vose & Company, Albany, New York*. 1853. Reprint, Albany, N.Y.: Early American Industries Association, 1983.

Whitehead, Russell F., ed. *The Architectural Treasures of Early America Series*. 8 vols. Reprints of *The White Pine Series of Architectural Monographs* (1914–1940). New York: Arno Press and the Early American Society, 1977.

Woodward, George E. *Woodward's Country Homes*. 1869. Reprint, Watkins Glen, N.Y.: American Life Foundation and Study Institute, 1977.

———. *Woodward's National Architect*. 1869. Reprint, Watkins Glen, N.Y.: American Life Foundation and Study Institute, 1977.

Woodward, George E., and Edward G. Thompson. *Woodward's National Architect; Containing 100 Original Designs, Plans, and Details, to Working Scale, for the Practical Construction of Dwelling Houses for the Country, Suburb and Village*. 1869. Reprint, New York: DaCapo Press, 1975.

———. *A Victorian Housebuilder's Guide*. Reprint of *Woodward's National Architect*, 1869. New York: Dover Publications, 1988.

Journals and Periodicals Containing Information on Building Design and Technology

APT Bulletin. Published quarterly by the Association for Preservation Technology International, this journal includes both general articles and case studies illustrating techniques for the conservation of historic structures.

Blueprints. Published by the private, nonprofit National Building Museum in Washington, D.C., this quarterly journal covers all aspects of design, construction, and function.

BR: Building Renovation. Published quarterly from 1992 to 1996 by Penton Publishing, Cleveland, Ohio, this was a trade journal for those engaged in the renovation and preservation of existing structures.

CRM [Cultural Resource Management]. Published by the National Park Service to "promote and maintain high standards for preserving and managing cultural resources," this occasional publication includes information of value to managers of historic sites and articles on building preservation and conservation.

Historic Preservation. Published six times a year as the members' journal of the National Trust for Historic Preservation, it includes articles on the field of historic preservation, features on specific preservation projects, organizations, or individuals, and a general portrayal of the role of preservation in American life.

History News. A quarterly published by the American Association for State and Local History as a membership benefit, it emphasizes concerns of historical agencies and societies but includes occasional information on preservation of historic buildings.

IA. Published biannually as a membership benefit by the Society for Industrial Archaeology, *IA* includes articles on industrial structures, sites, and processes, including processes related to the fabrication of building materials.

Information. Published by the National Trust for Historic Preservation, this bulletin is available only to members of the Preservation Forum, a special Trust membership category.

Each issue contains thematic essays on specific preservation subjects or issues.

Journal of the Society of Architectural Historians. Published quarterly by the Society of Architectural Historians, this academic journal contains articles about historic structures (mostly non-American) and reviews of current books on architectural history.

The Old-House Journal. Published six times a year, this popular magazine is intended primarily for private owners of older houses and contains information on a wide range of old-house problems and concerns.

Perspectives in Vernacular Architecture. Published occasionally since 1982 by the Vernacular Architecture Forum, each issue is a collection of papers presented at VAF meetings. Subjects are wide-ranging and generally treat vernacular buildings as cultural artifacts that reveal patterns of human behavior.

Preservation Briefs. Published on an occasional basis by the Preservation Assistance Division of the National Park Service, *Preservation Briefs* cover topics in building preservation and conservation and in procedures for rehabilitating historic structures according to federal standards. Some forty *Briefs* have been published; about twenty are cited specifically in this bibliography.

Preservation Tech Notes. Published by the National Park Service, *Preservation Tech Notes* "are designed to provide practical information on techniques and practices for successfully maintaining and preserving cultural resources," describing techniques that conform to established National Park Service policies, procedures, and standards.

Technology and Conservation. Published quarterly by the Technology Organization, Inc., in Boston, this journal emphasizes building conservation and the application of modern technology to historic structures.

Traditional Building. Published six times a year, this subscription journal discusses and lists sources for a wide range of materials and services applicable to preservation and restoration of historic structures of all kinds.

Historic Houses Open to the Public

Da Costa, Beverley, ed. *Historic Houses of America Open to the Public.* New York: American Heritage Publishing Company, 1971.

Chamberlain, Samuel. *Open House in New England.* New York: Bonanza Books, 1937, 1948.

Pratt, Dorothy, and Richard Pratt. *A Guide to Early American Homes, North.* New York: Bonanza Books, 1956.

Society for the Preservation of New England Antiquities. *House Guide* [various titles]. Boston: Society for the Preservation of New England Antiquities, various dates. A guide to the houses of the society in Maine, New Hampshire, Massachusetts, Rhode Island, and Connecticut.

Vanderbilt, Cornelius, Jr. *The Living Past of America: A Pictorial Treasury of Our Historic Houses and Villages That Have Been Preserved and Restored.* New York: Crown Publishers, 1955.

Wilson, Everett B. *America East: Its Architecture and Decoration.* New York: A. S. Barnes and Company, 1965.

INDEX